The Dark Side of Europe
The Extreme Right Today

The Dark Side of Europe

The Extreme Right Today

GEOFFREY HARRIS

Barnes & Noble Books
Savage, Maryland

First published in the United States of America in 1990 by
B A R N E S & N O B L E   B O O K S
8705 Bollman Place
Savage, Maryland 20763

First Published in the UK in 1990
by Edinburgh University Press

Library of Congress Cataloging-in-Publication-Data
is available from the publisher

Printed in Great Britain

Contents

Contents

Preface

BY GLYN FORD, MEP

As Chairman of the European Parliament's Committee of Inquiry into the Growth of Racism and Fascism in Europe (1984–86), I feel honoured to write the introduction to this book, itself a welcome and timely addition to the armoury of contemporary understanding of the twin, though not always identical, problems of fascism and racism.

At the beginning of the 1990s it is all too clear that the subject of this book is very much a matter of widespread public concern in many countries. In the mid-1980s I myself took the initiative to encourage the European Parliament to respond promptly to the success of the extreme right in France. The report which resulted from this initiative, detailed though it was, foreshadowed but could not have predicted the changing shape of events in European politics since then. For example, on West Germany: when the *Evrigenis Report* was written it concluded that right-wing extremism was only 'a minor part of Germany's politics' and that 'in the middle term organised German right-wing extremism has no chances in electoral politics'. That was before a series of developments which have turned the West German far-right into a much more dangerous force and which catapulted a far-right party, *die Republikaner*, led by Franz Schönhuber, into the European Parliament in the June 1989 elections.

When some of us in the European Parliament drew attention to the growing danger from 'the fascists in smart suits' our remarks were not, despite the mountain of evidence presented by the *Evrigenis Report*, always welcomed. Nor was it always understood when we pointed to the connection with the profound economic, political and social changes in Europe's structure which have been instrumental in producing some major shifts to the extreme Right. Geoff Harris's response to this situation was exactly the opposite. For him, it was crucial to recognise the depth of these changes, to observe what was new and to commence work on a serious analysis and description of the whole process. Thus it was precisely at this stage that he began to marshal the information so powerfully presented in this book which is a thorough survey of the problem from a European perspective. His participation as a staff member of the Socialist Group in the European Parliament's Inquiry put him in an ideal position to do this and, more importantly, to prepare this information for dissemination to a wider audience.

This study will help observers and activists to meet the challenges of a post-1992 Europe in which the prospects are that the far-right's growth will continue. Thus it should be seen as an attempt to come to terms with very deep political, social and economic changes in Europe, East and West, based on the warning signals already apparent in 1986.

Many of us in the European Parliament had been all too painfully aware of this new reality, the strength of which was confirmed by Le Pen's strong showing in the May 1988 French presidential election. After people finally began to take notice a new problem arose. How was this development to be characterised? Were the politics of Le Pen, the Front National and, indeed, the whole Group of the European Right (since 1989 The Technical Group of the European Right) a new species of fascism, or did they symbolise a new, if extreme, type of radical conservatism? Old ideas can appear in new forms and shapes and this, as this book demonstrates, was clearly the case with the Front National, whose politics are a mixture of neo-fascism and Poujadism, tailored to meet the needs of the last decades of the twentieth century.

Times have moved on somewhat since the days of Hitler and I am convinced that it is both illusion and delusion to restrict the label fascist to the isolated bands of cranks and nazi-uniform wearers who are unfortunately to be found in every European country. Of course these elements can be dangerous and are certainly capable of appalling violence, as the fascist terror campaign of the early 1980s in Italy, France and Germany showed. Racism as a means of political mobilisation became fashionable in many European countries during the 1980s. Already in West Germany *die Republikaner Partei* had been established in 1982 and this party was not slow to see the implications of Le Pen's racist demagogy and talent for propaganda for its own activities and began to work closely with the Front National.

The Republikaners' politics go much further than the populist racism which says that they 'will decide who is German' and demands the expulsion of foreigners. They would, for instance, scrap the West German state welfare system, they advocate a unified Germany with the same borders as in Hitler's time, they would abolish trade unions 'in their present form' and some members have proposed publicly that AIDS-virus victims should have their genitals tattooed.

In other countries, too, against a background of increasingly tight immigration and asylum policies, racist and neo-fascist parties benefited from the 'ripple effect' of Le Pen's successes. Like the Front National, they played up the alleged incompatibility between the new settlers in Europe and the European cultural background. As a staple of their propaganda, they made the facile equation between the numbers of immigrants and the number of unemployed in each country with the figures always juggled to fit each situation. They talked increasingly of the 'Islamicisation of Europe' and demanded that 'foreigners' should be encouraged to leave. A racist malaise spreads beyond the boundaries of the European Community to such countries as Austria, Switzerland and Norway. In Austria, the Liberal Party has been taken over by the far-right and its 'yuppie' leader, Jörg Haider, early in 1989 became leader of the Regional Government in Carinthia, where the Slovene minority faces increasing discrimination. In Norway, the far-right and anti-immigration Progress Party led by Carl Hagens collected over 13% in the September general election there.

The apparent stabilisation of Le Pen's support and the gains of the Republikaner have changed the complexion of the Technical Group of the European Right in the European Parliament quite drastically. Before June 1989, it was comprised of 10 Front National members, 5 members of the neo-fascist Movimiento Sociale Italiano-Destra National (MSI-DN), one member of the neo-fascist EPEN in Greece and a solitary British member, the Official Ulster Unionist John Taylor. This added up to 17 members. Between June 1984 and June 1989, the Group of the European Right saw two changes in its membership. Taylor joined after leaving the Group led by the British Conservatives and one FN member, Olivier d'Ormesson, resigned over Le Pen's statement that the Holocaust was 'a point of detail in the history of the Second World War'. At the time of writing, the same Group in the new Parliament has 17 members, this time comprised of 10 Front National MEPs, 6 Republikaner and 1 member of the Belgian neo-fascist Vlaams Blok, which ran a frenzied racist campaign in the Dutch-speaking part of Belgium under the slogan 'Our own people first!' and in the Euro-elections collected over 20% of the vote in Antwerp, building on earlier success in local elections.

For the moment, the *MSI-DN* no longer belongs to the Technical Group of the European Right, having registered deep differences with the Republikaner over the South Tyrol, where a German minority with a long past of extreme-right sympathies objects to being part of Italy. The strongly Italian nationalist *MSI* opposes this revanchism and has in consequence been excluded from membership of the Le Pen–Schönhuber 'Axis'. This has not been helped by internal struggles within the *MSI* over the succession to its former leader Giorgio Almirante, now resolved in favour of Pino Rauti, a founder member of the terrorist group Ordine Nuovo, and Member of the European Parliament. The row which has precluded the 21 right-wing extremists in Strasbourg from cementing unity is, in itself, important because it has involved the leader of a far-Right party from outside the European Community: Jorg Haider of the Austrian Freiheitliche Partei Österreichs (FPO). In the discussions between the FN, the Republikaner and the MSI, it was reported that Haider played a direct role. After all, the German minority in the South Tyrol wants 'Anschluss' with Austria.

The new shape of the far-Right in no way alters the material facts contained in this book. Quite the contrary, it adds to the central argument which is to draw attention to the burgeoning danger in our collective European midst. Europe must come to terms with the fact that it is made up of millions of disenfranchised and deprived immigrants, refugees and asylum seekers. In every respect, this 'thirteenth member' of the European Community is disadvantaged. Generally, it has no vote. It has more restricted access to social security and welfare systems. It endures higher levels of unemployment and poverty and obtains lower standards of educational provision. It has few advocates to speak up for it and is frequently the object of violent attention from the kind of racists who vote for the extreme-right parties and indeed are often members of such parties. At the same time, it is itself multi-national and multi-cultural and mostly originates from outside the European Community. In each country, this 'thirteenth nation' is different. In Britain, it is from Asia and the Caribbean. In Germany, from Turkey and Yugoslavia. In France, from North Africa. In Belgium, from Morocco and other parts of Africa. Above all, it is the consequence of the economic, social and political domination of large parts of the world by the Northern European states in the last two centuries.

If we want to learn anything from this book, the defence of this 'thirteenth nation' and the expansion of democratic rights to include it must be a starting point. At the very least this means a continuing and relentless campaign for the right to vote for all who have established their residence in Europe. It should also encompass the right to move freely without police harassment and state intimidation. And it should fully recognise the right of religious, cultural and ethnic minorities to their own identity.

These demands, which seek to accord basic human rights and dignity to our fellow citizens, are of course anathema to the political movements which form the subject matter of this book. They will remain so, whether racists argue from the pseudo-scientific position of supposed 'racial superiority' or from the new racism which emphasises 'racial and cultural separation'. For these people, racists and fascists, democratic rights are themselves unnatural except as a weapon to be used ultimately to uproot democracy.

We in Britain have been fortunate in that the anti-democratic nature of our home-grown fascists was understood some years ago, through the campaigns of organisations like the Anti-Nazi League and the diligent research of journals like *Searchlight*, resulting in the demise and split-ting of the once sizeable National Front into warring factions. Thus, though we still have a growing problem of racism, much of it fuelled by elements within the 'Establishment', we are not confronted with neo-fascist organisations that have a mass base. This does not mean that we in Britain can ignore what is happening on the continent. Indeed it is unfortunately the case that these disturbing developments are not limited to Western Europe. The breakdown of communist regimes in Eastern Europe has seen the re-emergence of openly anti-Semitic groupings in East Germany and Poland, for example. In the Soviet Union itself anti-Semitism has been used to attack reformers and rekindle Russian nationalism. So even the hopeful international situation resulting from *perestroika* and *glasnost* does not remove the causes for concern.

If this book performs any single function, it is this: to sound the alarm. By educating and informing, by telling us to sit up and start seeing what is happening around us, Geoff Harris has done us all a service.

Glyn Ford
Member of the European Parliament

One

Out of Oblivion

For many Europeans, 1945, the end of the Second World War, was the beginning of a new era: the 'Year 0' as a film by Roberto Rossellini depicted it. The political map of Europe was transformed as the American and Soviet armies raced towards Berlin and the last horrific fantasies were being lived out by Adolf Hitler and his dwindling entourage. Even as the war ended the full horror of the racist policies of Nazism was only gradually coming to light. As politicians and soldiers worked to devise new constitutional arrangements in many countries, in others civil war raged and around the globe a new and potentially ever more devastating conflict between 'East' and 'West' was in its initial phase. In countries that could afford the luxury many citizens preferred to take little interest in politics, concentrating instead on taking up their lives, having children, and rebuilding their communities. The tranquil conservatism of the 1950s in Europe and in the USA was to a great extent a natural response to the horror and insecurity of the 1940s. A new generation coming to maturity in the 1960s found it hard to live in what seemed a Western world cut off from reality. Security in the sense of personal well-being alone was not enough.

Long before the oil crisis of the 1970s and the consequential economic slump, the political atmosphere in Europe was changing. Reformist socialist and social democratic parties came into their own. The student rebellions of the 1960s reflected a growing crisis in European society and a growing feeling that the political system even when it adopted reformist policies, was not adequate to channel people's deepest concerns. The crisis of the 1960s occurred in a period in which the left appeared increasingly predominant. The democratic left was entering a period of unprecedented electoral strength and the revolutionary left appeared to have increasing support. In Germany in the 1960s, for example, the revolutionary left led the attack on social democracy, consumerism and what they saw as a sick bourgeois society. The extreme right was also angered by the dull destiny which history had appeared to reserved for their country. In other countries the youthful rebellions of the 1960s led to a crisis within conservative parties between those who wanted to turn back the tide of political consensus and those who wanted to challenge it. The factors that first led to the revelation of crisis in the 1960s were still there when in the 1970s economic decline made a difficult situation much worse. It was in this climate that racists, extreme right-wing terrorists, and neo-fascists found opportunities which many had thought would never arise again. By the 1980s political extremism was widespread and deep-rooted,and even if no major threat to parliamentary democracy exists it is clear that an increasing number of people are prepared to flirt with revolutionary politics of the right and left.

At the end of the 1980s, as unemployment rises and social and economic tensions make the 1960s appear a distant bygone age, it is right that all those attached to the maintenance of a democratic society be made as aware as possible of the presence in our society of those who would wish to try again, with new methods and new techniques, to succeed where Hitler and Mussolini failed.

That a country with the history and culture of Germany should have fallen prey to rule by a murderous gang was neither an inevitable nor a chance event. The crisis of European society at the end of the twentieth century comes after decades of rapid social changes: war, revolution, the end of empires, economic competition, a crisis of religion and culture. In the twentieth century Europe has destroyed itself as the economic and political centre of the world. The major countries have had a psychological crisis combined with the economic and social crisis: Britain, France, Portugal, and Belgium lost massive empires; Germany no longer exists as a country; Spain, moved rapidly from being a police state to trying to be a modern social democracy. The insecurity which many individuals feel as a result of these developments can be politically explosive when it is linked to a social and economic crisis reflected in young people's desperate search for jobs; in a crisis of the welfare state, in a feeling that crime is out of control. In such a situation people are bound to be attracted by the search for simple solutions and for scapegoats. In the late nineteenth century anti-Semitism became popular, respectable, and effective as a result of a developing economic crisis in certain parts of Europe. That crisis has not been resolved and now new scapegoats exist; political activists and writers are beginning to give a new credibility to ideas which, back in 1945, seemed to have been buried with Hitler in his bunker.

The Cold War was under way even before the Second World War was over and this partly explains why attempts to begin the new era by effectively punishing all those responsible were never completed. In the second half of the 1940s Western Europeans perceived a major threat from the Soviet Union. For many, education for democracy and denazification lost precedence because of the priority given to European defence. In Germany and Austria no denazification took place in the church, the law, the schools, or the police. The Nuremberg trials provided a symbol of what was, in fact, a comforting myth that Nazism was being destroyed. As Britain and the USA vied for the political leadership of Western Europe, many Nazis were able to escape justice. Russians and Americans took on scientists, bankers and policemen to help them in their conflict with one another. Adenauer and others strongly and successfully argued that the continuation of the trials of Nazi murderers would jeopardise Germany's support for the Western Alliance. In the USA those who had always maintained friendly contacts with Nazi Germany, for example some businessmen and right-wing ideologues, lobbied Washington, using similar arguments. Since virulent anti-communism, itself a key ingredient of the fascist appeal, was now becoming popular, it was hard to draw the line between those who used this argument sincerely and honestly and those who were merely continuing the same argument they had put forward in the 1930s in favour of a worldwide alliance against communism.[1]

The fact that many businessmen who had helped Hitler continued in business or that many Nazis escaped to South Africa or South America is well known and well documented. It would be quite absurd to argue that their survival represents a major threat to Europe, even if, as many rightly argue, war criminals should still be brought to justice. Similarly, it is not our purpose to analyse the rights and wrongs of the policy of abandoning denazification. What is less known and perhaps more important is that many of those who escaped did not just disappear into political oblivion, give thanks that they were still alive and settle down to a quiet expatriate existence under a new name. Klaus Barbie,[2] the 'Butcher of Lyons' and a notorious torturer, is a very good example of many who escaped from Europe with the help of the Odessa and American intelligence, and elements of the Catholic Church, and was thus able to continue his work for a new boss in Latin America. The way he prospered and survived is a perfect example of how virulent anti-communism poisoned elements of Western society, even as it was celebrating a great victory over Nazism. Nazi work on behalf of fascists in Latin America and South Africa is not a new discovery. However, what is often overlooked is that this sordid aspect of the post-war era is not something without vital relevance to Western Europe today. It is widely known that American intelligence helped bring a fascist to power in Greece in 1967. What is less appreciated is that fascist regimes in Europe and South America provided both a quiet haven and an undisturbed place of work for many who would seek to reintroduce fascism into Europe. Magistrates inquiring into the fascist terrorist outrages of the 1980s have frequently found themselves investigating people who spent long periods in one or several of these places.

It should not be imagined that we are speaking here of the odd fanatic who could not live with the idea of the defeat of Hitler or Mussolini, or with people like Oswald Mosley or Léon Degrelle, Hitler's followers in Britain and Belgium. Nor are we speaking of isolated fanatical terrorists who think that bombs and graffiti can give their perverted dreams a chance of coming true. In some cases we are speaking of people of vast wealth (not just Nazi treasure), successful businessmen, well known to the Western establishment and exercising significant political influence.

The careers of two men can be used to illustrate the extent to which being a Nazi or a fascist did not need to be a major barrier to developing a powerful role in Western society. Indeed, it is quite clear that for these men and many others whose role was less spectacular, their experiences and contacts made during the 1930s and 1940s provided the launch pad for their brilliant careers. Neither of these men's names is very widely known but they have clearly played a bigger part than many politicians from these countries whose names are well known to the public. The two men are Otto Skorzeny and Licio Gelli.

Otto Skorzeny (1908–75)

1935   was among the founder members of the Austrian Nazi party
1939   having been rejected by the Luftwaffe on account of his age, joined the Waffen SS as a technical expert
1943   as a result of his close relationship with General Kaltenbrunner the Head of the Reich Security Office, was made an SS Commander
        on 12 September personally took part in the release of Benito Mussolini from the Gran Sasso Hotel where he was being held prisoner by the new Italian Government
1944   was briefly Commander-in-Chief of all German Home Forces for twenty-four hours at the time of the 20 July plot against Hitler; he denies the allegation of ordering summary executions on this occasion
        in November was given responsibility for the sabotage section of the Reich Security Office. His job was to train foreign intelligence agents and terrorists to continue the war behind Allied lines. His agents were recruited from amongst extreme right-wing groups from France, Italy, Belgium, and Spain
        at this time his major preoccupation was to organise the escape arrangements for leading Nazis
16.4.45 surrendered to an American command post. During captivity he may have been recruited by American intelligence
1947   he was acquitted of having contravened the Geneva Convention

1948   escaped from an allied 'denazification camp'. He made use
        of the network for escape which he had himself started to
        establish. At this time he appears to have been recruited by
        American Intelligence and consequently travelled widely in
        Europe and Latin America

1950   set up home and business in Madrid from where he co-
        ordinated Nazi escapes. At this time he was appointed security
        adviser to various right-wing Governments in South America
        and was employed by the Spanish Interior Ministry

1953   helped reorganise the Egyptian security services under both
        Neguib and Nasser. The CIA helped pay his salary. The
        invitation to take up the job came from Allen Dulles, head
        of the CIA, via Skorzeny's father-in-law, Halmar Schacht
        (Hitler's Reichsbank president)

1960   press reports referred to his role during negotiations by the
        Federal German Government for Bundeswehr bases in Spain
        (still then under fascist rule)

1969   having been contacted via the German embassy in Bogotá was
        appointed security adviser to the Colombian government

1972   was named by Klaus Barbie (then masquerading as a Bolivian
        businessman under the name of Altmann) as head of a network
        of 100,000 Nazi sympathisers in twenty-two countries
        met generals from the South African army, one of whom was
        a former Panzer chief of staff

1973   took part in meetings with Italian fascists to plan the 'Rose of
        the Winds conspiracy' in which senior Italian secret service
        officers, such as General de Lorenzo, and extreme right agi-
        tators, such as Stefano delle Chiaie, attempted to overthrow
        Italian democracy
        in this year the *Washington Post* identified him as a 'major
        arms broker for Portugal (still under a fascist regime). He had
        apparently also been trafficking arms to African countries

1975   died in Madrid

Licio Gelli (1919–   )

1919   Born in Pistoia, Central Italy [3]

1937   joined Fascist Party and volunteered to take part in 35th Italian
        Black Shirt Division, fighting alongside Franco's army in
        Spain. He apparently saw his brother die in the Battle of
        Malaga

1939   fought in Albania and returned to Pistoia, where he wrote
        articles about his experiences in Spain and also a book in
        which he described Mussolini as a genius initiated into the
        mysteries of the spiritual evolution of man

1942   went to Caltaro in Montenegro where he took part in repressive
        action against partisans

1943   as fascism began to fall he apparently combined his position
        as an SS Oberleutenant with secret work for the communists.
        This double game enabled him to escape arrest and executions
        (documents illustrating this episode were published by a jour-
        nalist in Italy, Mino Pecorelli, in a magazine (*O.P.*) early in
        1979; on 20 March 1979 Pecorelli was assassinated)

1945   arrested in Sardinia, he gave the names of some fascists from
        Pistoia to the police. Evidence that he had tortured and mur-
        dered partisans was not considered sufficient for a conviction.
        In this period Gelli was apparently involved in helping leading
        Nazis escape to Latin America

1949   started travelling as a businessman. He was questioned by
        police as a suspected agent of 'Eastern countries'

1950   set up a bookshop and other business activities through which
        he built up contacts with Andreotti and other leading Italian
        politicians, as well as with the Argentinian Peron and the
        family of General Franco of Spain. He apparently worked
        with the Italian Communists as well until 1952 or 1956
        during the 1950s Gelli spent half his time outside Italy. He
        visited South America, building up contacts with extreme right
        elements. His network spread into Paraguay, Brazil, Bolivia,
        Venezuela and Nicaragua. He played a major part in the arms
        trade, including the sale of the Exocet missile to the fascist
        junta in Argentina
        whilst Gelli is considered by some to be politically very
        unsophisticated, it is clear that his main contacts were with
        those who were fanatically right-wing and anti-communist.
        He had contacts with Stefano della Chiaie and others linked
        to Barbie in Bolivia, with whom he was a business partner

1963   became a freemason and later head of the P2 (Propaganda-Due)
        lodge, which provided a cover for extreme right sympathisers in
        politics, business, and the secret service, but also included many
        other figures from Italy's political, commercial, and military
        elite. Branches exist in Latin America also

1971   Sandro Saccucci, a former parachutist, later MSI (Italian
        Social Movement) deputy, who disappeared from Britain,
        told an investigating magistrate about masonic involvement
        in the 'Rose of the Winds' conspiracy. (The magistrate,
        Vittorio Occorsio was later assassinated by a fascist hit
        squad)

1974   an attempt by the head of Italian freemasonry to dismiss
        Gelli failed

1976–81 at the peak of his power. He helped to encourage magistrates involved in investigating fascist bombings and is linked to Sindona (an Italian banker who faked his own kidnapping when his financial empire collapsed). After P2 was exposed, magistrates and parliamentary investigations heard from intelligence chiefs about his role as secret service informant, his links with the American Embassy in Rome and his role as a link man between Argentina's fascist regime and thé CIA. The Republicans' return to power in the USA in 1980 enabled Gelli to improve his contacts as Washington resumed the positive anti-communist policies of the Kissinger years.

1982   arrested in Geneva in connection with the crisis in one of Italy's leading banks, the Banco Ambrosiano.

1983   escaped from Champ Dollon prison on the eve of the start of his trial. He reportedly spent part of his time on the run in Paraguay, Argentina, and Brazil

1986   charged with Stefano delle Chiaie and other neo-fascists with direct involvement in the bombing of Bologna railway station. A mafia defector tells magistrates in Palermo of the links between the P2, the Mafia, and the extreme right in terrorism and the various attempted *coup d'états* of the 1970s

1987   December: condemned by a Court in Florence for subsidising an armed gang (in connection with the 1974 'Italicus' train bombing)

1988   February: extradited to Italy, held in custody in Parma. Allowed to live at home, even after his conviction in connection with the Bologna railway station bombings

From these men's lives it is clear that the abandonment of denazification, which may have contributed to West Germany's integration into the West, had some very unfortunate side-effects. This is far more than just a moral argument of the kind so easily dispensed with in a period of military confrontation. It is clear that since extremism breeds extremism, letting murderers go free, employing Nazis as secret agents or policemen, and supporting fascist regimes, does not mean that these people operate under even the, sometimes, limited civilising influences of the CIA. They continue to be fanatics and continue to encourage bloodshed. Their activities were consciously designed to poison the political atmosphere and encourage support for anti-democratic regimes. In allowing these activities to continue, Western intelligence agencies may have done lasting damage to Western democracy.

Another sad aspect of the history of the post-war period is apparent on the level of ideology. Contrary to what many Europeans continue to believe, in 1945 fascism did not evaporate with the defeat of the fascist regimes. In Spain and Portugal they were not defeated anyway. The ideology and objectives of fascism have been kept alive. As the true extent of Hitler's attempt to exterminate all Jews became known, a taboo descended on overt racist activities and on explicit support for Hitler and Mussolini. No possible political respectability or support could be gained by movements not prepared to accept that those two had not, at least, made some mistakes.

A lot of literature exists on neo-Nazism and neo-fascism but it is important not to overlook a substantial element of continuity in terms of personnel and ideology. In 1951 SS General Heinz Reinefurth, Barbie's opposite number in Poland, known as the 'Butcher of Warsaw' was elected Mayor of Wastermand, a small island in the North Sea. He had admitted that it was only lack of ammunition that had prevented him from killing Poles at the rate of more than 15 000 a day.

The American Consul in Hamburg told the American Secretary of State in 1949 that the German public had been renazified. He pointed out how Nazi propagandists, operating underground, argued, as their contemporaries now do, that stories of Nazi atrocities are exaggerations and lies spread by the Allies.[4] This theory coupled with racism and the idea that Europe can only be revived under fascist leadership provide the common elements with groups already at work in the other European countries in the 1940s and 1950s.

In Holland the National European Social Movement was founded in the immediate post-war period and was prohibited only in 1955. In Belgium the Belgian Social Movement was founded in 1950 to agitate for the rehabilitation and return of Léon Degrelle. Like their fellow travellers in France, they launched newspapers with small circulations. Even in Britain Sir Oswald Mosley returned remarkably quickly to the political scene after 1945.[5] Small book clubs and various organisations gave Mosley a base that provided audiences and enough people to stage rallies sufficiently significant to cause the Metropolitan police concern that they could not keep order on some occasions. On May Day 1948, 1500 members of the Union movement marched through Camden. That even a handful of people were prepared to march through the streets of a city which had been heavily bombarded for the first time in its history by a movement sympathetic to those who had ordered the bombings is rather extraordinary. Mosley's speeches were based on the idea that the shortages and rationing proved that the war had been a mistake.

As later in the 1970s counter-demonstrations far outnumbered the fascists participating in rallies and as the prospects for a new apocalypse receded, Mosley went into exile. He had, however, done enough to ensure that, as in other European countries, a framework would continue to exist in which ex-Nazis like Arnold Leese, or new converts like Colin Jordan, could carry on the fight.

In France in particular the national disgrace of collaboration and the Vichy regime placed a taboo on any overtly pro-fascist activity. Thousands of collaborators were executed. The extreme right in France has, however, a very well-established tradition, and by the early 1950s new groups had been formed such as 'Action Europe' and 'Nouvel Ordre Européen' etc.

It is important to emphasise that extreme right-wing ideology and racism even were more deeply implanted in France before the 1930s than in Germany. Such writers as Drumont and Maurras provided the intellectual respectability for French fascism. Anti-Semitism in contemporary French fascist propaganda is, in fact, the continuation of a well-worn tradition. The French philosopher Bernard Henri-Levy has argued in a book published in 1981 that fascism was really the ideology of France ('L'idéologie française'). He argues that after the war a new generation was taught something of a fairy story about the pre-war period and the extent of popular support for the Vichy regime. The slogan 'France for the French' used now by contemporary racist politicians like Le Pen, finds its origins in politics and philosophy in France over the last century. The attacks today on Badinter (the socialists' Justice Minister) or Simone Veil (a minister under Giscard) are as explicitly anti-Semitic as those on Léon Blum in the 1930s and on Pierre Mendès France in the 1950s. Moreover, the use of such slogans, and even legal condemnation for doing so, has not done political damage to those who campaign with these methods.

The turning point came in the mid-1950s, as defeat in Indo-china and Algeria provided a more fertile climate both for populist anti-parliamentarianism (Poujadism) and for violent activism. As will be seen, the ideology and personnel around Jean-Marie Le Pen and other leaders from the far right today was formed in this period even before General de Gaulle returned to power. It appealed to a feeling that France had been betrayed from within by Jews and others, and that an authoritarian nationalist regime should be installed.

In Italy, in spite of legal bans, former Mussolini supporters continued in active politics and the Italian Social Movement (MSI) was formed as early as 1946. Fascism, therefore, did not vanish from the Italian political scene in spite of the execution of Mussolini. As Paul Wilkinson has observed, Italy's defeat meant that the Allies had neither the resources nor the inclination to purge fascist elements from the Italian establishment, police, judiciary, church, etc.[6] A former head of the Private Office of the Minister of Propaganda of the Salò Republic, Giorgio Almirante, was leader of the MSI for many years and sat in the Italian and European Parliaments. In the 1980s he lost his parliamentary immunity and faced charges of helping fascist terrorists escape from justice. The Salò Republic was known as being one of the most brutal interludes in Italian fascism and it is in the person of Almirante that the continuity of European fascism is most evident. Whilst Almirante in the 1940s, as in the 1980s, continued his populist attacks on Italian democracy, appealing, like Poujade in France, to the small man (Uomo Qualunque, as the MSI's short-lived predecessor was called), others looked for a more revolutionary way forward. In 1951 Pino Rauti (who openly quarrelled with Almirante and was later linked to terrorism) and Julius Evola (the theoretician of black terrorism and racism) formed the Revolutionary Armed Fascists (Fasci d'Azione Rivoluzionaria). Such groups formed links even at this early stage with like-minded Europeans in Belgium and France, as well as with the SS Odessa network through which leading Nazis escaped into exile.

The situation on the far right in Italy, as in other countries, consisted of numerous different organisations. After such a dramatic collapse as had occurred in the early 1940s, internal tensions were inevitable, but these splits should not distract attention from the underlying continuity. Moreover the right-wing dominance of Italian politics in the 1940s and 1950s with the total exclusion of the left from power, reduced the political opportunities for fascists. The circumstances of the 1960s with some Christian Democrats trying to engage in an opening to the left and with the USA and many elements in the Italian elite totally opposed to any communist participation in the government, meant that fascists found sympathisers in high places. From the late 1960s they began a series of actions intended to overthrow the democratic system. In the wilderness years of the 1940s and 1950s such actions would have been pointless. The Italian fascists, therefore, argued a lot among themselves about the way forward and had difficulty coming to terms with the defeat of fascism: was it due to betrayal or internal errors?; would success come through careful manipulation of the democratic system or through revolutionary terrorism? This argument continued throughout the 1950s, until in 1969 Almirante took over the party leadership again, this time recommending a combination of both strategies.

The main problem that all fascists faced in undertaking political activity in the 1940s and 1950s was not a lack of coherent ideology or a sufficient grass-roots support for political activity. What they lacked was political respectability. Most Europeans knew what had happened last time such ideas had been tried and few were prepared to vote for it again. Moreover, as Mosley admitted when he went into exile, slump was not yet on its way. Indeed the 1950s were times of rapid economic growth and stability in which even the social democratic left was generally excluded from power. Fascists could not make much headway at a time when anti-communism was the keystone of most European countries' foreign policy. It was therefore hardly surprising that the 1950s appear in retrospect as the doldrum years of those parties explicitly committed to defending Nazi ideas.

In West Germany, in particular, this was a period of rapid economic growth. Former Nazi activists could make their way into a prosperous society and enjoy the revival of their country. A broad popular consensus developed which was so strong as to remove any opportunities or credibility for extremist parties. Until the 1960s the left represented by the SPD seemed to have no chance of power. It was, however, a short-lived period of an apparently new era and West Germany, like Britain, France, and Italy, was soon to be shaken by attacks on this consensus from various sources and by the quick emergence and re-emergence in the 1960s of movements disdainful of the very stability and well-being that was becoming more widespread. The superficiality of any idea that Nazi ideas were completely dead in West Germany was confirmed by opinion studies and election results. In 1971 a poll revealed that 50 per cent of the people thought that 'National Socialism was, in principle, a good idea poorly put into practice.[7] The figure was 26 per cent as recently as 1977. In 1979–80 a further study found that 13 per cent of the electorate had a right-wing extremist picture of the world, whilst 37 per cent appeared to be highly susceptible to right-wing extremist thinking. In the light of this evidence it is clear that any emergence of Nazism as an electoral force will depend on particular circumstances of time or place. A study on school children in Berlin just after the recent breakthrough by the Republican Party in January 1989 found that 11 per cent supported the extreme right.[8]

During the 1950s only a few hundred thousand votes could be picked up by right-wing extremist parties. This figure may have been lower than its potential level because of the disunity in this area of the political spectrum. The coalition of forces around the National Democratic Party (NDP) formed in 1964 and the particular circumstances of the 1960s led to a vote of 1.5 million (4.3 per cent) for the neo-Nazis in 1969. The party did particularly well in economically weak parts of the country and where the Protestant tradition was stronger. Between 1966 and 1968 the party had seats in five regional Parliaments, its highest score being 9.8 per cent in Baden-Würtemberg in 1968. This was the time when the limits to the German economic miracle first became apparent. The two main parties, the Christian Democrats and Social Democrats formed a grand coalition from 1966 to 1969, leaving a space in which the NDP could operate. More right-wing CDU, in Bavaria CSU, voters were naturally uneasy at this development in particular as it led to a much less hostile attitude to the Communist regimes of the East. As the economic situation improved and the CDU/CSU shifted to the right as the only opposition to the SPD/Liberal coalition, the opportunity for the NPD rapidly evaporated and the party failed in 1969 to win the 5 per cent of votes necessary to get seats in the Bundestag, the Federal Parliament in Bonn. The rapid emergence of the NPD confirmed, however, that there was a significant market in the electorate for its ideas. In the 1980s the CDU/CSU is once again in power and its failure to deliver what the extreme right hopes for may be the reason for the electoral successes of the neo-Nazi Republican Party. The immigration issue, drugs, law and order all provide fertile ground for those who would campaign for racist, authoritarian policies.

The public humiliation of the former Speaker in November 1988 for a speech which appeared to glorify Hitler and accept the need for the Jews in Germany to accept a less-powerful role in society might please all those anxious to kill off the ghosts of the past. Such incidents, however, confirm that Chancellor Kohl will never be able to satisfy the extreme right. Moreover, as one Jewish leader rather wryly observed after Speaker Jenninger had resigned: the fuss was perhaps exaggerated and unhelpful as Jenninger was saying only what many Germans still think. Such incidents, coupled with the evidence of opinion surveys, anecdotal evidence, and the reports of the Office for the Protection of the Constitution suggest that as in other countries fascism, whilst marginal, is not a spent force, and that circumstances could provide racist political agitators with the opportunity to make further political impact.

Indeed, the 1989 success of the Republicans comes at a time of disillusionment with an aimless and uninspiring Centre-Right coalition in which hard-line conservatives do not feel their views are represented. The fact that it is illegal to be openly in favour of Nazism merely forces the extremists to be more sophisticated in getting their message across. The Republicans' leader, Franz Schönhuber, served in the SS and is himself a former CSU member and indeed as soon as the Berlin result became known a tough debate took place among Christian Democrats as to whether the perception that they had not been tough enough on immigration had given the extremists their chance. The presence of policemen among those elected in Berlin to sit in the Federal Parliament for the Republicans is also significant as is the fact that the coalition government's failure to deal adequately with the drugs and AIDS problems featured prominently in Republican propaganda. Similarly, it should be noted that the party openly expressed admiration for Le Pen. The issues raised by the extremists are different from the usual battle slogans of either mainstream left or right. Moreover, these issues will remain important in the years ahead, as 1992 causes economic problems and, indeed, if economic growth does pick up it will necessitate further immigration to Germany. The fact that nearly half a century after the defeat of the Nazis, a party led by a former member of the SS should be able to score any kind of electoral success is not a freak event to be

discounted. The opening up of the way to German reunification will provide fertile ground for right-wing extremists. European integration will
bring fears that Germany's dignity and superiority is being undermined
and détente will bring more people into the country as the right to leave
communist countries freely is accepted. The Republicans will be stopped
from growing only if other right-wing parties can convincingly attract
their votes, but, as we shall see from the experience of France, even this
is a problematic strategy. It did, however, work in the late 1960S, the
previous occasion on which neo-Nazis scored electoral success in West
Germany. The price would, of course, be the breakdown of consensus
politics. It is in this disturbing context that apparently isolated events
take on deeper significance – racist slogans on the streets, racial attacks,
videogames glorifying the holocaust and so on cannot be ignored as
social problems irrelevant to politics. There is also the matter of where
the money is coming from to keep political extremism in business. The
Financial Times reported in January 1989[9] on the activities of another
neo-Nazi party, the Deutsche Volksunion, which found the resources
for a direct mail shot to 28 million voters in preparation for the June
1989 Euro-elections. This operation cost about 6 million DM. The fact
that the DVU has such funds available is as disturbing as the political
message they seek to spread.

In the June 1989 Euro-elections the Republicans achieved their aim
of breaking into West German politics on a national level. They took
2 million votes, or over 7 per cent. On this basis they could hope to
win seats in future federal elections and hold the balance of power in
the Bundestag.

The Republicans (REP) were founded in 1983 in Bavaria. The Party
soon became a magnet for members of other extreme right groups and
'new right' intellectuals. It was careful to deny any explicitly neo-Nazi
objectives and in his maiden speech in Strasbourg Schönhuber claimed
to be not a Nazi, but a German and a European patriot. In fact, its
image varies from region to region, and from its public to its private
activities. Its leader's previous status as a television personality and its
very well-produced television spots are only part of the explanation of
its success. As well as its ability to play on anxieties and issues other
parties prefer to leave alone, it has clearly benefited from the death
of Franz-Josef Strauss, whose nationalistic conservatism provided an
alternative home to those with extremist sympathies. In Bavaria, where
the REP took 15 per cent of the vote in the Euro-elections, CSU leaders
have complained of the REP stealing its ideas. It is, however, clear that
the REP goes further than the Christian Democrats, with its explicit
emphasis on the priority of German reunification as an alternative to
European integration which the mainstream German Christian Democrats accept. The rise of the REP has coincided with evidence from the

Office for the Protection of the Constitution of increased activity on the extreme right and its electoral success has been followed, particularly in Bavaria and Berlin, by an increase in racist violence. That the REP is not an isolated phenomenon with no relevance to Germany's past is apparent from its 22 per cent score in Rosenheim in Bavaria, the town where Herman Goering, one of the leaders of the Third Reich, was born.

The REP is no less irrelevant to Germany's future role in Europe, particularly with the impact of 1992 and Gorbachev's call for a Common European Home. A disturbing sign of the times came in the summer of 1989 when Chancellor Kohl and President Von Weizacker came under right-wing pressure not to attend commemorative events in Poland to mark the anniversary of the German invasion of September 1939. If such pressure leads West Germany to reopen the issue of its Eastern borders, the whole of the West German/Soviet *rapprochement* could be put at risk. Whatever happens, it is clear that the rise of the REP raises questions which will have to be answered, if the momentum towards Western European integration and *détente* with the Soviet Union is to be maintained.

Before going on to look more closely at the elements of continuity and discontinuity in European fascism, it should be made clear that I am not arguing that fascism is about to make a dramatic return to power anywhere in Europe. It is however my view that the idea that fascism was killed off in the 1940s is a dangerous myth of which Europe should be aware. The activities of the National Front in Britain and the other tiny groups in other countries are significant because they have ensured that fascism as an idea did not die with the military defeat of fascism. The 'pathological' solution, i.e. waiting for all Nazis and fascists to die, is not enough. It is quite obvious, in the 1980s, that as an electoral and social force or as an underground movement fascism is not dead. It may be only a shadow of the past, but it is a shadow which is cast menacingly across society and politics in Western Europe, not least because it can reduce the overall level of tolerance and democratic pluralism in society as other parties try to contain the success of the extreme right by taking over some of its ideas, a development obvious both in France and Germany in the course of the 1980s.

If we look at racism in Europe today and recall the importance it played in Hitler's rise to power, and observe how racism against blacks and Jews continues to play a major part in the activities of the extreme right, it is clear that a major challenge to European democracy and pluralism has to be faced. As the report of the European Parliament put it:

> Europe will never forget the bloodshed and humiliation that were
> the expression of racism under the totalitarian regimes. And it is

significant that Europe is now building its future on the basis of reconciliation and cooperation among its constituent nations. The Community approach means, by definition, the renouncement of nationalist rivalries. Even more obviously, it means the rejection of all racist tendencies within the European context. But, having thrown its doors wide open after the war to newcomers of a variety of ethnic origins who came here, individually or in groups, either to join in the work of reconstruction and development or seeking in its lands refuge, freedom and justice, Europe today presents a much enriched ethnic and cultural picture. In a world tending increasingly towards a global village, the pluralism so characteristic of the community of European nations is gradually acquiring a new meaning. Like all great changes in history, this transformation is not without its problems and painful shocks. When the stresses of an economic and social crisis accompany the friction that inevitably results from the shaking down together of people differing in their ethnic origins, culture and religious beliefs may, indeed, by their content, tradition or particular political orientation be directly opposed, there is always a danger that a climate of intolerance or xenophobia may arise and occasionally prove alarming in its manifestations. Conscious of its responsibility, Europe must face this challenge frankly and clear-sightedly, with the kind of political integrity and moral courage which have marked the best hours of its history. The European synthesis which is now underway can only be achieved in accordance with the principles of which historical Europe, now partially united within the Community, has always regarded itself as the inspirer, creator and guardian.[10]

Continuity and Change in European Fascism

Ideology, organisation, and a particular political culture can be seen as the key elements in the continuity of the history of European fascism. Semi-secret societies, book clubs, pressure groups, paramilitary clubs, and political parties can keep going for a long time if they can keep convinced that their ideas have a chance of success. In the 1950s and 1960s the glories of the Nazi and fascist regimes were not so remote, and indeed in some countries in Europe and South America similar regimes remained in power. The electoral successes of the 1970s and the 1980s, patchy and marginal as they may be, have been enough to convince those operating on the edge of political oblivion that they will one day make it back into the big time. Small groups also need an ideology to give them a sense of purpose, and an organisation providing an ability to operate with a minimum of effectiveness to enable them to embed themselves in the political culture of their society. Fascists have succeeded in doing all this. As any political movement has to accept, the rest – success, failure, power, or total defeat – is primarily a matter of circumstances and the skilful exploitation of political opportunities. In that sense internal arguments or electoral defeat is not something with which only fascists have to learn to live. Paul Wilkinson writes of the 'puzzle' surrounding the survival of fascism as an idea, but goes on to argue that 'the people involved in leading the new fascist movements . . . were by and large those who had been small fry in war-time, middle-range officials and local party organisers'.[11] This is a highly questionable viewpoint, especially as Le Pen or Colin Jordan were not Nazis during World War Two and so many modern extreme right-wing activists are very young. It does, however, fit Almirante or Franz Schönhuber of the West German Republican party, which scored 7.5 per cent in West Berlin in January 1989. The latter had fought in the Waffen SS.

As Anne Dummett of the Runnymede Trust in Britain has put it:

> There are times when it seems as though fascist ideas have won,
> although fascist weapons lost. Racism, contempt for the powerless,
> the exaltation of the nation as good above all other goods, the
> use of terrorism: these were the political ideas which repelled
> all decent people, which it seemed had been defeated, and which
> are now resurgent.[12]

All the studies of this problem have to face up to the difficulty of providing a definition of fascism, especially as it is sometimes used as a generalised term of abuse, both within and between political parties which do not challenge the democratic system. No such definition is offered here. The common elements of fascist parties can however be seen as

extreme nationalism
rejection of pluralism and therefore parliamentary democracy
opposition to liberalism and communism
opposition to capitalism as a freely operating market economy
the use of violence
the attacking of particular targets, e.g. racial or sexual minorities
the defence of discrimination and the rejection of the idea of equal
basic human rights

It is clear that in expressing ideas to be found in *Mein Kampf* modern writers have to cling to political respectability. One way of doing this is to reformulate the basic message of racism. The core of supposedly scientific criteria and ethnological terms can provide a convenient cover. Numerous modern writers refer to 'Indo-European civilisation', 'the incompatibility of different races', or the 'intellectual

superiority of the white race'. A form of social Darwinism known today
as sociobiology is widely used by academics who, in many cases, do not
appear remotely perturbed to find their ideas quoted in extreme-right
publications. Moreover, whilst anti-Semitism remains significant the
primary target of racists is now the visible minority population present
in most parts of Western Europe and a convenient scapegoat for urban
social and economic problems.

During the 1970s a major rethink took place among many conservative parties, leading eventually to the intellectual predominance
of Thatcherism and Reaganism. Separately but contemporaneously a
'European New Right' moved out into the open to rehabilitate the roman-
tic nationalism of the late nineteenth and early twentieth centuries. They
attacked the pillars of liberal society in terms reminiscent of the fascist
era. In France, for example, the GRECE (Groupement de Recherche et
d'Etudes pour la Civilisation Européene) has openly admitted to being
engaged in a cultural war,[13] trying consciously to achieve the cultural
predominance which Gramsci argued was a necessary precursor of
any revolution. Alain de Benoist, for example, argues in favour of
differentiated anti-racism taking into account 'the relative differences
between individuals and between groups of individuals'. He denies
arguing that one race is necessarily superior to any other, but argues
that assimilation is not possible. Such writers directly quote Jensen and
Eysenck on IQ differences between blacks and whites. Similarly, Jensen
and Eysenck are quoted in publications of the British National Front
whose leaflets are circulated in schools telling children of the scientific
evidence that whites are superior to blacks.

Such ideas are not remotely new. The gas-chambers were the direct
political consequences of genetic theories advanced by such as Fischer,
Bauer, and Lenz in the 1930s. The continuity of such ideas and the fact
that they have now entered into contemporary popular culture has been
carefully exposed by Stephen Rose.[14] In 1931 Fischer and his colleagues
wrote that

> In general the negro is not inclined to work hard in the present in
> order to provide for well-being in a distant future.

In 1969 Arthur Jensen criticised the American 'Great Society Program'
to help blacks, arguing that 'the number of intelligent genes seems lower,
overall in the black population, than in the white.' In 1971 H. J. Eysenck
argued that 'whenever blacks and whites are compared, with respect
to IQ, obvious differences in socio-economic status do not affect the
observed inferiority of the blacks very much.' Numerous publications
and articles have followed. GRECE has its own journal, *Elements*, of
which the British version, *Scorpion* reproduces such theories and argues
that the notion of being 'a European would have to be based on the notion
of identity and opposition to what is non-European'.[15] Such opposition

in a country like Britain with so many black citizens has fairly obvious implications.

The other key element in the effort to make fascism once again respectable comes in the form of historical revisionism. Not only do fascists now parrot Hitlerite racial theories, but they also deny that the consequences of such theories were really so devastating. In short, they claim that the whole history of holocaust as it is now embedded in Europe's political consciousness is nothing more than a gigantic hoax. This is a different issue from the historian's debate over how far Nazism was an exceptional political theory or Hitler was pursuing traditional German foreign policy objectives.

As has been pointed out, the horrors of the extermination camps were such as to make it difficult for many even to believe that such brutality was possible. Many, at the time, first thought that the stories of the concentration camps were just communist propaganda. This is not the place to consider how best the history of the twentieth-century should be taught, or whether it is appropriate to emphasise what is only one of the many holocausts of this century alone. It is, however, clear that the truth about the consequences of racism in Germany provides many people with something of a discouragement from flirting with similar political doctrines.

This does not mean that contemporary Nazi sympathizers do not, when they enter the political arena, try to dress up their views to avoid reference to the past and to concentrate public hostility on contemporary problems such as immigrants taking away jobs and houses from the citizens of a particular city or country. The very fact that Le Pen's Hitlerite sympathies were unknown to the wider public and even to a lot of the media and the political professionals is, as we shall see, a result of his ability to express his views in relation to the present situation and future prospects. The challenge for right-wing extremists is merely a question of how to present the same basic racist and anti-democratic philosophy in terms of its relevance to people's perceptions of everyday problems, as indeed any successful political campaigner must do. What is disturbing is that the lifting of the taboo in discussion on racial theories has coincided with a conscious attempt to whitewash Hitler and deny the holocaust.

The falsifiers of history have been at work throughout the post-war period, but in recent years there has, according to the Institute of Jewish Affairs in London, been an increase in such literature. Some argue that the whole holocaust story is nothing more than a mercenary effort designed by Jews to extract money from Germans. As early as 1948 Maurice Bardéche[16] in France openly defended Hitler and the collaborators. Accusing the Western Allies of collusion with communism, he wrote of systematic distortion of the facts. In 1950

Paul Rasinier followed in similar vein, arguing as others do now that the holocaust 'story' was just propaganda. Robert Faurrison, a Lyons University lecturer, took up the cause again in the 1970s and his works were circulated via GRECE and extreme-right political groups.

A steady stream of such literature in Germany has expressed similar views. Indeed, it can be argued that the failure to complete the denazification process appeared to confirm the claim that a lot of the revelations of 1944 and 1945 about Nazi massacres were just propaganda. For those who wished to distort the truth, the numerous failures to convict because of lack of evidence could be conveniently given a particular explanation. Defence lawyers'[17] arguments, that murderers were only obeying orders in the same way as Allied commanders in the midst of battle, are now echoed in such publications as Richard Verall's *Did Six Million Really Die?*. In the 1940s American Congressmen had attacked the Administration's denazification policies, arguing that it was a Jewish and communist conspiracy.

In California, more recently, a former member of the British National Front became director of an 'Institute of Historical Review' which publishes the works of Faurrison and others. It publishes a journal and advertises in the Liberty Lobby weekly, *Spotlight*. In Britain there is an outlet via the Historical Review Press, whose publications are advertised by the extreme right. The wide availability of such publications illustrates the danger of a well-funded and well-organised intellectual movement gaining ground. The target is clearly the uninformed minds of the young, and the aim is to make prejudice acceptable, and indeed marketable. Nazis are to be converted through these writings into the heroic victims of history, killed fighting against communism and the decline of Europe.

The opportunities for historical revisionists are likely to increase as time passes, memories fade, and as new holocausts appear to make Hitler's massacres appear less exceptional. Indeed, since the main aim of the extreme right is to gain power rather than to whitewash Hitler, it would appear quite possible that racists and fascists will find the memory of national socialism less of a liability as time passes. It is, however, not only in terms of ideology, scientific racism, and historical revisionism that the continuity of European fascism can be observed. It is also evident from the structure of extreme-right organisations and the message they seek to put across.

As in the past, fascist groups operate on the basis of control by a strong leader with a small inner circle. The message for the general public is not the same as the one circulated amongst party members. This can be both a political tactic and a legal necessity. The aim is not necessarily immediate mass mobilisation or electoral success. It is the creation of tension, the incitement of hatred and the sapping of confidence in democratic society which is the real objective. Hitler successfully dissociated himself from his own thugs during his rise to power. Similarly, in the post-war period, Italian fascist ideologist Julius Evola argued that politics was the task of a small elite which could, through propaganda, manipulate the masses and prepare the ground for a seizure of power.

Similarly, the political culture on which modern European fascism feeds is clearly not something new. The mixture of virulent anti-communism and racism remains the key element. The slogans used today are very similar to those used in the pre-war period and can be guaranteed to appeal to a public far wider than those fully committed to fascism. When Le Pen's 'National Front' argues that 2 million unemployed means 2 million immigrants too many, he is playing with figures and popular fears. Moreover, he is echoing slogans of the 1930s when he points out that Simone Veil (a former Minister and former President of the European Parliament) is not really French: he knows exactly what he is doing, just as he did in the 1950s when, as a hard-up ex-M.P., he sold an LP record of Nazi songs, the cover of which emphasised that Nazism had triumphed via electoral success. In February 1984 the pro-Le Pen Newspaper *Present* published an article by Romain Marie (now a Euro-MP) criticising 'the tendency for Jews to monopolise all the highest positions in the Western nations'. Such slogans confirm that in looking at racism and fascism in Western Europe today we are not looking at something new, we are looking at an extremely well-established tradition which is now reasserting itself. Today it uses the question of immigration as its primary self-justification and appeal, but its personnel, methods, philosophy, and aims go back to the origins of European racism.

It is, however, appropriate to try to understand both the similarities and the differences between now and the 1930s. As is obvious, the facts of the war and its aftermath force modern fascists to revise their appeal. Moreover, the economic establishment which, eventually, gave its blessing to Hitler and Mussolini and benefited enormously from their policies (in spite of their propaganda whilst in opposition) shows no signs of openly giving its blessing to anti-democratic solutions to current problems — at least not in Western Europe. In Latin America and many developing countries this is, unfortunately, not the case. Italy is not Chile, even if the P2 and their circle could not see that obvious reality. It remains necessary, however, to find some explanation as to why there has been an increase in racist and fascist activity and appeal in recent years. The ideas of fascism survived the war, but it was only the deepening crisis of the 1970s and 1980s which gave it an opportunity to expand its audience.

Partly this is a product of economic decline and unemployment, and the continuing failure of orthodox parties to find lasting solutions. There is nothing remotely novel in Jensen's sociobiology. What is new is the political climate which has, once again, become receptive to such ideas. The rise of unemployment, plus the presence of immigrants or guest-workers (whose low wages helped make the earlier boom possible), is clearly a key element in a new and more unstable political situation. It is, however, also hard to deny that the rise of the extreme right is part of a changing political atmosphere, to which it has also contributed. Conservative politicians in Britain, for example, particularly Margaret Thatcher, have openly played on popular fears of being 'swamped' by immigrants and have deprived the National Front of most of its votes. We have now a Catholic Church whose leadership appears to be fixed on an explicitly conservative political role. Infiltration of the British Conservative Party by the extreme right is at a level which would never have been imaginable ten or fifteen years ago. These are signs of new political times. It is pointless to speculate about the prospects, but one issue which has clearly changed the political climate is an issue which will not go away: that is the issue of race.

Richard Thurlow has traced in detail the rise and fall of the wider electoral popularity of the National Front in Britain in the 1960s and 1970s.[17] British fascism had regrouped in 1967 within the NF, which represented the convergence of neo-fascist and racist politics. In spite of internal splits over how fascist it should be and attitudes to Oswald Mosley, it is clear that it was the issue of immigration that enabled it to seem, for a time, capable of breaking the mould of British politics. The main reason for its expansion came in the refusal of the Conservative Party leadership of the time to pander to growing xenophobia in Britain. Enoch Powell had been sacked by Edward Heath from the Conservative Opposition front bench for a speech in 1968 predicting that rivers of blood would flow as a result of immigration. Indeed, Heath began to lose his hold on sectors of his party precisely because of his honourable position on this matter. When Powell predicted the apocalypse and referred to old ladies having excrement pushed through their letter boxes he was bringing the hate-mongering style and fundamental racism of the extreme right into the mainstream of public debate. This provided the NF with its first substantial opportunity to step out of oblivion. In 1965 a Labour government had passed a Race Relations Act which made incitement to racial hatred a prosecutable offence. Ironically, it would appear that this legislation, like the taboos on certain historical references in France or Germany, actually forced neo-fascists like John Tyndal to express their basic views in more carefully chosen words within a presentation superficially more rational. That racist propaganda only circulated through book clubs advertised by the NF did not prevent it from influencing certain sections of public opinion but it did make the circulation of such propaganda legal. The fact that even in the 1960s the internal struggle went on between those who wanted a revisionist form for expressing fascist ideas and those intent on political violence does nothing to undermine the unfortunate truth that the immigration issue and the social and economic context provided racists with the political opportunity for which they had waited so long. Moreover, as we shall see the rise of the NF signified that votes could be won on the issue of race, and later other Conservative leaders expressed themselves differently from Edward Heath on this matter. In this sense, Powell and the NF did, in fact, contribute to the breaking up of the political mould which has taken place in Britain since the mid-1970s.

The experience of Britain is by no means unique or separate from the rest of Europe, when in many places it is racism as a popular sentiment and as an instrument of policy which has provided the main new political opportunity for the extreme right. It should be emphasised that encouragement by established political parties of the belief that immigration is a problem preceded the rise of racism in the form of racial attitudes and racist political campaigns. As Anne Dummett has put it: 'the resurgence of fascist ideas in many European states has come after many years of discriminatory behaviour and hostile attitudes towards certain racial groups. It has followed prejudice, not led it. The new parties seek to exploit an existing situation rather than to create one'.[18] In Germany, France, Holland, Belgium, as well as in Britain, the extreme right is using racial prejudice to enlarge its following. The advantage for Le Pen or the British NF is that they do not have the burden of historical guilt that Germans bear, and this enables them to give a freer rein to their views than their Nazi contemporaries in Germany. As, however, a recent book by a journalist who toured Germany disguised as a Turk[19] has shown, there is clearly a wealth of racial prejudice in West Germany on which political extremists could feed. The clash in 1986 between the Christian Democratic government and the Social Democratic opposition concerning legislation to cut the flow of political refugees shows that race is clearly a potentially major political issue in Germany. Similarly in Italy, Arab terrorism has led to a growing rejection of immigrants in general.

The case of Italy is particularly instructive as the reports of racism appear to have come as something of a surprise in a country in which, even during the fascist era, this had not been a major political issue. In fact, during the 1980s, as other countries have tightened up controls on immigration, Italy's frontiers have remained very much open. Immigrants often arrive with tourist visas and then disappear into the 'black' unregulated part of the economy, itself very substantial anyway. As in Germany, employers in agriculture as well as in industry have been attracted by the possibility of employing people on very low wages without coming under pressure to pay for social security, health cover and safe working conditions. Until the 1980s, Italy had been primarily a country of emigration. The absence of a colonial past and the miniscule Jewish population are both factors which help explain the relative weakness of the tradition of political racism so much more deep-rooted in France and Germany.

The first major racist incident came in 1979 when three neo-fascists set fire to the clothes of a Somalian who was asleep in the Piazza Navona. The Somalian burnt to death. In the following decade the total number of immigrants is estimated to have doubled, now reaching a total of between 1 million and 1.5 million. The rapidity of this process explains why those parts of the big cities which have taken so many immigrants are, as in other European cities, an obvious terrain for racist propagandists keen to politicise xenophobia. By the end of the 1980s racist incidents are becoming so regularly reported in the press that there is sometimes a feeling that the media exacerbates the situation. In the spring of 1987, 30 000 residents of the Rome suburb of Ladislopi rebelled against the presence of 'foreigners'. This target included not only Africans and Arabs but also Soviet Jewish refugees and Gypsies. They blocked the streets of their suburb for three days in a successful example of direct action against the establishment of a Gypsy campsite. Many of the Gypsies had come from Yugoslavia producing a situation as in Germany in which there is a clear contradiction between Western Europe's willingness to accept refugees and popular xenophobia in society. In June 1988 there was a national outcry when an Eritrean maid and her twelve-year-old son were thrown off a bus in Rome by a white man who shouted that seats on the bus were reserved for whites. In 1987 a hotel full of immigrants in San Lorenzo was attacked by a mob brandishing guns and breaking windows. No one was prepared to help the police with their inquiries. In 1988 a group of anti-racist activists took legal action against an official in Genoa who had been systematically refusing licences as street salesmen to black people. It was ironic that a sector of economy notorious for tax evasion should have suddenly been prepared to complain against unfair competition. Indeed, such problems do not arise when it comes to allowing people to do dirty jobs illegally in hotels, kitchens, or factories. Here we see the first seeds of the institutional racism which has become so entrenched in other parts of Europe.

Within the MSI a new leader, Fini, had been keen to follow the example of Le Pen and to use immigration as a political campaigning issue. Similarly, in Italy there is conscious emulation of the racism of the British skinheads. The works of Evola and the historical revisionist school are used in Italy even though the country has such a weak tradition of anti-semitism. It may, however, be the case that Italy's body politic is even less inoculated against this kind of propaganda precisely because it has no specifically Italian historical precedent. As we shall see in detail later, the most dramatic actions of the Italian extreme right have been terrorist murders. This is, however, not an entirely separate matter. Maurizio Mirelli, who now publishes neo-Nazi and revisionist pamphlets, has served time in prison for his part in riots in 1973 Milan, during which a policeman was killed. The anti-Semitism of the political activists may be less important than anti-Arab and anti-African racism but it is certainly not to be ignored. Inevitably propaganda that immigrants bring in AIDS and take Italians' jobs is becoming more widespread. Racist slogans are commonplace in football grounds. In December 1987 the Italian writer Umberto Eco was challenged in court when he accused neo-fascist groups of being behind the appearance in Bologna of particularly inflammatory racist graffiti. The magazine which published his article followed up with evidence showing that political agitation was being stepped up by the extreme right.[20] Early in 1990, one of the most outspoken critics of the MSI's flirtation with Le Pen, Pino Rauti, a fascist who has always mistrusted the electoralist strategy, became leader of the party. In the European Parliament, MSI members have echoed Le Pen's views on the issues of immigration and the danger of Europe being undermined by the acceptance of a multiracial destiny.

Altogether the evidence from Italy suggests that with 50 000–100 000 new immigrants expected each year, a political problem of major proportions is only now just beginning to emerge. As in France in the 1970s, the left is dominated by a bitter struggle for dominance, with the socialists growing in strength at the expense of the communists. The possibility that disillusioned voters in a country already facing chronic economic, social, and urban problems (particularly housing) could turn to a party echoing Le Pen's views can no longer be discounted.[21]

The way such social problems can, in particular circumstances, spill over into politics is apparent in many countries. In Antwerp in 1988, 17.7 per cent of the votes in local elections went to an openly racist and extremist party, the Vlaams Blok (Flemish Bloc) which had publicly announced its agreement with Le Pen on the immigration issue. In May 1988 in Denmark, 9 per cent of the votes in a general election went to the Progress Party, which, although originally a populist anti-tax movement, has scored its biggest success following the adoption of the language of racism - complaining that Denmark is becoming a new Lebanon and that political refugees should not be allowed to profit from Denmark's generous social security system. This party now has sixteen MPs in the Danish Parliament. In Norway another Progress Party picked up 13 per cent of the votes in the general election in 1989. Whilst the situation in

Copenhagen, Oslo, Milan, Marseilles, London, and Berlin is certainly very different and each faces distinct economic and social problems, it seems clear that the rise of racism and its effects on the political system cannot be seriously analysed without looking at the European context.

In most European countries, evidence of xenophobia and racist violence has preceded racist political activity. It is for this reason that possible dangers facing European political systems in the 1990s cannot be assessed only by analysing election results or, even, the often very disturbing opinion poll evidence. It is clear that hostility to immigration, rather than anti-Semitism or explicit neo-Nazi or fascist slogans, has provided the extreme right with its best political opportunity for decades. We are not only dealing with a phenomenon present in many parts of Europe but also with something very much linked to the way Western European society is now developing, in particular in terms of the evolution of its population and the plans for the establishment of a single economic area in the 1990s.

The prediction of demographic trends, at least beyond the next couple of decades is an extremely uncertain exercise. It is, however, at present the case that the population of the European Community (EC) was 321 million in 1985; according to United Nations predictions it will be around 331 million in 2010 and 329 million in 2020.[22] During these decades, unless people start having more children, the average age of the population will rise. In this sense immigration will be an advantage for the European economy especially if it is a planned, understood, and accepted fact of European life. If, however, this is not the case the population explosion taking place in Africa, coupled with political instability in developing countries and the attraction of relatively high wages in Europe, could lead to a massive influx of immigrants with inevitable social and political tension. Whilst it is true that the visible minorities are the main targets of racist attacks, the atmosphere is also influenced by other immigrants, most notably refugees, including those from South-East Asia and Eastern Europe. Britain has been only partially affected by this phenomenon in spite of the impression sometimes given in order to justify restrictive policies and the kind of treatment that was reserved for Viraj Mendis, the Sri Lankan refugee who was somewhat unceremoniously expelled in January 1989. In the mid-1980s other European countries were admitting far more refugees, but in reality Europe has taken less than 5 per cent of the total world refugee population. These issues should be faced with objectivity and with a clear rejection of the language of the extreme right.

A. Sivanandan has written of the danger of moving from an 'ethno-centric racism to a Eurocentric racism, from the different racisms of the different members states to a common market racism'.[23] This is certainly a danger and would be consistent with Nazi and fascist philosophy.

The whole 1992 project is sometimes, not unreasonably, presented as a chance for Europe to recover political and economic influence in the world; something which it has certainly lost. However, it is precisely this loss of confidence and self-esteem to which the extreme right appeals. The social problems which the restructuring of Europe's economy will inevitably create will also feed the kind of anxiety about the future to which the extreme right claims to offer a response. European integration will also inevitably lead to the more rapid communication of ideas and symbols, which explains why the racism of the skinheads in Britain or Le Pen in France quickly creates copy-cat movements in other parts of Europe. 1992 must not therefore, be just about enhancing Europe's sense of superiority. It is too early to be either pessimistic or complacent. The international success of movements like 'SOS-Racisme' is itself as significant as the Le Pen phenomenon and, as we shall see, within the European institutions themselves there is a growing awareness of what is at stake. A coherent European response to racism and fascism is needed, not just because these problems reflect issues fundamental to the kind of Europe that will emerge in the 1990s but also because the extreme right itself has its own vision of a united Europe which must be exposed and rejected.

Fascists and the European Idea

The idea of European Union has rarely been used as a mobilising slogan, although outside Britain and Scandinavia it has been broadly supported by most political parties, even if in a rather nebulous fashion. In Italy and in other countries, extreme-right groups use the European idea as part of their political graffiti. The common symbol of the Celtic cross can be found in publications and banners and on walls throughout Europe. Other Europe-wide political movements have spent years trying unsuccessfully to find common symbols and slogans for use, for example, during European Parliament election campaigns. In some respects the extreme right have had fewer difficulties.

The idea of Europe has been constantly present in fascist propaganda since the 1940s. Oswald Mosley's journal was called *The European*. In 1944 the magazine *Nouvel Europe* (NEM) was founded in Belgium. It is still published, and serves as a convenient link between extreme right-wing writers and the extreme fringes of more traditional political parties, like the Christian Democrats and liberals. It campaigns against both capitalism and Marxism. Its editor is on the editorial board of the publication of GRECE based in France.[24] A constant theme of their work is the need for a renaissance of Europe.

In Spain the same sort of function is performed by CEDADE (Circulo Español de Amigos de Europa), supposedly a documentation centre for studies on Europe, but in fact a meeting place of Spanish and European fascists. As was confirmed by the European Parliament's Committee of Inquiry,[25] it was founded in West Germany in 1965 by leading personalities from the Hitler and Mussolini regimes. The 1983 report of West Germany's Office for the Protection of the Constitution stated that:

> Links between Spanish right wing extremists and their counterparts in Germany and Western Europe went primarily through 'Circulo Español de Amigos de Europa' (CEDADE) which despatched neo-Nazi propaganda material to the Federal Republic of Germany. On the 50th anniversary of Hitler's accession to power on 30 January, CEDADE published under the title '50th anniversary of national socialism' a special issue which was also distributed in the Federal Republic. [p. 150]

This organisation still apparently serves as a publishing house or other Nazi groups and its own publications propound 'pan-Europeanism' as well as anti-Semitism.

In France in 1951 two former SS men (one French and one Swiss)[26] started the New European Order, which published the *Combat Européen*. Among the constituent elements of France's National Front is the Faisceaux Nationalistes Européens (FNE, formerly FANE), a neo-Nazi organisation which campaigns explicitly in favour of fascism and 'European nationalism'. Its publication *Notre Europe* (*Our Europe*) reports regularly about neo-Nazi activities in different European countries. It has not hidden its links with German neo-Nazis such as Michael Kuhnen.

The idea of Europe is not just a convenient cover for continuing contacts among extremists. It is a key element in the continuity and coherence of post-war fascist thought and action drawing as it does on national socialist ideals of a European brotherhood and crusades against both communism and decadent democracy. The idea is that Europe should be liberated from the double domination of the USA and the Soviet Union, and in this way the European race could be purified from these external multiracial influences. The combination of nationalism and Europeanism, which many mainstream politicians fail to achieve, thus comes easily to racist and fascist ideologues who see in today's social and economic crises the justification of their original approach. European co-operation between fascists is, therefore, not something new or something particularly difficult or irrelevant to current social and political realities. Ever since the 1940s, when the idea of European unity seemed to many people almost self-evident, it provided a convenient starting point for the first neo-fascist groups. In Sweden, in 1951, the 'European Social Movement' was founded, and then, as we have seen, the New European Order continued on the same theoretical basis. Like CEDADE, this organisation still has branches in various European countries. In the spring of 1986 *Scorpion* in Britain urged its readers to become European in spirit.

The precise issue of the European Community is, of course, different. It was not founded to oppose American hegemony, and it is firmly committed to pluralist democracy and to the free market. In their subtle combination of Europeanism, nationalism, and racism, fascists do not let themselves get distracted by technicalities such as the Treaty of Rome. In many countries they even oppose the process which that Treaty set in motion, or merely refer to it with disdain and to its petty obsessions as confirmation of Europe's crisis of identity.

This version of Europeanism is, of course, a continuation of the pre-war ideology expressed by Hitler and particularly by Strasser. The 1984 report of the German government's Office for Protection of the Constitution points out how much importance has been given to the ideas of Otto and Gregor Strasser, who rivalled Hitler as leaders of Nazism in the 1920s and who saw the whole idea as a form of 'anti-imperialism'. In the 1940s Italian fascist writers like Julius Evola and Adriano Romualdi argued that Europe could never be really united without a revival of fascism. They saw in Hitler's vision of Europe's racial unity a way of overcoming the narrow boundaries of traditional nationalism, and they saw in the French, Danish, Dutch, and Belgian volunteer members of the Waffen SS a proof that Europe could really be united. This is the origin of the idea of a New European Order as a heroic ideal to be dramatically contrasted with the dull routine of European unity Brussels style. In the 1950s the 'Ordine Nuovo' broke with the MSI, arguing that it was not sufficiently anti-American and emphasised its own vision of European independence and unity. In the 1960s Franco Freda, who provided the theoretical justification of the fascist terrorism of the 1970s, appeared to question this vision. He argued[27] that modern fascists had more in common with the popular fighters of Vietnam against the Americans than with the Spanish fascists who were so closely tied to the USA and the Catholic Church. He opposed the Europe of businessmen, Jews and parliamentary democrats, and in his opposition to both Marxism and bourgeois capitalism argued that the first step could come only through a national revolution, to be followed by alliance with genuinely non-aligned anti-imperialist countries.

In the 1980s the almost permanent crisis of the EC seemed to confirm that Europe is still not sure what role it should play in the world, and that there is an unresolved problem of how to assure economic development within the limits to growth of the modern economy and the modern nation state. The adoption of the 1992 target itself provides the extreme right with another issue on which to mobilise and to campaign for their vision of a racially pure and united Europe.

The problems of European political integration were very precisely foreseen by Sir Oswald Mosley, who from the 1940s advocated a form of European nationalism, without running away from the fact that this would not be possible without a supranational European state. This would, of course, be a corporate state as Mussolini had instituted, but there would be both a European Parliament and a European government. This was in tune with what a lot of people in the 1940s were saying, even following the total defeat of Hitler and Mussolini, after which overt glorification of their arms and methods could not be openly expressed. Hitler had failed in his attempt to lead Europe in its resistance to domination by the new superpowers of the USA and the Soviet Union because his methods had been wrong. He should have used political methods, appealing to a genuine European idealism. Mosley saw in European Union a voluntary framework in which both socialism and mercantilism would function. In October 1948 he proposed that as a first step to the creation of 'Europe a Nation' there should be elections based on universal suffrage for a European assembly. Unlike the timid European leaders of the 1970s who eventually arranged such elections, he cut through all the squabbles about a common electoral procedure, arguing that 'every European shall be able to vote for any other European'. Mosley had apparently come around to the view that fascism had been too nationalistic and that the decline of Europe would continue unless a new European patriotism could be born. The racist element remains in this vision, as it does today, as Mosley was assuming that Africa would remain under European control and European greatness would be apparent from its continuing enslavement of the black people who inhabit it. Indeed, Mosley in 1948 endorsed a form of 'genuine' apartheid to be organised on a continental scale. As Robert Skidelsky has observed, Mosley's vision of European unity had its origins in Mussolini's propaganda of the 1940s, and, for example, the manifesto of Mussolini's Republic of Salò, which called for the creation of a European Community.[28] Giorgio Almirante, formerly deputy chairman of the Group of the European Right in the European Parliament, was head of the private office of the Minister of Propaganda of the Salò Republic.

It is interesting to note that in spite of Mosley's rather modest role in post-war British and European politics, his writings meant that he was a respected figure on the extreme right. Like Gelli and Skorzeny (with whom he was in contact), he met Peron. He met Julio Valerio Borghese, who, with P2 backing, was later to attempt a coup in Italy. He got to know Almirante. His memoirs reveal that he was impressed by the appreciation of his ideas about Europe which he received from SS veterans. In 1962 he met MSI leaders, as well as German and Belgian fascists, in Venice.[29] Were these activities those of a man completely out of touch with political reality, or just one who was like many 'idealistic' about European unity, and just a little ahead of his time? For as time has passed, new circumstances have led to a revival of many of the ideas he and others were associated with, even if for reasons of presentation the fact of historical continuity is not emphasised by those who now carry on the struggle against what they see as the decline of Europe.

Notes

1. See Tom Bower, *Blind Eye to Murder*, (André Deutsch, 1981).
2. See L. de Hoyos, *Barbie* (W.H. Allen, 1985).
3. See G. Piazzesi, *Gelli* (Garzanti, 1983).
4. See Bower, op. cit.
5. See Martin Walker, *The National Front* (Fontana, 1977), pp. 25-6.
6. See Paul Wilkinson, *The New Fascists* (Pan, 1983), p. 55.
7. Richard Stöss, 'The European Problem of Right-wing extremism in West Germany' *West European Politics* II, 2, April 1988 p. 38
8. The *Guardian*, 1 February 1987.
9. *Financial Times*, 14 January 1989.
10. D. Evrigenis, *Report of the European Parliament Committee of Inquiry into Racism and Fascism* (January 1986, European Parliament Doc. A2–160/85).
11. See Wilkinson, op. cit. p. 66.
12. See Anne Dummett, Document presented to the European Parliament Committee of Inquiry *Evrigenis Report* Annexe 4, C1.
13. See *Dix ans de Combat culturel pour une Renaissance*, published by *GRECE*, Editions 'La Source D'or', Paris, 1977.
14. See Stephen Rosen, Document presented to the European Parliament Committee of Inquiry, *Evrigenis Renort* Annexe 4, pp. 1-5.
15. See *Scorpion,* Spring 1986.
16. See *The Extreme Right in Europe and the United States*, Anne Frank Foundation, 1985, pp. 18–23.
17. See Bower op. cit. p. 394.
18. Richard Thurlow, *Fascism in Britain 1918-1985* (Blackwell, 1987, p. 275 ff.
19. See Anne Dummett, Document presented to the European Parliament Committee of Inquiry, *Evrigenis Report* Annexe 4, p. 1.
20. Gunter Wallraff, *The Lowest of the Low*, (Methuen, 1988).
21. *L'Espresso* 12, April 1987 and 6, December 1987.
22. Giorgio Bocca, *Gli Italiani sono razzisti?*, Garzanti, 1988.
23. *L'Europe Multiraciale*, Documents Observateur No.4, February 1989 p. 160.
24. A. Sivanandan, 'The new racism', *New Statesman* 4 November 1988.
25. See Anne Frank Foundation, *The Extreme Right in Europe* pp. 43–4.
26. *Evrigenis Report* para. 161.
27. See M.J. Chombart de Lauwe, Document presented to the European Parliament Committee of Inquiry, *Evrigenis Report* Annexe 4, p. B4.
28. See Franco Ferraresi *et al. La Destra Radicale* Feltrinelli, Milan, 1984, p. 39.
29. See Robert Skidelsy, *Oswald Mosley*, Macmillan, 1975, p. 484.
30. See Serge Dumont, 'L'ordre noir', EPO, Brussels, p. 183.

Two

The Borders of Right-Wing Extremism

The absence of clear dividing lines between different historical periods is reflected in the absence of clear lines of demarcation between political ideas and movements. It has become commonplace for left-wing parties to be denounced for excessive tolerance towards extremists on their fringes. This is not an imaginary problem, as the recent history of the Labour Party in Britain has shown, but it should not be assumed that extremist activists and ideas do not pose similar problems at the other end of the political spectrum. As John Tomlinson has shown[1] political extremism is a problem, even in a country like Britain with a long history of political stability and parliamentary democracy. He argues that an attempt should be made to recognise the distinction between 'radicality' and extremism' . He sees the extremists as those whose critique of society is revolutionary rather than reformist. Extremists do not really expect to convince a majority of their views but adopt a strategy which is either extra-democratic or even anti-democratic. In a democratic society revolutionaries can only hope to succeed in a period of major crisis and upheaval. In the meantime they are obliged to adopt a strategy which is 'parasitic, exploitative and provocative'.[2]

In this sense they live off and alongside broader political movements or certain widely held feelings, and at the same time undertake actions, such as the fomenting of violence or the circulation of propaganda, which they hope will create greater sympathy for them in public opinion at large, or win them recruits. Just as revolutionary socialists have attempted to hide behind the broad democratic legitimacy provided by membership of the Labour Party in Britain, so groups on the far right of the Conservative Party are the targets for infiltration. The problem of defining the borders of extremism, in this case right-wing extremism, cannot, however, be solved in terms of neat dividing lines. Indeed, even if infiltration is no doubt practised by extremist groups, what is more obviously a cause for concern is the convergence of views on certain issues between extremists and others who would not naturally be defined as belonging to this category. If the would-be revolutionary socialist groups in Britain can be described as parasites dishonestly seeking legitimacy within a democratic socialist party, this image does not in practice apply so simply to right-wing extremism. For example, the conscious exploitation of neo-fascist terrorists by parts of the Italian establishment groups in the P2 lodge was something quite different from a parasitical relationship. Similarly, the way in which mainstream politicians play on anti-immigrant xenophobia to win the votes at election time of those who have swallowed the ideas of racist propagandists reverses this image completely. Simplistic models that equate all kinds of extremism do not, in fact, improve our understanding of what is really going on in society or in the body politic. This does not mean that the threat of totalitarianism is not present at both ends of the political spectrum, but this reality alone does not explain why right-wing extremist ideology should have proved so durable. Racism is only a part of this ideology but it is central to it and Dr Martin Luther King was quite right to see it as a form of cancer which, if not controlled, destroys society. Such a cancer can be destroyed only by conscious moves to eradicate it, not by attempts to try to live with it, or, worse, to use it to sustain a supposedly democratic political movement. The experience of Britain is particularly instructive.

On the one hand there has been since the late 1960s a conscious attempt by members of the National Front (NF) and others to infiltrate the Conservative Party. When Enoch Powell launched his anti-immigration tirade in 1968 he was supported by mass demonstrations obviously organised by extreme right-wing political activists. At that time he was a leading member of the Conservative Party, but was disowned by his party leader Edward Heath. In the last twenty years, however, the Conservative Party has evolved, and the young man who attended an MSI Conference apparently on behalf of the Monday Club is now a Conservative MP. Even more important than all the talk of 'Maggie's Militant Tendency' is the way Mrs Thatcher took the votes which the NF had been building up during the 1970s, using a major pre-election speech in 1979 to express her sympathy with those she said felt 'swamped' by an excessively large wave of immigration. In 1979 the Labour Government fought the general election having been forced into a defensive position on the race issue. In January 1990 Norman Tebbit, a disillusioned ally of Mrs Thatcher, rejected the possibility of any immigration from Hong Kong, pointedly referring to her 1979 speech.

Racism as an electoral strategy

The impact of Mrs Thatcher's remarks on the extreme right was dramatically illustrated by the revelations from Ray Hill about life inside an extreme right-wing party.[3] He estimates that by 1977 the NF had built up a membership of around 20 000 at a time when the party had been able to get over 10 per cent in some local elections. In stopping this remarkable progress, the remarks of Mrs Thatcher appeared to have had as important an impact as the activists of anti-Nazi groups. The ground was cut from under the feet of the NF at a stroke and the Conservatives improved their image with a part of the electorate which Heath had, perhaps unwittingly, lost through his open denunciation of Enoch Powell. In the 1979 general election, the NF's vote declined dramatically. In a careful study of this phenomenon by Marian Fitzgerald for the Runnymede Trust,[4] attention was drawn to the way in which the main political parties in Britain have fished for racist votes. This factor has been accentuated by a feeling that the 'black vote'is of secondary importance. Inner city riots and concern about law and order can be used to appeal indirectly to racist sentiments. Labour's leaders have handled the 'Black Sections' issue with remarkable insensitivity, perhaps calculating that alienating black activists will cost Labour less votes than would have occurred had some compromise on the issue been arranged.

Not only did the Conservative Party raise its profile on the race issue at the end of the 1970s but, having become the party of government, they maintained a line on race and immigration issues which has effectively prevented any revival of the electoral fortunes of the NF or any other extreme-right party. A new Nationality Act was passed in 1981. As Christopher Husbands[5] has pointed out, by 1983 Labour was in such disarray that, having the advantage of the Falklands victory, the Conservatives did not need the race issue in the General election of that year. In the run-up to the 1987 election, specific measures were taken to show that the Conservatives were sticking to a hard line on immigration. New visa requirements, designed to discourage refugees, proved an effective policy. Local labour councils were denounced for their positive efforts to deal with rising racism in the big cities. The NF has thus been deprived of any significant political opportunity, but, in the light of this analysis and the experience of other countries where racism remains a potentially important political issue, it is not hard to imagine the consequences of a change of government policy, especially if in the 1990s a new Conservative leader were to adopt a less strident tone on the race issue.

In the post-Thatcher era the experience of France will be very relevant, as it is clear that extremists have benefitted from the disarray on the right in a period of socialist rule and have succeeded in making a major impact on electoral politics. In January 1988 Jacques Chirac launched his Presidential Election campaign with a commitment to a referendum on the reform of the nationality laws in order to make it harder for immigrants to become French citizens. A more provocative and divisive issue for a national referendum would be hard to imagine, but it was clear that the RPR Presidential candidate was trying to cut the ground from under Le Pen in the way Mrs Thatcher had done to her own extremist competitors in 1979. An unwillingness to risk losing votes to Le Pen was already apparent in the 1986 elections for the National Assembly. In a televised debate between the then socialist Prime Minister Laurent Fabius and Jacques Chirac it was impossible not to notice how the socialist speaker purposely passed up the opportunity to challenge in any way the tough remarks of Chirac about law and order, and immigration. In this way a new consensus could be seen to emerge as efforts were made to take votes from Le Pen and to avoid losing votes by saying anything that might offend the xenophobic sentiments in the wider electorate. Indeed, Fabius perhaps unintentionally accepted the view that criminality and immigration go together in arguing that the socialists had already sufficiently strengthened the law to deport people who were a threat to public order and security. Later he expressed understanding for those who criticised his presentation of these issues.

In the next chapters we look at the Le Pen phenomenon in France as the most dramatic illustration of the strength and potential of the extreme right, and at right-wing terrorism. It should, however, be stressed that racism and terrorism are not ends in themselves. They are used by extremists in an attempt to create the conditions in which they would hope to be able to widen their support amongst the population at large. Moreover, since the relative success of extremists is a reflection of a crisis in society, the analysis of the strengths of right-wing extremism cannot clearly be limited to adding up election results or estimating the number of paid-up members or activists that different movements can rely upon. In most countries racism has been the main source of support for these movement and precisely because not all racists are by any means right-wing extremists or fascists it is essential not to underestimate the importance that the propagation of racist ideas can have for the functioning of democracy and the development of political parties and society in general. In this sense it is clear that the rise of the extreme right is a reflection of deeper problems which should not be ignored just because the chances of the extreme right itself taking power at present seem so remote. This is all the more necessary given that, in the 1980s, there has been a strengthening of right-wing parties in general leading to an almost total eradication of the social democratic dominance of Western Europe in the 1960s and 1970s.

Since the late 1960s there has been a conscious cultural revival by what has become known as the 'new right' in a number of continental countries. In Britain and the USA there has been a dramatic recovery in the electoral strength of conservative parties, and within these parties there has been a clash between the traditional leadership and what have become known as 'neo-conservatives' most dramatically and effectively represented Mrs Thatcher. It would be a mistake to assimilate all these phenomena – the new right, neo-conservatism, the extreme right, neo-fascism – as if they were all part of a single body of thought. On the other hand, the differences should not be stressed to an extent which becomes artificial. It has been argued that one of the most significant developments in the last twenty years has, in fact, been the trend towards the elimination of such differences. Although democratic conservatives or Christian Democrats have quite clearly rejected the European fascist tradition, there are still many issues on which the right as a whole can be seen to be quite united. For example, it was not, at first, the natural reaction of many German Christian Democrats or Belgian Liberals to isolate Le Pen totally when he arrived in the European Parliament. Similarly, where governments have adopted tough policies to restrict immigration and encourage repatriation they have, in fact, responded to campaigns initially launched by the extreme right. In the opposite direction, Le Pen has sought to combine his appeal to the French traditions of racism and xenophobia with an adoption of enthusiastic support for Reagan and Thatcher and their liberal free-market economics. On the one hand, we see mainstream parties trying to occupy all or part of the electoral territory of the extreme right; on the other, we see the extreme right seeking respectability by trying to adopt part of the package of the neo-conservatives. The relationship could prove extremely unhealthy for European society.

This is particularly the case given the extent of racism and xenophobia in contemporary Europe. The relationship between xenophobia, racism, and incitement to racism is extremely difficult to define. Race, itself, is a concept which defies definition. In fact, there is no scientific justification for the view that within the human race as a whole, different races actually exist. The concept of different races is something human beings have constructed in their own minds. If, however, races do not exist this does not mean that racism is therefore an imaginary problem. In this context racism is taken as the claiming of superiority by one identifiable group over another. Where the claim is based on political, social or cultural differences clearly it is not an issue of racism. Where, however, the claim to superiority is based on imagined innate characteristics resulting from the biological or genetic origins of a particular part of the human race, racism can be said to be apparent. Dialogue between racists and anti-racists is often almost impossible precisely because the former use the term race as if it were, in fact, a meaningful biological concept. As Stephen Rose has explained,[6] racists see the term race as a purely technical one which can be used to differentiate between different 'subgroups of a species characterised by a particular set of gene frequencies'. They see that races are definable to the extent that there are real and meaningful boundaries preventing interbreeding. The scientific basis of racism is questionable as an objective means of analysis but in practice racism is a way of seeing society and the world and therefore race is a social description since the contrasts between people of different colours, nations, or social origins cannot be defined in terms of biology. Racism is, of course, not the only political theory based on a spurious scientific foundation. In many periods of history different ideas are presented as the unchallengeable and unalterable truth, and in that sense racism is not unique.

Since the nineteenth century, when the ideas of Darwin became current, there has been a constant interchange between political ideas and supposedly objective scientific writing. Racism most conveniently provided a moral basis for slavery and colonialism just as today the anguish of individuals or sections of society can be suddenly removed as people convince themselves that racist ideas permit certain political or social actions. It is precisely because the supposedly scientific basis of racism was well established long before Hitler emerged on the scene that his political programme could gain acceptance. Similarly, the rehabilitation of such ideas in recent years does not mean that Nazism will dramatically re-emerge, but it does mean that political debate is bound to be influenced if the basic tenets of racism gain wide acceptance as scientifically valid. This can be seen from the way that ideas about differences in IQ level identified by scientists are taken up by politicians. Le Pen has achieved success through a careful use of such ideas combined with historical revisionism and open appeals to xenophobia. Inside 'new right' publications, attempts to rehabilitate scientific racism are taking place. The argument is that the decline of Europe is precisely the result of refusing to recognise the supposed realities of differences between races. The new right, therefore, sees itself as leading a crusade for the renaissance of Europe free from the polyglot influences of multi-racial USA, Marxism, and racial intermingling. Their theories can be conveniently combined with arguments about wasteful public expenditure. For if the ideas about IQ differences between races are accepted then social or educational policies aimed at providing equal opportunities for all are really a dishonest waste of money. In Western Europe the argument that men and women should be treated as complete equals has become widely accepted only in the last few decades, and even here social and economic realities lag far behind legal and constitutional provisions. Stephen Rose quoted[7] Enoch Powell who argued passionately that 'societies can be destroyed by teaching themselves myths that are inconsistent with the nature of man', and Patrick Jenkin, a British Cabinet Minister in the 1980s responsible for social policy who was convinced that 'if the Lord had intended us to have equal rights to go to work he would not have created men and women'. When Ronald Reagan and Margaret Thatcher attack the 'race relations industry' as if special laws and institutions were just a waste of money designed to featherbed bureaucratic careerists, they echo the language and philosophy of racist extremists who also consider 'anti-racism' as an aberration. It is words like these which provide encouragement for those on the political fringes who base their whole approach to politics on what they see as a scientifically justified natural order. They also influence public opinion more generally to sympathise with such ideas. Indeed, the extreme right draws much of its inspiration from writers who are considered academically quite respectable but take their ideas to their logical conclusion in a way which mainstream politicians would not do. This means, in practice, that racist ideas can gain much wider credence than can be judged by merely looking at levels of support of parties openly campaigning on a racist platform.

It is hardly surprising that there should be in modern Europe a sense of racial superiority towards people from continents which only a few decades ago were parts of Empires controlled from one or other European country. Indeed, the decline of these empires is one of the salient political facts of European political history in this century; as important if not more important than, the nationalism that led to two world wars. Moreover, it is the disappearance of these empires which many of the right regret. Some consider that a united Europe could lead to a recovery of that dominance. It is not apparent, for example, that in the 1960s much of the strength of the extreme right in France came from those who felt deeply the loss of French colonies in North Africa. It might be assumed that as time passes such inevitable nostalgia will become less potent, but this is not necessarily the case. The rapid evolution of European society in the post-war and post-colonial era creates an inevitable crisis of change and uncertainty in which it is appealing to look back to earlier, supposedly more satisfactory, situations. Mrs Thatcher frequently refers to Victorian values, unfortunately overlooking the fact that this was an era of mass poverty, imperialism, and extremely painful social change. Racism feeds precisely on people's distorted vision of a world and a sense of having been cheated of the dominance to which they feel entitled. It is, therefore, clear that support for some kind of European renaissance based on racism has support well beyond the confines of the extreme right which first took up the idea early in the twentieth century.

Racism can, of course, take very different forms: racialism and prejudice by individuals; institutional racism, whereby organs of the state are seen to discriminate between different parts of society. Racism is, therefore, a much larger phenomenon than the political threat posed by parties openly practising racial incitement and encouraging racial hatred. It is not my purpose here to try and measure the dimensions of this problem. It has, however, without doubt, decisively worsened since the onset of the economic crisis in the mid-1970s. Mass unemployment has created despair and insecurity amongst millions of Europeans, and many Governments have felt obliged to carry out cuts in social welfare provisions. In such circumstances the presence of ethnic and cultural minorities has offered a ready scapegoat for a whole range of social problems: rising crime, lack of housing, unemployment, health service problems,and so on. Le Pen is not the only politician to have consciously played upon the anxieties inevitably developing in such a situation. The political strength of the extreme right is as much a matter of concern as the climate of racial violence which has developed in many parts of Europe. Different minorities have faced disturbingly similar problems. The blacks in Britain, the Turks in Germany, even the Vietnamese in many countries, including Ireland, have been the victims of racial violence, part of which is politically motivated and organised. This is an unfortunate social and political reality in many European countries.

In Austria, for example, whilst there is only weak and sporadic organised right-wing extremism, there is growing xenophobia. It is not always expressed openly although polls have shown growing hostility to foreigners even whilst the number of foreign workers in the country has been declining. It is the deteriorating economic situation which explains the evolution of part of public opinion. Xenophobia remains an example of irrational prejudice, since the relatively limited areas of unemployment to have emerged in Austria are not those where many foreign workers are involved. Foreign workers have been employed mainly in unskilled jobs not affected by the crisis. In 1989 a Socialist-Christian Democratic coalition faced a major electoral challenge as the extremist wing of the Liberal Party under the leadership of Jörg Haider used nationalism as an effective basis for major electoral advance.

In Holland racial violence and the activities of racist political organisations are also part of a much wider problem. In particular, there has emerged an implicit consensus that the minorities are, by definition, problematic, troublesome, and superfluous. The authorities condemn violent racist incidents and the activities of overtly racist organisations, but at the same refuse to recognise the extent to which racism is profoundly rooted in society. In this context Philomena Essed, a Dutch writer[8], has stressed the importance of racism as an everyday experience for people from minority groups. Indeed, their perception of the extent of racism in society is probably a more helpful guide than any opinion survey. Expressions of racism are thus perceived in all aspects of normal life: looking for a home or a job; relations with colleagues and neighbours; how one is treated in shops or on public transport. Racism in these contexts can be just as upsetting as reading racist slogans on the walls of your home, or being harrassed as you walk the street, let alone the extreme experience of being the victim of a racially motivated physical assault. All these incidental examples of racism are a reflection on the state of society and a signal to their target that they are unwanted. From this point of view different examples of racism: political speeches, actions by officials or the police force, discrimination — are part of a whole. It is in this context of a major social problem that the extreme right undertakes its political activities. In Holland there is an active extreme right-wing political party, the Centrum Partij, which argues a very simple line: '500 000 foreigners in our country and 500 000 unemployed'. A similar slogan was used in the 1930s and again today by the Front National in France. Within this party there is a hard core of convinced Nazis, but around them exists a heterogeneous range of members and supporters. Their racist political activity takes place in the social context described by Philomena Essed. Whilst their ideas reflect a feeling across a wide range of society, politically they are not considered respectable particularly because of their connection with Nazism. Precisely because the situation in Holland is not so dramatic as in Britain, Germany, France or Italy, it is perhaps a better illustration of the extent of sympathy for racist ideas in Western Europe today.

A similar picture emerges from Gunter Wallraff's book about his experiences when he disguised himself as a Turk in order to experience the realities of West German society.[9] He finds himself working in conditions of great danger, where safety regulations are ignored, trade unions are of little value, job security is non-existent, and where his German co-workers often do not hesitate to insult or to discuss in front of him the pros and con'¹s of Hitler's final solution. On the walls of factories where he works he has to bear the additional humiliation of seeing slogans about 'Germany for the Germans' and so on. Again, a picture emerges of extreme racist sentiment and of a society that treats immigrants with contempt even if electoral support for parties which say precisely what many people think is limited possibly because, unlike in France, the taboos of the post-war years cannot yet, if ever, be completely lifted. In other European countries the resurgence of fascist ideas follows long periods in which discrimination and hostility to foreigners has become commonplace. It is a product of prejudice, not its source.

The issues of migrant workers, immigrants, and other visible minorities are complex ones. It is, however, impossible to deny from these examples in different European countries that hostility to immigrants has had a major influence on government policies since the 1960s. In the years of crisis since 1970 racism has, however, increased in violence and political potency, in spite of attempts to pander to it. This does not mean that the extreme right enjoys inordinate influence. What it does mean is that racism remains endemic in European society, it can be politically exploited, and most often the response of governments has been to take it into account rather than to join actively in efforts to eradicate it. Since they know the economic reasons which brought so many migrants to Europe; since it is also obvious that because the migrants are doing jobs others do not want to do; and since many migrants are settled permanently in Europe, the response of much of the political establishment is both dishonest and short-sighted since it cannot be possible to destroy racism or even limit it by accepting the central arguments put forward by racist politicians.

This is particularly true of Britain, where immigration controls were introduced in the early 1960s, to some extent as a response to violent riots against black people partly sponsored by Nazi sympathisers. Sending all the blacks home was not really a practical proposition or acceptable to Britain's liberal conscience. Britain has seen both voting rights given to immigrants and anti-discrimination laws, but unfortunately more significant has been nationality legislation and immigration laws which affect only a relatively small number of people but are designed precisely to assuage the hostility to immigrants of a substantial element of public opinion. As Anne Dummett has put it, immigration controls are only meaningful politically if they operate on 'the assumption that the fewer black people there are in the country, the better'.[10] This is precisely the point made in every extreme-right pamphlet or slogan; it is the heart of their appeal and governments may find that if social problems continue in spite of immigration controls they have merely fed the flames of racism.

A dramatic example of the way extremist ideas and language can become part of the common currency of politics came in the 1987 Belgian General Election campaign. Joseph Michel, a Christian Democratic Minister, was quoted as having told an interviewer that the Belgian people were 'facing the risk of befalling the same fate as the Roman Empire which had been overwhelmed by barbarians'. In the case of Belgium this was meant to refer to 'Moroccans, Turks, and the Islamic people'. When the surprised journalist asked if he was serious, he replied: 'I cannot call them anything else. They are people who come from a long way away, who have nothing in common with our civilization'.[11] When news of this extraordinary outburst broke, the Minister's office first denied the quotation, but, when tapes were played on Belgian radio, he confirmed what he had said but insisted that he was using the word in an etymological sense to refer to people who were different, and therefore did not intend to express hostility to anyone. He was sorry if anyone had felt personally offended. As protests poured in from embassies in Brussels, the Minister apologised, but it was clear that he had given a signal that racism had entered the political mainstream. These remarks were particularly deplorable as they came in a country plagued by xenophobia and racist violence, where, for example, people booking taxis often insist that their driver should not be an immigrant.

The significance of the Minister's words was not lost on the extreme right, which immediately circulated leaflets inviting the public to mass rallies under the slogan 'Stop the Barbarians'. This is a classic example of how irresponsible remarks by supposedly respectable politicians provide encouragement and a sense of legitimacy to the extreme right. In the 1987 Belgian general elections the extreme right did well in Flanders and, as we have seen, followed this up with even greater successes in the 1988 municipal elections. In the June 1989 Euro-elections the firm implantation of the extreme right in parts of Flanders enabled the Vlaamse Block (VB) to elect its first member of the European Parliament. This party is the direct political descendent of the prewar Nazi 'New Order' movement, and, following its first electoral successes, the VB became the umbrella under which various militant extremist groups could gather and, indeed, hide. The Party, whose main successes came in Antwerp, where it took 17.7 per cent in the October 1988 local elections, based its programme on Flemish nationalism and popular racism. Antwerp is a city with a large immigrant and Jewish population (in spite of the holocaust) and so the new and old versions of political racism could be conveniently and effectively combined in the propaganda of the VB. By June 1989 the VB had achieved a 100 per cent increase in support during a twelve-month period and took 214 000 votes in the Euro-elections. Like the FN and the REP, the VB claims to have 'humane and responsible' policies for repatriation of immigrants. Like the REP in Bavaria, the VB draws on a strong desire for regional independence. The local socialist MEP, Marijke Van Hemmeldonck, who had lost many members of her family in the holocaust and who had served on the European Parliament Committee of inquiry, saw the VB's success as part of the explanation for the relatively poor result achieved by the Flemish Socialists. As in other countries, it was clear that the level of support for the extreme right varied considerably in different localities and its appeal was less significant in areas where immigration was not a major concern.

The response of the Prime Minister, the Flemish Christian Democrat Wilfred Martens, was to encourage greater efforts to build up racial harmony in his country. This contrasts with the approach of many Liberal and even Christian Democrat leaders in the French-speaking part of Belgium, Wallonia. In this region there have been only limited electoral successes for the extreme right as the mainstream right-wing parties have been openly competing for the racist vote. In one commune of Brussels, the Mayor, Roger Nols, has actually provoked riots by taking part in a public meeting with Le Pen. British Liberals were embarrassed when it was pointed out in 1984 that Nols was standing for the European Parliament on the Belgian Liberal Party list. Certainly, these episodes show how difficult it is to establish the frontiers between the extreme right and some other political parties. Chirac and Thatcher, albeit with little more sophistication, have also played on xenophobic fears during election campaigns, probably without realizing the way in which their electoral opportunism can damage society. Perhaps they are unaware just how much modern European society and democracy is in danger of being undermined by racism.

Their words and the immigration controls which such politicians always emphasise as the answer to the 'problem' confirm prejudice, encourage xenophobia, and provide encouragement to extremist groups. Immigration is seen as a negative fact not a result of economic necessity or an opportunity for cultural enrichment, let alone as a frequently repeated historical phenomenon. Anne Dummett explained to the European Parliament inquiry how racist violence erupted in Britain in the early 1960s and how this was immediately followed by the first significant immigration controls. These were designed to stop racism, but in fact proved to be an encouragement and legitimisation precisely because immigration controls inevitable make those immigrants who have settled already feel unwanted, or at best, outsiders. Racists then take up the campaign for repatriation. Whilst planned immigration is necessary, racism cannot be challenged by policies which are themselves motivated by or are at least a response to racism amongst the electorate.

Similar developments have occurred in West Germany, where the popular press has continued to encourage people to believe that German culture is being swamped or diluted by foreigners. Simplistic linkages are made between unemployment and immigration. In 1982 the Social Democrat–Liberal coalition took measures to reduce or delay arrival of migrants' dependents. Inevitably this led the opposition parties, the CDU/CSU, to press for tougher measures. The implementation of this legislation was accompanied by a wave of racial violence against the Turkish workers. The German government has continued with a very high-profile tough policy, particularly with regard to political refugees. Some Turks were sent back to face jail or torture, and in one dramatic incident a young Turkish refugee committeed suicide by throwing himself out of the window of a Berlin courtroom where he was facing a deportation hearing. Another example of the insidious relationship between racial violence and irresponsible politicians who refuse to confront it, came in December 1985 after a group of skinheads brutally murdered a young Turk in Hamburg. Rather than denounce racism, the Hamburg CDU preferred to see the attack as nothing more than 'normal' juvenile criminal delinquency. Closer observation of developments in Germany and in other countries confirms that xenophobia and racial violence reflect widespread racist sentiment which some politicians prefer not to offend.

The insidious way in which extremism can poison democratic politics is apparent from the events following the Republicans' electoral success in Berlin at the beginning of 1989. Attention quickly turned to local elections in the state of Hesse, where the even more openly neo-Nazi NPD presented the extremist challenge. The German Interior Minister, Zimmerman, explicitly accepted in the run up to the vote that the only way to halt the rising tide of hostility to foreigners was to restrict the flow, especially of those illegally seeking asylum. The political atmosphere in West Germany had been seen to change dramatically between January and March 1989, when the vote in Hesse took place. Daniel Cohn-Bendit, now a leading Green Party figure, wept in public as a sign of his shock at being the object of open anti-Semitic denunciations.

The NDP is now led by a thirty-six-year-old former Luftwaffe captain Udo Voigt, who based the Hesse campaign on attacking the SPD's positive attitude to immigration. The Christian Democrats attempted to stop the slide to the NDP by adopting a similar approach. Within Germany, and within the European Parliament, they rejected the right of immigrants to vote. The tactic failed dramatically. On 12 March the NDP got 6.6 per cent and elected seven councillors to the Frankfurt City Council. By accepting some of their arguments, the Christian Democrats had only provided a helping hand to extremists and as in France, the only immediate result was an electoral victory for the left.

Tensions within democratic conservative parties

The frontiers of the extreme right also extend into the political mainstream through phenomena other than racism. The role of secret societies such as the P2 lodge in Italy is only the most dramatic example of co-operation of extremist elements and parts of the establishment. The cultural offensive of 'the New Right' in France is equally significant. In Germany and Austria as well it is hardly surprising that sympathy with Nazi ideas should linger on, since it was into the Christian Democrat and Liberal parties that many Nazi party members moved in the second half of the 1940s. The Austrian Liberal Party (FPO) was formed in 1976. It was based on the 'association of independents', a movement which had served as a rallying point for former national socialists.

There have inevitably been power struggles between the nationalist and liberal sections, with the former successfully resisting attempts to remove from the party manifesto references to the German ethnic and cultural community. There is an overlap between membership of the Liberal Party and that of extreme right groups. It was against this background that a remarkable incident occurred just a few weeks before the fortieth anniversary of the end of the Second World War. Walter Reder, a war criminal and former SS leader, was returned to Austria at the end of his thirty-five year sentence for his responsibility in the mass murder of 1800 people at Marzobotto. On his return home he was quite unexpectedly received personally by the Liberal Minister of Defence, who also arranged for him to be lodged at an Austrian army barracks. The dismay caused by this incident, both in Austria and in Europe more generally, did eventually lead to the Minister's resignation. The nationalist section of the FPO supported the Minister, and the fact that the incident ever occurred is adequate testimony to the way some leading elements in Austrian political life consider the events of the 1930s and 1940s. On 1 February 1985, he narrowly survived (98–80) a vote of censure after he had provided what Austria's Chancellor considered to be a correct, sincere, and honest apology. This apology kept an unhappy coalition in power a little longer in Vienna, but contributed to damaging the country's international reputation. A man in such a senior position would not have acted in such a way towards a convicted war criminal if he had not intended to give a signal to public opinion. Austria is a country where SS veterans' meetings often take place; where brochures denying the holocaust circulate;and where the extreme right has, over the years, kept up international contacts with South Africa, Chile, and the Spanish Falange. The fact that Austria should have elected as President a man who for decades chose to cover up his role in the war years must itself also be disturbing. In this case it would appear that for some voters international concern at the contents of the reports about Waldheim's real military status was itself a provocation rather than a reminder of any need to keep former Nazis out of power. It would even appear that attacks on Waldheim have served only to strengthen his support. It is clear that the country's failure to face up to its own past has not prevented a resurgence of xenophobia and anti-Semitism. The fiftieth anniversary, in 1988, of Germany's takeover of Austria by Hitler was marked with particular ambivalence. Peter Handke,[12] an Austrian author, pointed out that what is disturbing about Waldheim 'is not so much his war record as his moral inadequacy'. Former soldiers apparently 'cannot admit that they were victims of a criminal who led a criminal war'. The tendency to rally round Waldheim as he was attacked and even banned from entering the USA means, in Handke' s words, that 'now there will be no cleansing'.

In trying to estimate the extent to which the views of the extreme right have any credibility beyond the numerous, relatively small, political movements openly committed to Nazism and fascism, it would, unfortunately, be a mistake to look only at those countries where these ideologies were once much stronger. Moreover, it would also be a mistake to imagine that the continuing support for such ideas is a result of the work of those who have, in some sense, kept the faith which inspired them in an earlier historical period. The leadership of the

MSI in Italy was briefly passed to a man in his mid-thirties, a fascist who was not alive during Mussolini's lifetime. The football hooligans or racist bullies who openly wear Nazi insignia are not necessarily operating on the basis of some consciously adopted ideology, but this does not mean that they totally lack political awareness.

The fact that football hooliganism is commonplace in so many parts of Europe cannot be ignored. Not only do the the gangs chant similar racist slogans and carry similar Nazi insignia, there is also clear evidence of international agitation by fascists. Given the overlap and conflict between the revolutionaries and the electoralists, it is hardly surprising in Italy, for example, that the MSI should feel obliged to deny any connection with fascist agitators in football grounds. We are not, moreover, dealing with separate but similar events in different countries. In 1988 a Louvain University professor presented a report to the Belgian Interior Ministry detailing the facts not only about how Belgian hooligans model themselves on their British equivalents but also how they work together, visiting each other's grounds, exchanging views, and meeting on the fringes of political events such as the annual Flemish nationalist rally in Diksmuide. The British NF's 'League of Louts' now also has its European version.

Racist violence and hooliganism are both a reflection of a social problem and the result of political activity. It is no secret that Nazi groups look for recruits in football grounds, and perhaps it is not so surprising given that violent gangs were at one time the original sources of the strength of the Nazi and fascist movements. Among such groups there are all the ingredients for such activity: gangs are based on blind faith and commitment to a particular group; aggression towards strangers; the cult of a strong leader; reliance on brute force; exhibitionism and a feeling of belonging which gang members have perhaps failed to experience in the rest of their lives. Across Europe today there is enough youthful frustration, feeling of marginalisation, insignificance, and isolation – all of which are a response to the modern urban environment – mixed with xenophobia, and sometimes, but not always, with unemployment. It would be much too convenient to dismiss all this as a product of Thatcherite language and economics. It may well be an unfortunate reality that the British Conservative Prime Minister's ideological agenda does appeal to racism and national chauvinism, but it is also the case that the kind of search for a white, male working-class identity is a problem which existed before and will, perhaps to an even more damaging extent, exist after the Thatcher era. Certainly, introducing special controls on access to football grounds will not solve the problem.

Europe is living with explosive material embedded in society. Some observers see in hooliganism a potential following for an authoritarian charismatic leader. No such leaders at present exist and it would be impossible to estimate how serious such a danger might be. Moreover, in a society where violent crime is hardly a rarity, it would' be a mistake to concentrate on this particular phenomenon of football hooligans and take it out of its overall context. For the purposes of our attempt to estimate the existing strength and potential of right-wing extremism it cannot, however, be ignored.

The strength of extreme political views among young people may be greater than imagined. This at least is the message which comes across from a recent study undertaken in Britain by the Economic and Social Research Council (ESRC).[13] Britain is a country where Nazism has never been very strong, except in limited periods and particular social situations. Apart from Mosley, the leadership of the extreme right has never appeared remotely able to provide a credible challenge to the political system. Since the advent of Thatcherism the united electoral strength of the extreme right has evaporated. Professor Harry McGurk of the university of Surrey refers in his introduction to the ESRC report to the 'political innocence, naivety and ignorance of Britain's young people. The overwhelming majority of British youth appear to be politically illiterate. They have no conception of the structure of society, of how the economy works, of the characteristics of different political systems'. Surprisingly, in a period of relative polarisation, they find it hard to see the philosophical or policy differences between the main parties. The report contains a cry of alarm about Britain's education system, which 'allows such ignorance and prejudice to be so widespread among young people', and finds that, as a result of this ignorance, overt racism would appear to be 'endemic among white youth in Britain'. In a society with very high youth unemployment it is hardly surprising that sociological research should reveal that most of the young unemployed see unemployment in terms of the 'failures of the system'. Such a cynical attitude towards politicians and institutions is perhaps inevitable, but the findings of the ESRC research team with regard to adolescents and politics are perhaps more remarkable and more a cause for serious concern. Even among young people identifying themselves as Labour supporters 'racist themes were often intermingled with economic ones'. They felt that times were better when they were younger and when there were fewer non-whites living in Britain. At the same time, some of the support attracted to the centre, including the SDP, reflected a kind of anti-political view that there should anyway be only one party. To the dismay of its leaders the SDP may have attracted support from those who saw it as offering a kind of 'extremism of the centre' in a country where the political system was seen by some to be failing. Most remarkable, however, was the increase from 7 per cent to 14 per cent (between 1979 and 1982) as the level of support for fascist parties (the National Front or the British Movement). If second choices are included, then the 1982 results indicated that over 30 per cent were expressing some sympathy for a fascist party. Again, the statistical aspect is secondary to the light it sheds on the evolution of British society and politics. The ESRC study quite rightly points out that this evolution cannot really be explained as a direct result of the activities of fascist political agitators. Unemployment appears to have been the single most significant factor; on the other hand, this is not the only factor and, indeed, there is no evidence of support for fascist parties being disproportionately higher amongst young people with unemployed parents.

The study would appear to suggest that the fear of unemployment is just part of a more general climate characterised by fear about the future and a lack of positive expectations, with young people showing a particularly high level of political alienation and disillusionment. It is also certain that such disillusionment has not provided any significant level of support for the extreme left. Where young socialists have trouble 'making contact' with working-class youth, the extreme right acts as the spokesman of their gut feelings about their lives and the society in which they are growing up.

The results of this study make it all the more inappropriate to ignore the links between young people's political outlook and the activities of extreme-right activists whose strength is a reflection of the problem. Racist violence in the playground is not a separate phenomenon from co-ordinated extreme-right actions. During the Thatcher years the far right has, anyway, drifted away from overt party politics towards more effective, ways of attracting support. For example, a pop group 'Screwdriver' led by a former NF militant Ian Stuart has organised 'white power' rock concerts where skinheads and Nazi symbols set the tone. Stuart's activities are nothing more than a low-life version of GRECE's attempts at cultural counter-revolution. They accept the limits of nationalism (just as Mosley did) and put the emphasis on European co-operation. As Ian Stuart has put it: 'music is a potent force for putting over our message. I believe we should try to do so on a European scale, as Britain is no longer strong enough to stand alone for the nationalist cause'.[14] His ideal would be a kind of street-based skinhead version of the European Movement. Indeed, as a response to the activities of the left it could be that identification with Nazism becomes the most up-to-date version of youthful rebellion. Reports of co-operation between football hooligans, of international participation in 'rock against communism' concerts, reflect a small part of European political life, but it would be unwise to dismiss these phenomena as insignificant. Unemployment and xenophobia are European phenomena and the incidents of racial violence regularly reported in the British press find their counterparts in other countries. Given this unfortunate reality, it would appear unlikely that the political attitudes highlighted by the ESRC study are in any way unique to Britain.

Alongside the social and economic crisis during which racism and xenophobia have grown, there has been a remarkable revival of the right in Western Europe. There is an overlap between this phenomenon and the activities of extremist groups who see Reagan and Thatcher as having sold out on the right-wing revolution for which they hope and strive. We have already referred to the importance of the overt racism of Enoch Powell in the 1960s. He opened up to public view the deep divisions within the Conservative Party which have been overcome only as a result of the overwhelming dominance of Thatcherism. As David Edgar[15] has put it: 'what is now called Thatcherism was originally known as "Powellism": bitter-tasting market economics sweetened and rendered palatable to the popular taste by great creamy helpings of nationalist custard'. He quotes Peregrine Worsthorne who stated in the *Sunday Teleqraph* of 2 June 1983 that it was to Powell's 'great voice' that credit should go 'for shattering the Butskellite glacis, the dissolution of which led to the avalanche'. It is because Mrs Thatcher reaps such benefits from the activities of Powell, who was at the time the hero of the extreme right, that it is impossible to treat the rise of Thatcherism as something totally distinct from the strengthening of right-wing extremism in recent years. Thatcherism which provides a kind of 'popular authoritarianism' makes unnecessary the activities of P2 type organisations, or those revealed in Peter Wright's book about the attempts by the secret service to destabilise the Wilson administration.

As the new right began its challenge to the consensus politics of Edward Heath, there was a clear overlap between conservative counter-revolutionaries and the extreme right. For example, Mary Whitehouse's campaign against pornography co-operates in London with leading NF sympathisers like Dowager Lady Birdwood. Powell's 1968 'Rivers of Blood' speech was followed in 1972 by Monday Club/National Front co-operation in opposition to the Heath government's acceptance of 30 000 Ugandan Asian immigrants. At this time various organisations of the 'libertarian right' flourished, in which businessmen, intellectuals, former secret servicemen, and politicians co-operated to mount an ideological onslaught on what they saw as the Heath-Wilson consensus. The left, at the time almost totally immersed in internal party conflict, completely ignored this important phenomenon and therefore failed to grasp the significance of the 1979 general election result. They failed to see that the revolution of the 1960s could spark a counter-revolution, and it was not until the. mid-1980s that the successful activities of the Salisbury Group or the National Association for Freedom became apparent. In particular, the idea that many people actually wanted a stronger government to bring order to the country which was perceived as lacking any sense of direction would have been ridiculed in the era of consensus. After a decade of Mrs Thatcher in power it is clear it was precisely this aspect of her appeal that delivered her such a string of victories. At the same time a series of events has enabled the theories of the extreme right to enter the mainstream. Race riots could be blamed on those who had encouraged the 'illusion' of Britain as a multi-racial society. Militant trade unionism appeared to justify a strengthening of the role of the police. The Falklands War provided an opportunity to revel in military glory. A political atmosphere has developed in Britain in which the counter-revolution called for initially by the extreme right is being gradually implemented by a mainstream political party. During the 1980s the Conservative Students Organisation has become the playground for right-wing extremists. In this sense, it is remarkable to observe that at the level of some university students extremist ideas have become as widely acceptable as a simplistic version of fascism has become popular amongst working-class youth. In this context the Falklands War was seen by one Conservative activist as 'the ultimate orgasm' when, finally, these ideologies could find themselves in 'harmony with ordinary people'.

Within the young Tory right there has also been an advance by libertarians with ideas about legalising heroin or lowering the age of consent for homosexuality. Their view is that the individual should be given virtually complete responsibility for his or her own action. This contrasts sharply with the more dominant puritan, moral authoritarianism born in response to the 'swinging sixties'. In spite of the conflict that these elements face with the party leadership, it would be absurd to underestimate the popularity of such ideas.

At the fortieth anniversary conference of the Young Conservatives in Eastbourne, in February 1988, the dark side of Britain was on public display. It is worth reflecting on the relative importance the media has given to Labour's problems with the militant tendency. Indeed, the comparison in the way in which Britain's two main parties have dealt with extremists in their ranks is perhaps instructive. The militant tendency has been officially condemned; the Labour Party's youth section subjected to a radical overhaul with rule changes forced through to exclude key figures. The party leader has personally confronted this challenge. This was Britain's official opposition party cleaning itself up. In the meantime, the government party actually shied away from a clash with young extremists. In the run-up to the 1987 general election the then party Chairman, Norman Tebbit, chose to give advice about the need to confront this problem. In practice, Thatcherite elements have been working in alliance with the extremists and libertarians to browbeat traditional moderate conservatives into submission. That a young man nasty enough to describe Harold Macmillan as a 'war criminal' should ever be a member of the Conservative Party is shocking enough; that he should be considered as a possible Chairman of the Young Conservatives should be intolerable to the party leadership. Norman Tebbit's actions have not solved the problem anyway. In 1988 Ken Henderson, a former neo-Nazi parliamentary candidate, took over the leadership of the Young Conservatives in the West Yorkshire town of Todmorden. He emphasises his admiration for Enoch Powell and his rejection of the concept of a multiracial society. The difficulty for the party establishment is that whereas the militant tendency is clearly an 'entryist' organisation with a completely different ideology and aims from the party leadership, the difference between Mrs Thatcher and her own young extremists is harder to define. Labour's extreme left openly detest Neil Kinnock, whilst for the Conservative's young extremists Margaret Thatcher is their heroine and inspiration, and so far she does not appear to be disappointing the extremists in the way that Reagan, Bush, Kohl, or Giscard certainly do.

Having noted how the rise of racism in the 1960s opened the way for a swing to the right in the 1970s, it is particularly significant to note the present campaign by the new right against what they call 'anti-racism'. Having rehabilitated social biology, they are now moving on to attack those who favour an active policy to counter the effects of the racism and xenophobia which their writings have sought to legitimise. The attack on anti-racists enables responsibility for racism in society to be shifted away from the national authorities on to local councillors and the immigrants themselves. Rather than attempt to face the problems which lead to racial violence, institutional racism, and discrimination, the new right accuses the anti-racists themselves of being the cause of social problems because of their distorted, unhealthy views of what society could be.

Many people in Britain might claim that all this is quite irrelevant to right-wing extremism in modern Europe. The sad fact is that so many of the ideas put into practice now and campaigned for by the new right are precisely those for which the extreme right originally campaigned. The heady mixture of libertarianism and authoritarianism is particularly attractive as it provides a key to creating a massive electoral appeal which either element alone could not attract. The particular importance of Thatcherism is not just its success in Britain but the impact it has in other countries, where the centre of gravity also is shifting to the right and mainstream political parties are sometimes occupying ideological territory hitherto occupied only by extremists.

Counter-revolution

The links between mainstream conservatives and active counter-revolutionaries are not just the product of social change and a successful ideological battle, they are also partly a result of more shady efforts by intelligence agencies, businessmen, and others who decided in the 1960s that the 'left' had to be fought with much more resolution. The mentality which led the USA to back a fascist coup in Chile, or which led the British secret service to plot against a Labour Prime Minister was widespread in the 1960s and 1970s. There was, of course, no worldwide conspiracy mounted, but various organisations were set up to play a part in the hoped-for counter-revolution. Some of them overlapped with groups and individuals which had always remained faithful to fascist ideas. It was in this atmosphere that the P2 lodge operated. A remarkable illustration of the overlap between mainstream and extremist political activity *came in* April 1982 when President Reagan felt it appropriate to salute publicly the work of one of the key figures of the shadowy world of the 'New Right' and post-war fascism.[16]

The man whose 'ideals and values' Reagan praised has been particularly active as a bridge between international fascist groups linked together in the Northern league and the intellectual circles of the neo-conservatives. His name is Roger Pearson. Born in 1927, he had begun his political career in India, where he edited from 1956 a publication called *Northern World*. This was anti-Semitic and was put on sale through Colin Jordan, a leading British fascist. The publication carried adverts for *Nation Europa*, one of the contact journals set up by former Nazis and sympathisers after a 1951 Malmö conference. Maurice Bardeche and Oswald Mosley naturally contributed to *Nation Europa*. In 1958 Pearson helped establish the Northern League, which aimed to foster the interests of friendship and solidarity of all Teutonic nations'. It was not really a political party but a meeting point for Nazi sympathisers long before any kind of revival seemed likely. It was also, more sinisterly, a channel of communication for Nazi activists around the world. Among its recruits was Hans Gunther, whose racist writings had, in 1941, earnd him the Goethe medal from the Hitler regime. In 1959 Pearson wrote, echoing Mosley and forerunning Le Pen, that 'what we have to learn and learn quickly if we as Europeans are not to be annihilated as a species, is to begin to think in terms of ethnic identity and pan-national concepts'. The league had contacts with the NF and the Ku Klux Klan. At meetings in Brighton in 1969 and 1970 Martin Webster and Colin Jordan were present.

In the 1960s Pearson moved to the USA where he took up an academic career concentrating on anthropology and eugenics. In 1960 *Northern World* was described in a similar publication as aiming 'to make whites aware of their forgotten racial heritage, and to cut through the Judaic fog of lies about our origin and the accomplishment of our race and our Western culture'. The publication's title was changed to *Western Destiny* after a brief period in which it had the simple and meaningful title of *Folk*. One of the contributors was Austin App, who had been a

pioneer of historical revisionism and the denial of the holocaust. Alain
de Benoist, who later led the work of the Nouvelle Ecole in France in
trying to make racism respectable, also contributed.

In the 1970s Pearson became active in the World Anti-Communist
League (WACL) which held its 1978 conference in Washington under
his chairmanship. Giorgio Almirante personally represented the MSI
at this conference, where the Nouvelle Ecole and the Liberty League
were also present. Pearson was in this way able to play a further key
role in using ultra-conservative pressure groups to further anti-Semitic
and fascist interests. Indeed, in 1980 there was a row inside the WACL
about the way Pearson was bringing neo-Nazis into the organisation. In
spite of this his career was capped with a public act of praise by no less
a person than Ronald Reagan. The President wrote to thank him for
sending him a copy of the *Journal of Social, Political and Economic
Studies*, an ostensibly conservative publication.

Pearson ended his career as a successful academic in various universities, where presumably he felt at home in the new era following the
neo-conservative revolution. It would be absurd to assume that a man
who had spent twenty years as a racist activist had changed his views.
All that had changed were the political circumstances in the USA, and
elsewhere. In keeping alive certain views which were so unfashionable
and even taboo in the 1950s and 1960s, he had made a significant contribution to the history of ideas. Reagan's letter illustrates the difficulty of
finding a dividing line between neo-fascism and neo-conservatism, but
cannot be used to argue that the two are identical. Having spent decades
on the fringes, it must have been very encouraging for Pearson to be told
by the President that with his latest publication he was 'performing a
valuable service in bringing to a wide audience the work of leading
scholars who are supporters of a free enterprise economy, a firm and
consistent foreign policy and a strong national defence'. Amongst the
associate editors of this publication is James Angleton, former head of
the CIA. In the 1960s Angleton had worked closely with Peter Wright
and the British Secret Service, and was a typical exponent of the view
that the CIA had the moral right to destroy unfriendly governments
even when they had been democratically elected. He had played a key
role in trying to form a unified Western intelligence organisation under
CIA control.

The WACL, through which Pearson passed on his way from obscurity
to respectability, is one of various bodies which provide a respectable
front behind which Nazi sympathisers can hide their real views. It had
begun life in 1967 as a private body which was, in fact, financed by the
Taiwan-based Nationalist Chinese Government. It has always been well
connected with American and other intelligence agencies. Its finance
still comes from the South Korean and Taiwan Governments, as well

as from the 'Moon' international organisation. Its 1986 conference was held in Luxembourg under the chairmanship of John K. Singlaub, a former CIA covert guerrilla warfare chief. At this conference[17] there were representatives of RENAMO, the anti-Machel group from Mozambique, which, with South African connivance, had brought the country to famine and collapse. The Nicaraguan contras also participate in WACL activities since under Singlaub it has become an effective link between various anti-communist guerrillas and ideological groups. Singlaub has been a leading figure in the campaign to get the USA to support the contras officially, a policy which President Reagan has also insisted upon. In 1986 Singlaub was linked to Eugene Hasenfus, the American mercenary shot down over Nicaragua. At the Luxembourg meeting rebel groups from Afghanistan, Cambodia, Burma, Iran, and India met to exchange ideas and perhaps to advise each other on arms procurement. Alongside these were representatives from the Romanian branch of the WACL, who openly referred to their previous involvement in the Nazi Iron Guard, recalling that then 'there was a new spirit, we were building a new Europe'.

In 1973 Geoffrey Stewart-Smith, a former Conservative MP and at that time leader of the British branch of the WACL, had pulled out of the organisation, seeing it as nothing less 'than a collection of Nazis, fascists, anti-Semites, sellers of forgeries, vicious racialists, corrupt self-seekers, Kuomintang geriatrics and Ukranian anti-Russian racialists'. Stewart-Smith's deputy at the British chapter of the WACL had been Ian Grieg, a leading figure in the Monday Club, particularly active on the subject of 'counter-subversion'. The WACL had grown rapidly by the early 1970s, by which time it had ninety national chapters and five regional groups. The rabid anti-communism of the organisation means that its driving force comes from those countries where a direct clash has, or is, taking place. Chiang Kai-shek from Taiwan, Presidents Van Thieu and Lon Nol from South Vietnam, Anastasio Somoza from Nicaragua, and Stroessner from Paraguay have all been personally linked to the work of the WACL.

Clearly, the international standing of the organisation would have been undermined had Stewart-Smith's criticisms been ignored. When Singlaub took over in 1985 he ordered the expulsion of the Mexican Group, the Tecos, a fanatically anti-Semitic group which is widely believed to have been behind the massacre of students at the time of the 1968 Olympic Games in Mexico. The WACL continues, however, to be a meeting ground between respectable conservatives like Jeanne Kirkpatrick, former NATO officers like the Belgian General Close, and the British General Sir Walter Walker, and other more shadowy figures directly involved in helping anti-communist guerrilla movements. The General Secretary of the British WACL is the Dowager Lady Birdwood, a member of the Conservative Party and herself not unfriendly towards the National Front.

Rabid anti-communism used as an excuse for terrorism and dictatorship is one of the key elements in the ideology of the extreme right. In the 1980s the language used by President Reagan has, on occasions, been indistinguishable from that used by the extreme right during the preceding decades of *détente*. His absurd comparison between the Contras in Nicaragua and the American founding fathers ignores the brutal strategy of the Contras, who use terrorism as a key part of their attempt to defeat the Sandinistas and receive aid from drug traders. In practice, Reagan and Thatcher have ushered in a new era of collaboration with the major communist countries. As recently as 1984, however, Reagan sent a message to a WACL meeting in San Diego, California, praising its work in attracting attention to the heroic freedom fighters of our time. He was referring to the Afghan rebels and to the Contras.

Singlaub, as head of the WACL, has in fact played a key role in bringing financial and military aid to the Contras. He had spent all his professional and political life in the front line of the war against communism.[18] After helping the resistance in France, he served later in the 1940s as a military adviser to the Kuomintang before it was defeated in China. During the Korean War he was CIA deputy station chief in Seoul. Between 1966 an 1968 he organised the secret 'non-conventional' part of the American intervention in Vietnam which undertook secret operations in North Vietnam, Cambodia and Laos. In 1977 he successfully mounted an open challenge to President Carter over the plan to remove American troops from South Korea, where he was head of the 8th Army. His emergence as one of the key figures in the channelling of aid to the Contras was the continuation of his life's work. At the same time the WACL campaigned, alongside Reagan, against the 'betrayal' of the Contras by Congress. In practice, the Congress decision has led to the privatisation of the war against the Sandinista government. In this way plans developed inside the Pentagon have been put into effect by secret intelligence operators financed by private donations from various American companies.

At the same time as this operation has been continuing, the WACL has not in reality totally broken with the extreme right. As the reports of the 1986 Luxembourg conference show, the counter-revolutionaries of Nicaragua are seen inside such groups as the WACL as part of the same family as extreme right groupings challenging communism in Eastern Europe.

Given the way in which ex-Nazis, fascist dictators, secret agents, and drug traders have worked so closely together in certain countries, it is hard to see the supposed purge of the WACL as anything more than a half-hearted public relations exercise. In 1986, for example, a Belgian Christian Democrat Senator and trade unionist, Jose Demarets, became

President of the WACL.[19] He has always been on the extreme right of the Social Christian Party (PSC) alongside Paul Van den Boeynants and Joseph Michel. As a junior Minister Demarets was advised by a man who told the press that it was necessary to infiltrate the big traditional parties in order to struggle more effectively against socialism, which is really responsible for the current crisis. In 1980 Demarets had intervened with Van den Boeynants in order to get a job for one Paul Latinus, who later became a founder member of the mysterious Westland New Post (WNP). The WNP, a neo-nazi grouping, has been linked with the Belgian Secret Service and may be linked to the Brabant killers who undertook massacres in supermarkets possibly as part of a strategy of tension to counter efforts to reduce the power of the left or of anyone who tried to limit the influence of certain elements of the secret police.

The flavour of the WACL is also apparent from a *Searchlight* article of April 1987 reporting the arrest of General Guillermo Suarez Mason, who, in 1980, had become chairman of the Argentinian chapter. Also at the Buenos Aires conference where he was elected were General Videla (at the time Argentina's dictatorial President), Roberto d'Aubuisson (leader of the extreme right in El Salvador and closely linked with anti-communist death squads), and Stefano delle Chiaie (the Italian fascist terrorist). Mason's arrest in 1987 was in connection with numerous charges of murder, kidnapping and torture.

Equally extraordinary and in many ways even more significant, however, are the links between the WACL and the Unification Church of 'Reverend' Moon. In the Far East and Latin America the Moon organisation has built up massive funds for political activities. Sun Myung Moon sees himself as the world leader in the war against communism and still dreams of a 'march on Moscow'. He would be difficult to take seriously as a political figure if his organisation had not become so powerful. His right-hand man for political work was Colonel Bo Hi Pak of the Korean CIA and a person well known to Ronald Reagan and John Singlaub. Moon's political pretensions originally caused some problems within his native South Korea. The WACL held its first meeting in Seoul, the South Korean capital, in the 'Freedom Centre', which had been set up by the Unification Church, but Moon did not succeed in getting complete control of the WACL. He was more successful in Japan, where Moonists do control the organisation. Moon invested 1 million dollars in the 1970 WACL conference; conferences in Seoul and Taiwan having been directly financed by the governments of the countries concerned. During the 1970s Bo Hi Pak developed the Church's contacts around the world.

His contacts in Latin America were built on the views that a 'battle of ideas' had to be waged against communism, and that since this battle was going on throughout the world it required a worldwide organisation. On this basis, Bo Hi Pak has had contacts not only with Ronald Reagan but also with soldiers and politicians throughout Central and Latin America. He described General Stroessner, the Paraguyan dictator, as a 'special man chosen by God to lead his country'.[20] CAUSA, the political front for Moon in South America, held a seminar in the Paraguayan capital Asunción following which, through the good offices of the chairman of the Paraguay chapter of the WACL, CAUSA was able to put on political education courses for members of the Stroesner Party. In Bolivia Bo Hi Pak was also among friends. It has been rumoured that the coup which brought General Garcia Meza to power had been announced previously by Moon himself. The Bolivian dictator offered the colonel a dinner in his honour and again CAUSA was allowed to undertake political education work for the supporters of the dictatorial regime. Moon's organisation has been linked to the preparation of the 1980 coup in which Klaus Barbie also provided expert assistance. In 1984 it emerged from the Bolivian government that Moon and CAUSA had offered 4 million dollars to finance the coup and that the American Air Force had flown in 50 000 books published by the Unification Church. Not surprisingly CAUSA has also held political seminars in Chile and in Argentina during the dictatorship of General Videla. It has been particularly supported by Archbishop Plaza and other reactionary elements in the Argentinian Catholic Church which have used all their influence at home and with the Vatican to fight 'liberation theology'. It should be understood that we are considering here the work of an organisation with billions of dollars to spend, with an ideology looked upon positively by the American administration and some of the world's most powerful multinational companies. Whilst these organisations are linked to marginal groups in some countries, they should not be dismissed as irrelevant even to the political developments in Europe which are our main concern.

Much of the strategy of these groups is concerned with taking power in the media so as to influence the development of public opinion without openly revealing their fanatical political views. The attempt by the Moon organisation to establish the *Washington Times* as a challenger to the more liberal press in the USA is hardly an isolated event. In Uruguay and other Latin American countries similar enterprises have been undertaken; 150 million dollars were originally invested in the *Washington Times*. In 1978 Moon was behind the establishment of a world conference on the mass media which has held seminars the world on the ideological war against communism. Its meetings have been addressed by Singlaub, Jacques Soustelle, and General Ky of South Vietnam. In 1984 the French newspaper *Le Canard Enchâiné* revealed the links between Moon's Time Tribune Corporation and the French media magnate Robert Hersant, and in Italy P2 influence has been seen behind major corporate battles for control of the media.

In 1975 Cardinal Marty, Archbishop of Paris, spoke out against the activities of the Moon organisation, but this was for its so-called religious activity. This activity has also been specifically denounced in a report to the European Parliament[21] but few people in Europe are aware of the political aims lying behind the pseudo-religious front. During the 1980s mainstream politicians in Western Europe have been directly in contact with Moon front organisations without always realising how they are being used. This is sometimes a result of the fact that the return to fashion of *extreme* language about the communist menace has led, as we have shown, to a blurring of the dividing line between the extreme right and democratic conservatism. It is also to be hoped that the concentration of economic conservative power in the Far East is not to be followed by a strengthening in the influence of the ideological fanaticism which is being financed from that part of the world.

In 1982 the French writer Jean-François Revel addressed the Moon organisation's fifth conference on the world media. In 1983 at Cartagena, Colombia, journalists from the *Figaro* Magazine were present, as was Jean Marcilly, a personal friend and author of a sympathetic biography of Jean-Marie Le Pen.[22] Colonel Bo Hi Pak naturally saw in the campaign against Euro-missiles an emanation of the communist threat and in 1983 undertook a tour of Europe under the grandiose title of the 'European Peace Movement Fact Finding Tours'. He took 500 journalists to Paris, Bonn, Berlin, and London. Jacques Toubon in the name of Jacques Chirac, the Mayor of Paris and leader of the Gaullist RPR, offered a drink in honour of the participants. Chancellor Kohl, tipped off via the press as to the real nature of the tour, refused to receive the participants officially. In 1984 in Montevideo the first Pan-American conference of CAUSA was attended by a French Gaullist parliamentarian, Yacinthe Santoni, reportedly attending at the request of Jacques Chirac. Philippe Malaud, a French UDF member of the European Parliament, who played an active part in trying to block the work of the European Parliament's Committee of Inquiry into the Rise of Racism and Fascism in Europe was also present. In July 1986 the *Sunday Times*[23] revealed links between senior aides of Mrs Thatcher and the Moon organisation. An American group which monitors the activities of the Moonie cult revealed that the Global Economic Action Institute was funded by the Moonie organisation. It is dedicated to the free market economic philosophy and holds political and economic conferences in all parts of the world. Julian Amery, MP has served as chairman of the London branch of the Institute. Brian Griffiths, from Mrs Thatcher's Downing Street Policy Unit, resigned from the institute as soon as he heard of the involvement of Moonie funds. Professor Alan Walters, at the time a Thatcher adviser, argued that the work of the institute should be judged on its merits and that it had helped enhance awareness of world economic problems by bringing together experts from around the globe. He called for a more tolerant attitude towards Moonism. The Moonies have continued to be a source of funds for the activities of right-wing activists within the Conservative Party. In January 1989 it was reported[24] that London Young Conservatives worked with a group called 'Western Goals' which is, in turn, part of the World Youth Freedom League, based in Washington. The league's secretary-general does not deny receiving 'several hundred thousand dollars' from the Unification Church. He now claims to have split with the Moonies, having become aware of their 'ulterior agenda'. The plans for a conference in London in April 1989 went ahead in co-operation with the WACL and with the specific intention of organising a strong anti-communist network for 'all of Europe, both captive and free'. Among those working on this event is one Mrs Yaroslav Stetsko, wife of the wartime Nazi Prime Minister of the Ukraine.

The founder of the moonie cult has been jailed in the USA for tax offences, but as Walters remarks and the continuing links with Tory fringe groups show, few people who have been involved in its political or economic activity are aware of the political fanaticism which lies in its origin. If the strength of the following for the religious side of the Moon operation is a reflection of social problems within Western society, the strength of its political operation is a sign of a changing political climate. The anti-communist zeal of Taiwan, South Korea, and South Vietnam in the 1960s has found stronger echoes in Europe and the USA than at the time when such organisations as CAUSA and the WACL were being established. Given the massive economic take-off that has occured in Taiwan and South Korea, it is hardly surprising that political organisations with big business support have been able to call upon funds running into billions of dollars. Few of the Americans or Europeans taking part in the apparently innocuous conferences organised by such bodies will be aware of their direct contact with American and South Korean intelligence organisations, fascist dictatorships, or religious cults. The ideological and cultural offensive of the extreme right in recent years has, however, been successful precisely because in many cases the origins or objectives of particular publications or pressure groups are kept well hidden. Moreover, as public opinion has swung over to the libertarian right and leaders like Reagan have rehabilitated the rhetoric of rabid anti-communism for electoral purposes, it becomes quite impossible to find any clear border between right-wing extremism and other less-openly fanatical elements.

It is, however, the case that when a leader like President Reagan sends letters or holds public meetings with Singlaub, Pearson, or Bo Hi Pak his advisers at least know what is going on. Indeed, nothing has shown more the dangers of taking the rhetoric of anti-communism seriously than the revelations about the activities of elements of the Reagan administration which have come out during the Irangate hearings. The mentality of Colonel North is the same as that which inspired British secret agents to fear Soviet infiltration of the British Labour government.

Racism and fanatical anti-communism have been part of the propaganda of fascism throughout this century. Both strands of thinking are shared in political parties and public opinion well beyond the ranks of the extreme right. What, however, should be a genuine cause for concern is the way in which, in the USA in particular, fanatical anti-communism has been accepted as a badge of political respectability and has, as we have seen, constituted a bridge between conservatives and the extreme right, through a labyrinth of front organisations and a common fund of shared ideas and prejudices. It was on this basis that Licio Gelli could develop enormous power from a position of obscurity and despite his fascist past. Similarly, the adoption of a certain tolerance of xenophobia or discreet use of racist slogans by conservative politicians leads to a poisoning of democratic politics to the extent that those who adopt such tactics probably underestimate. In both cases, democratic politicians are playing with fire. The role of the Front National in France and right-wing terrorism in Italy and elsewhere has shown just how devastating that fire could be.

Notes

1. John Tomlinson, *Left, Right: The March of Political Extremism in Britain,* John Calder, 1981.
2. Ibid. p. 11.
3. Ray Hill with Andrew Bell, *The Other Face of Terror,* Grafton, London, 1988.
4. Marian Fitzgerald, *Black People and Party Politics,* Runnymede Trust, 1987.
5. Christopher Husbands, 'Extreme Rght-wing Poltics in Great Britain' *European Politics,* II, 2, April 1988.
6. Stephen Rose, *Evrigenis Report,* Annexe 5.
7. Ibid. p. 59
8. P. Essed, *Evrigenis Report,* annexe D, pp. 2–3.
9. Wollrauf, op. cit.
10. A. Dummett, *Evrigenis Report,* Annexe C, p. 2.
11. *Le Soir,* 31 October 1987, p. 2.
12. Quoted in *Time,* 1986, p.11.
13. *What Next: An Introduction to Research on Young People,* ESRC, London, 1987.
14. The *Independent,* 16 September, 1987.
15. *New Socialist,* September 1983 p. 19.
16. *Searchlight* 11 September 1984.
17. *New Statesman,* 31 October 1986
18. Jean François Boyer, *L'Empire Moon,* La Découverte, Paris, 1986.

Ch. 17.
19. *Article 31* (Paris), 23 p. 110
20. 'L'Internationale Moon' *Le Monde Diplomatique*, February 1985.
21. EP Doc. 1-47/84.
22. *Le Pen sans Bandeau* Editions Granger, Paris, 1984.
23. *Sunday Times*, 6 July 1986, p. 3.
24. The *Guardian*, 9 January 1989.

Three

The Le Pen Phenomenon

'I prefer my daughters to my cousins, my cousins to my neighbours and my neighbours to strangers.' It was with these words on French television in February 1984 that Jean-Marie Le Pen showed his usual skill in acting both as a spokesman for prejudice and as someone able to express racist ideas as if they were commonplace self-evident truths. During recent years when his party, the Front National (FN), has achieved unprecedented publicity and electoral success, he has continued to show the same ability to outrage the establishment by expressing popular feelings rarely echoed by mainstream political leaders of the right, the centre, or the left.

When, in September 1987, he achieved international fame with his claim that the gas-chambers were nothing more than a detail of the history of the Second World War, he was continuing in the same vein, combining the attractions of a trouble-maker, a mouthpiece for prejudice, an entertaining television performer, and a would-be President of France. The immediate impact of his remark on that occasion, the expressions of outrage from across the spectrum of opinion in France, international condemnation, were somewhat surprising. Le Pen's political views and origins are well known, the parties he has belonged to, his speeches and writings all show him to be continuing a well-established French political tradition of racism and xenophobia. As Michel Rocard pointed out in 1987 the only thing that was surprising about his 'gaffe', if it was that, concerning the gas-chambers, was the surprise expressed by so many observers.

It is hard to accept that what Le Pen said during a memorable interview on RTL was really just a slip of the tongue. This is not only because of Le Pen's own political background but also because of a careful reading of the text of his interview.[1] The interviewer asked him first about the view held by many people that he, Le Pen, is a racist. He was asked if he would condemn the views of prominent revisionist historians who questioned the existence of the gas-chambers, and he was asked about the presence of neo-Nazi activists at a Joan of Arc Festival meeting organised by the FN. He immediately responded, denying personal responsibility for organising the meeting and accusing the media of a moral swindle because of the way they cut film of the meeting to link it with a neo-Nazi march. He was then pressed about the views of Faurisson and Roques and first stated that he was not familiar with their views, adding that anyway he was in favour of freedom of expression. He insisted on the extraordinary power of the truth, which has nothing to fear from lies and insinuations. It was for this reason that he expressed himself as 'hostile to all forms of prohibition and regulation of thought'. With regard to the history of the Second World War he referred to various controversial questions relating to this period of history and he went on to say that it took fifty to sixty years to discover the truth about the Lusitania, and that he faced certain problems: 'I do not say that gas-chambers did not exist. I have not been able to see for myself. I have not especially studied the question. But I do believe that it is a point of detail of the history of the Second World War.' When the shocked interviewers expressed horror that he could consider the death of 6 million people as a point of detail, he replied that the fact of the holocaust could not be considered as 'a truth, revealed, in which everyone must believe as a moral obligation'. Such matters were for historians. When asked about the fact that an overwhelming majority of historians did not see any reason to question the truth of this horrendous episode, Le Pen stated: 'there were many dead, hundreds of thousands, perhaps millions of dead Jews and also people who were not Jews'. He launched into his usual tirade about media interviews being turned into inquisitions on irrelevant issues. It is clear from the text of this interview that the interviewers did not conceal the purpose of their line of questioning as many interviewers do. Given the opportunity to dismiss the revisionist school of the history of the holocaust, Le Pen went out of his way not to do so, using words which made clear where he stood on the issue.

The immediate impact of this particular interview was an enormous hullabaloo in the French and the international media. Weeks later opinion polls showed Le Pen still sitting on top of 12 per cent support (above his 1984 Euro-elections score). Wishful thinking or selective polling taken immediately after the interview had given the impression that he had, at a stroke, lost 20 per cent of his supporters. The issues of immigration, insecurity, and the failure of the French political establishment, however, remain potent and no politician has yet successfully challenged him on this ground. It is for that reason as well that Le Pen's gaffe may have been a more clever move than his opponents would admit. For, as a profile in the *Independent* put it: 'Few of those who are attracted to Le Pen because he is opposed to Arab immigration will care what he thinks about the Nazi gas-chambers. And no one who is concerned about the Nazis would have been likely to vote for Le Pen in the first place. When today's issues return to dominate the debate, the row about gas-chambers will be forgotten but Le Pen will be much better known'.[2] This is also the case because Le Pen's aim is to appeal to voters in the 1980s who may be attracted by his anti-Arab xenophobia and are not directly concerned about the role of the Jews, past or present.

A French news magazine has carefully reconstructed the events that followed.[3] Even as Le Pen was completing the interview his followers were signalling to him from inside the studio; perhaps as a result Le Pen appeared to act as if he knew he had made a mistake, accusing the presenter of the programme of 'a staged attack and intellectual terrorism'. That evening Le Pen met with his advisers in an attempt to manage news coverage of the affair. Most significant was the reaction of other political parties on the centre and right.

One declared that Le Pen had reached breaking point with the other non-socialist parties. Others clearly were concerned not to say anything that could lose them votes from Le Pen supporters. In Marseilles the UDF leader, Jean-Claude Gaudin, who clearly feels obliged to work with the FN, had to face members of his own party insisting on a clear denunciation. The response of Gaudin and others was that local electoral deals were not the equivalent of a moral contract obliging the UDF to agree with all the statements of the FN's national leadership. One FN Euro-MP, Romain Marie, quoted in the same French news magazines stated that 'the affair about revisionism was put up by left wing people some of whom are Jews'. Pressed on the issue, he replied by referring to the dead in Vietnam, Afghanistan, Ukraine, and Nicaragua. As far as Marie was concerned, the methods of Goebbels were being used to try and crush the FN by people who refused to face the Soviet menace, the spread of pornography, and so on.

One of the more conservative Gaullist politicians, Charles Pasqua, the Interior Minister, used the occasion to appeal to the Gaullist inheritance of the resistance and to condemn Le Pen explicitly. In this he was joined by former Gaullist Prime Ministers Jacques Chaban-Delmas and Pierre Messmer. Pasqua claimed that he was the man to beat Le Pen because of the measures he had taken on immigration and anti-terrorist policy. A few weeks before the Le Pen interview Pasqua had asked for a secret service study of anti-Semitism in France. He therefore felt that he was doing more to fight Le Pen than 'those who please themselves by ritual incantations and who in the past have not shown much proof of a very great moral sense . . . having aligned themselves with the lackeys of Stalin who had deported 20 million people and had ordered the murder of several other million. . .'[4]

At the end of the week following the interview Le Pen gave a special press conference, at which he denounced the whole incident as a plot by the 'immigrants trade union' and the 'human rights professionals'. He insisted that a detail is no more or less than 'a part of the whole' and that his words had, therefore, been unfairly represented.

The ambiguous role played by various politicians of the centre and the right anxious either to keep favour with those who think like Le Pen in order to get his second preference votes or to occupy his electoral. territory reflects a continuing reality of French politics in the 1980s. To some extent even the French socialists' attack was pitched not on the immoral nature of Le Pen's views, but on the need for local electoral pacts with the FN to be broken. The former French Prime Minister Laurent Fabius denounced Le Pen as a fascist and welcomed the unanimous disapproval which Le Pen's remarks had achieved. He immediately took the opportunity, however, to attack also those prepared to consider electoral alliances with Le Pen.

The most sincere and disinterested attacks on Le Pen came from human rights and anti-racist organisations who had been denouncing Le Pen and the wider problem of racism in France long before he became an electoral force.

Judging by Le Pen's high score in the 1988 French Presidential elections, it is clear that in terms of the evolution of his public standing, it would be wrong to exaggerate the significance of this particular incident. Months after the interview there was no sign that Le Pen support was dropping, although in October 1987, it was announced that Olivier d'Ormesson had resigned as chairman of the Committee collecting the signatures from French notables necessary to enable Le Pen to be a candidate for President. D'Ormesson was a former Christian Democrat MEP who was re-elected in 1984 on Le Pen's list. He justified his resignation as a response to Le Pen's view on the holocaust.[5]

The limited electoral damage caused by this event suggests that one of the problems those who wish to challenge Le Pen must face is that of appearing to cry wolf too often and too soon. As the French philosopher André Glucksman had told the European *Parliament Committee of Inquiry:*

> If you keep crying wolf in the end when the wolf really comes no one will believe you. If you keep crying fire, fire, in the end when a real fire breaks out no one will believe you . . . we have a rather extraordinary phenomenon in France today, which is that 80 per cent of people who are neither communist or supporters of Le Pen talk about nothing but Le Pen. I suggest that we in Europe are all in danger of talking about the fascist danger because we have nothing else to say . . . Words create things, and it is because of the absence of discussion about European integration, about the development of democracy in every country, that there is a fascist danger, not because of a few fascists.[6]

The alternative view was also put to the European Parliament by Mme Pau-Langevin of the French anti-racist group MRAP. She claimed that:

> It would be wrong to underestimate the danger even if today we are apparently dealing with a party that claims to be democratic. Here too history has taught us that people start out by taking power in the most democratic fashion possible but that the ideology of hatred knows no reasonable limits. When the starting point is contempt for man and hatred of man there is no reason to stop half-way.[7]

The purpose of our analysis is to see whether Glucksman was right or whether the phenomenon which Le Pen represents is best dealt with in a less direct manner than simple condemnation. This will require an examination of Le Pen's programme, political origins and ambitions and an examination of the social and political situation in France. As we have seen, the extreme-right is not a purely national phenomenon without European or international aspects. It is, however, also the case that development in the fields of racism and historical revisionism in France will inevitably influence the development of European politics.

Le Pen's electoral success gives encouragement to those in other countries who agree with him. In a Europe supposed to be in the process of political integration interest in each others internal affairs is naturally inevitable and desirable. As Professor Alfred Grosser put it: 'If it is at all justified to take seriously the threat to democratic liberties, today it is the German people who have a right to be concerned about France's future rather than vice-versa, contrary to what we have been used to thinking'.[8]

In examining the Le Pen phenomenon in its contemporary French context, a certain caution is needed about the use of certain words. In particular, it is necessary not to get trapped into the fairly theoretical argument about whether Le Pen is, or is not, a fascist. Since the 1940s the word fascist has become a word most often used as a term of polemical abuse. Numerous overlapping phenomena are covered under general terms: the far right, the extra-parliamentary right, the new right, etc. Different individuals and events have contributed to a particular political tradition, Bonapartism, Boulangism, Pétainism, Poujadism and now Le Penism. In practice, there is no single extreme-right tradition anyway and attempts at over-simplification are likely to prove counter-productive from both a political and analytical point of view. Indeed, it seems quite likely that it does more harm than good to compare the FN with fascist and Nazi parties. Le Pen's response at the end of the interview on the holocaust showed how little advantage there is in putting Le Pen in the position of a victim, whether it be of legal action, media attention, violence, or whatever. Using the term fascist too glibly

provides an opportunity for those who are appealing to some of its ideas
to hide behind a jungle of semantics about whether fascism is really a
left-wing idea and so on. As we shall see, there is no doubt that among
Le Pen's followers and ideas there is a great part of the French fascist
tradition. It is, however, the case that his support for NATO, for liberal
economics, and his apparent rejection of autarky makes him closer to
Reagan than to Mussolini. Indeed, this would explain part of his success.
If those who want to fight fascism use the word too widely they end up,
as Glucksman suggested, undermining their own cause. It should also
not be overlooked that Le Pen's open appeal to anti-Semitic traditions
has not deprived him of, at least some, Jewish support.

Historical comparisons with the rise of Hitler, if they have any
value, should be used to try and understand how someone with such
monstrous ideas had achieved such electoral success. Why was it that
the contents and implications of *Mein Kampf* were ignored? It was
precisely because Hitler found the ability to express his ideas in an
anodyne and inoffensive manner. It is this that the new right and
Le Pen appear to have understood. The challenge now is to attack
the implications of Le Pen's statements whilst dispensing with the
hyperbole which plays into his hands. Given the anger his carefully
chosen words inspire, this clearly is not an easy task for his compatriots.
As was apparent in the work of the European Parliament's Committee of
Inquiry, accusations of semantic manipulation and political illiteracy are
easily made. Moreover, since fascism is not the only totalitarian political
idea around in modern Europe, those who wish to fight fascism must
also carry conviction in their challenge to totalitarianism in general.

The British public would probably never have heard about Le Pen's
notorious interview had it not been for the fact that the FN leader was
scheduled to attend a fringe meeting at the 1987 Conservative Party
Conference. Sir Alfred Sherman, who had apparently long ago lost
the confidence of Margaret Thatcher and Norman Tebbit as a result of
his views, wanted to invite Le Pen to Brighton in order to open direct
contacts between the FN and the Conservative Party. Sherman echoed
Le Pen's view that during the RTL interview he had been tricked by the
media and misrepresented by left-wing and Jewish bodies. He clearly
shares Le Pen's views on immigration, insecurity, repatriation, and other
subjects. Le Pen's invitation to Brighton, is part of a general attempt
to strengthen his quest for political respectability. The left would gain
nothing by suggesting that Sherman, let alone Thatcher or Lord Plumb,
are fascists. It is, however, clear that a political climate exists in Britain
as in France in which ideas once uttered only in the political wilderness
are now receiving extraordinary prominence. Sherman's invitation to Le
Pen reflects his view that Thatcherism is failing and that even more
radical ideas should be acted upon. It is, perhaps, at least worth noting

that Le Pen cancelled his trip to Brighton for fear, he said, of causing unwarranted difficulties for Mrs Thatcher. After Le Pen's high score in the 1988 Presidential election, Sherman was still arguing that since Le Pen had got one in seven votes, British people should try to understand his views and to see the difference between racism and patriotism, and between xenophobia and concern for national identity.

Le Pen continues to show an ability to surprise which experts on his movement find hard to understand. His views on the holocaust and his exploitation of xenophobia are an integral part of his political message and his personal background. The continuity of right-wing extremist history in post-war Europe is confirmed by the career of Le Pen. In casting doubt on the facts on the holocaust, Le Pen not only rides a tide of historical revisionism but also continues with a theme which was very important to him during his years in the political wilderness. Indeed, part of his, now considerable, wealth came from a record company catering for what was apparently a reasonably lucrative market in nostalgia for the Nazi era. He presided over a company (SERP), founded in 1962, which published certain items described as 'historical material'. This material included records with speeches of Hitler and other Nazi and fascist leaders, plus appropriate songs. On one record sleeve Le Pen wrote: 'These are the songs of the German revolution, Adolf Hitler and the National Socialist Party came to power through legal elections. They thank their ascent to a mass movement which was popular and democratic. These circumstances are generally forgotten.'[9] In fact, Le Pen has a past during which he has been convicted on various occasions for trying to deny Nazi war crimes as well as racial incitement.

André Glucksman has explained that the denial of the holocaust is an essential part of racist and fascist language. He explained to the European Parliament Inquiry that the concealment of the truth about mass murder may be sought in various ways: either simple concealment or trivialisation. In the latter case spokesmen argue that since war is so terrible, war crimes are a relative problem, not a question of apportioning blame either to individuals, groups, or ideas. The report of the European Parliament pointed out that a taboo seems to have been lifted. It quoted Theo Klein, chairman of the Conseil Représentatif des Institutions Juives de France (CRIF), who argued that there probably is no real increase in popular anti-Semitism, it is just that 'today some feelings surface more easily'.[10] This process can be linked to a wave of historical revisionist writing.

The revisionist school of history clearly represents a major trend of thinking on the French extreme right. This school of thought originates with the past war neo-Nazi groups. In 1947 Bardèche published various works defending the politics of the collaborators, arguing that they had succeeded in saving the French race from extinction. He attacked the

Allies in particular for the fabrication of evidence about the concentration camps and for collusion with the Soviet Union. This tradition was continued and revived significantly by Robert Faurisson, who treated the issue as a purely academic one about which doubts can be expressed. It is remarkable but necessary to add that, in the defence of freedom of thought, left-wing intellectuals like Serge Thion and Noam Chomsky have argued that such doubts should be freely expressed. It is, however, clear from Le Pen's remarks that the intentional creation of doubt about history is intended to generate a climate in which right-wing extremism can flourish. The French historian Edgar Morin has argued that since it became clear in the 1970s that concentration camps had also been a key element in Stalin's regime, the tendency to relativise Nazi crimes has strengthened. As the reality of the gulags entered into public consciousness, the image of the Nazi regime as uniquely diabolical has been undermined. The naïvety with which some on the left had always defended the Soviet Union undermined their ability to teach the public lessons about the holocaust. Morin, like many others, argues that little will be achieved by censorship but that it is a mistake anyway to get bogged down in a debate around certain people's views of historical facts when it is the whole nature of Nazism, fascism, and racism that has to be challenged. It is the philosophy that lies behind the desire to deny the evidence of the gas-chambers which needs to be confronted rather than simply trying to get revisionist historians to recognise and admit the truth. Le Pen's remark is not, therefore, significant as his contribution to historical studies but as part of the anti-Semitism implicit in his political message and this, in turn, is only part of his primary aim, which is to legitimise racial hatred in general.

Le Pen naturally challenges his critics to quote explicit examples of his anti-Semitism. He even has right-wing Jewish supporters in France, Britain, and the USA. It is, however, clear from the way that he denounces certain Jewish politicians at his rallies that they are particular hate figures. Simone Veil, Laurent Fabius, Charles Fiterman, and Jack Lang are his prime targets. In 1958 he told a former socialist Prime Minister Pierre Mendès-France that patriots felt an 'almost physical revulsion in his presence'. More recently he attacked the leader of 'SOS-Racisme' saying that 'if Harlem Desir gets a good press and receives subsidies it is because he is half Jewish'. Earlier he had explained that one of Giscard's Ministers who had challenged his views on immigration was in fact 'only a Frenchman of recent date'. It was, therefore, hardly surprising to find FN supporters giving moral support to Klaus Barbie during his trial in Lyon in 1987.[11]

If anti-Semitism is an undercurrent in Le Pen's media interviews, it is more explicit at rallies and in speeches by other FN leaders. Here the traditional themes of the post-war far right are given free rein, with attacks on people of mixed blood and so forth. During a 1983 election campaign in Brittany Le Pen took his theme about cousins and neighbours one step further, arguing that 'tomorrow if you are not careful they [the immigrants] will move into your house, eat your soup, sleep with your wife, your daughter . . . or your son.'[12] Hatred against Jews and immigrants is the message underpinning Le Pen's demand for 'France for the French'. At a rally in 1983 organised by Romain Marie, a discussion was organised on the colonisation of France by the four superpowers: the Jews, Protestants, Freemasons, and Communists. These were symbolised in 1983 by Badinter, Rocard, Hernu and Fiterman, all conveniently Ministers in the socialist-communist coalition of 1981–3. This kind of attack is clearly extremely reminiscent of those directed at the left in the 1930s. Romain Marie, now a FN Euro-MP, at least has the merit of being explicit. Writing in 1984, he criticised 'the tendency for Jews to monopolise the highest positions in Western nations. For example how can one fail to notice that in television there are far more Aarons, Ben Syouns, Naouls, Druckers, Grumbachs, Zitrones than there are Duponts or Durands'. He added: 'The modern world is experiencing a new intrusion of the Jewish phenomenon . . . Marx and Rothschild are by way of being two sides of the same coin'.[13]

If anti-Semitism is not the main theme of contemporary extreme-right propaganda, it is primarily because the immigrant is a more visible, convenient, and effective target, and the immigration issue produces a more substantial opportunity for mobilisation. It is, however, clear that no one should have been surprised by the recent confirmation of Le Pen's views. He has frequently stated that it is necessary to draw a curtain on the past and work to a common European future. The shock caused by particular statements merely reflects his ability to draw a curtain on his own past. In this sense the shock was somewhat artificial. What was not artificial was the consternation which accompanied his first major electoral advances in 1983 and 1984. As we shall see, they were closely linked to his successful exploitation of trends in French society of which historical revisionism and xenophobia were just a part.

The 1984 European elections

The 11 per cent score achieved by the FN in the 1984 Euro-elections in France was the party's first major breakthrough in a national election. It certainly marked a step in the direction of political respectability which, hitherto without success, the far right had been seeking for the best part of the previous four decades. This apparent breakthrough was not the lucky break of a newcomer but the culmination of years of effort and organisation throughout a period on the margins of electoral politics.

Before looking at the nature of Le Pen's campaigns in the 1980s, it is worth recalling the political landscape in which he was operating.

The Euro-elections came just over three years after the victories of the left in the 1981 Presidential and parliamentary elections. The centre-right opposition was still in disarray with a plethora of leading figures vying with each other for the all-important nominations for the 1988 presidential elections. The disarray of the right was accompanied by a crisis of the left. Hopes of a rapid turnaround in the economic situation following the 1981 victory of the left had been dashed. The communists had left the government but had lost so much credibility that they could not be a serious focus of opposition. Even within the Socialist party there was a split between those who accepted the need for economic retrenchment and the acceptance of the monetary discipline resulting from the European Monetary System (EMS) and those who wanted economic growth, devaluation, and a dose of protectionism. A great deal of Le Pen's success could, at first sight, be explained away by his ability to attract votes from those disappointed with the record of the left in power but unable to identify with the unconvincing and divided opposition. This success was made possible by, rather than being a direct consequence of, the lifting of taboos against the extreme right dating back to the liberation of France in 1944. In this sense Le Pen was part of a general development in French society. The absence in France of someone to represent the radical, neo-liberal Thatcher/Reagan philosophy also left a convenient space for the FN to occupy. Whether this occupation is temporary or permanent remains to be seen. Whatever view one takes it is clear that Le Pen's advance must say something about French society in the 1980s.

The analysis of where Le Pen's 2 million votes came from revealed, in fact, that only a minority consciously identified with extreme right-wing views. Most were ideologically nearer to the traditional centrist (UDF) and Gaullist (RPR) parties. It is clear that in attracting votes away from them, Le Pen had successfully exploited the issues of immigration, law and order, and unemployment. He also came across as a more rigorous and outspoken opponent of the left. This successful expression of racist sentiment in respectable language, plus his almost Churchillian mixture of tough and humorous speaking styles, put him in a position to denounce all the other parties as if they were all part of the same establishment club. In this way the bitter rivals of twenty years of French politics — Mitterrand, the socialist: Marchais, the communist; Giscard, the centrist: and Chirac, the Gaullist, were humorously dismissed as the 'gang of four'! Superficial attacks by the Socialist Party leader, Jospin, and others, that Le Pen was no more than a windbag merely played into his hands as they pointed to a gap between public consciousness of the importance of certain issues and the general view of the political establishment.

The 1984 Euro-election advance did not, however, come out of the blue. The result followed a series of electoral successes over the previous two years: 11 per cent in a municipal election in the 25th *arrondissement* in Paris; 17 per cent in Dreux in September 1983; 9.4 per cent in a by-election in Aulnay; and 12 per cent in another by-election in Muray. Le Pen had himself scored 51 per cent in a by-election in his home town of Trinité-sur-Mer in Morbihan, Brittany in December 1983. The 14 per cent score in the 1988 Presidential election should be compared with the extreme right's inability to get beyond 2 per cent of the votes before 1981.

In spite of the FN's by-election successes, the Euro-election result apparently came as a surprise to French political observers. National opinion polls had underestimated the likely vote for Le Pen's list, predicting a 6–8 per cent score in the week before the vote. He himself expressed no surprise at the result. Indeed, the failure of the political establishment to see what was developing in their country is itself symptomatic. In the previous year *la classe politique* had got into the habit of dismissing his successes as the result of temporary, local factors (high immigration, local following for candidates, etc.). Many dismissed his campaign as a re-run of the Poujadist movement of the 1950s: the classic revolt of the little man, the *petite bourgeoisie*. They closed their eyes to the fact that he had even, before June 1984, gained a national audience and following because he came across as an effective spokesman for a major current of opinion. In this sense Le Pen's success is more interesting for the light it may shed on the future of France than on its past. This is particularly so given the inevitable attempts by other parties to attract votes away from the FN. The Euro-elections were conducted on a national list but the presidential election was conducted on the basis of two rounds of voting, and so, assuming Le Pen could not overtake his non-socialist rivals, they would want and need his votes during the second round of voting. He knew this just as well as they do. Therefore, politicians at all levels and in all regions of France know that his forces have become part of every political calculation. In this sense Le Pen has already achieved his primary aim of breaking into the closed circle of the four other parties. This is especially the case following the demise and splits in the French Communist party, some of whose disillusioned voters have swung to FN.

In the 1984 Euro-elections Le Pen was also assisted by the fact that the UDF and RPR fought on a joint list headed by one of Le Pen's hate figures, Simone Veil. She may be a former President of the European parliament but as a result of the propaganda of Catholic fundamentalists, she is known as 'Mrs Abortion' because of the law she piloted in France

when she was a Minister under president Giscard. Since the public also
know that the UDF and RPR are in a permanent state of rivalry, the joint
list was particularly unattractive to the kind of voters at whom Le Pen
was aiming. Moreover, since Mme Veil is an avowed centrist she was
an easy target as, in the FN's language, 'a left-wing lady'.

The ability of Le Pen to shake up French politics is strengthened by
the heterogeneous make-up of his electorate. Exasperated middle-class
voters wanting a strong leader are nothing new or special in France,
but distrust of the political system from voters of the professional
classes must be disquieting. Often, but not always, Le Pen's votes
were concentrated in the heavily industrialised urban areas populated by
immigrants. Areas where *pieds noirs*, former residents of the colonies,
are concentrated also show strong support for Le Pen. These two factors
explain why, for a time, Le Pen also had his eyes set on winning
control of the town-hall of Marseilles. Marseilles was traditionally a
socialist stronghold. In other former left-wing strongholds (for example
Montpellier in the South and Thionville in the old industrial heartland of
the East) immigration has clearly been the key to the swing to the NF.

It is also interesting to note that whilst over 50 per cent of Le Pen's
voters had voted for Giscard in the 1981 run-off with Mitterrand, 30
per cent had actually voted for Mitterrand. With over 10 per cent of
the vote in forty-four *départements*, the FN was clearly much more
than a temporary, local phenomenon. Indeed, Le Pen could undermine
all voters' attachments to their 'natural' allegiance by saying that they
should not allow themselves to be treated as voting fodder. He also
cut across party lines with his defence of 'freedom', playing on the
individual's fear of being swamped, not just by immigrants but also
by an all-powerful but not very effective government. In this sense he
reflects a political culture which demands freedom for citizens to defend
themselves when law and order is inadequately guaranteed.

Finally, it should be recalled that the Euro-elections are not about
choosing a government and turn-out is relatively low. The traditional
parties know that the posts to be filled in these elections are not very
powerful. The electoral system may also play a part, voters feeling able
to vote for Le Pen under proportional representation, particularly given
the single national constituency for French Euro-elections. This may
also explain why Le Pen dropped from over 14 per cent in the May
1988 Presidential election to under 10 per cent in the parliamentary
elections a few weeks later, and maintained a high level of support
in many regions during the March 1989 municipal elections. This
provides an obvious opportunity for the party of protest. That said,
it is clear from the preceding analysis and what has followed since
1984 that the result was not a freak. Its predictability is also apparent
from the changing political climate in France during the previous year,

during which Le Pen was able to capitalise on the disarray within all the other parties.

Le Pen had already shown the ability to capitalise on other parties' willingness to play around with racist feelings in the electorate. One of the first dramatic examples of racism entering the mainstream of French politics came in spring 1983, when the communist mayor of a Parisian suburb personally drove a bulldozer into a tenement building housing immigrant workers from Africa. This move was seen at the time as an open attempt to stave off the direct loss of votes from white workers switching their allegiance from the communists to the extreme right, perhaps because of disillusionment with the role of communist Ministers then in power or because of the growing sense of crisis in the big cities. Later the Communist Party explained away the incident as a demonstration of its opposition to the formation of ghettos, but in retrospect the incident could not have come at a worse time as it led to an end to the self-discipline of the mainstream parties which had hitherto deprived racism of even a minimum of electoral respectability.

The most significant of the various election results in 1983 was that in the town of Dreux. In September of that year the FN broke through to score 17 per cent in a municipal by-election in Dreux, a Northern suburb of Paris. The RPR and UDF were forced to work with the local FN in order to defeat the socialist mayor. The socialists were identified locally as responsible for the high level of immigration. The RPR and UDF presumably thought that Dreux was an exceptional case and, therefore, felt able to ignore Mme Veil's public opposition to such an alliance. The alliance enabled Jean-Pierre Stirbois, the secretary-general of the FN, to become the deputy-mayor of a town where 25 per cent of the people are immigrants. This gave the FN its long-awaited badge of respectability. In 1989 municipal and parliamentary elections in Dreux the FN did even better than in 1983.

The successful emergence of a party basing part of its appeal on xenophobia cannot be considered separately from the growth of racial violence since the early 1980s. This was already a sign of the times. The FN campaign used the immigrant as the classic scapegoat. Experts heard by the European Parliament Inquiry showed that the slogans used were a direct echo of those used in the 1930s. The slogan that 2 million unemployed equals 2 million immigrants was by no means new, but it was the circumstances of mass unemployment in the 1980s which provided the occasion for it to be used again. During the 1950s to 1970s, when immigration was constantly rising, the circumstances did not turn traditional xenophobia into an opportunity for political mobilisation. Le Pen made himself the spokesman of what in the USA is known as the 'poor white'. This, again, is a sad reflection on the state of France, a country which has traditionally been a haven for immigrants from all over the world. The immigrant population in France increased steadily during the post-war period up to the mid-1970s. As in Western Europe generally, immigrant workers concentrated in areas where manual jobs are available, causing problems of political and social integration. Poor education of French children is blamed, on occasions, on the presence of large numbers of immigrants' children in the class. The FN's ability to exploit the situation politically in France has implications for other countries where immigrants are blamed for rising crime and unemployment. Before the Euro-elections this wave of xenophobia was quite apparent.[14]

As the European parliament reported,[15] by March 1984, 45 per cent of immigrants had perceived an increase in racism. In October 1982 the public was shocked by the murder of a young Arab in a Nanterre transit centre. In November 1984 two Turks were the victims of a senseless murder at Château Briant in Loire Atlantique. These murders, coupled with rising tension in inner cities and the successful exploitation of xenophobia by Le Pen, are further signs of a very unsatisfactory situation. The electoral circumstances may be particular to France, but it is clear that the increase in racial attacks is not. As in other countries, reports of crime create an overlap in the public mind of the issues of law and order and immigration. It would be no exaggeration to say that an explosive situation could be developing in France, with Le Pen successfully feeding and living off the development of a form of 'collective irrationality'[16] such such as underpinned the rise of other extreme right-wing movements in the pre-war period.

Another example of Le Pen's ability to speak for the crowd rather than addressing it from above can be seen in his highly provocative handling of the AIDS and homosexuality issues. His ability to speak the unspeakable makes him some people's hero. Again, he knows he is touching on the collective fear and anxiety of millions of people and speaking for them in a way that a respectable politician would never do. In this way he poses as the defender of moral order. He denounces those who, he claims, would proselytise in favour of homosexuality. Linking this to the 'problem' of the relative decline of the population of France at a time when immigrants and the third world are 'over-breeding', he argues that homosexuality could bring France to the 'end of the world'.[17] In an interview in 1987 he claimed that since 75 per cent of people carrying the AIDS virus were virtually condemned, to death they should be isolated from the rest of society in 'sidatoriums' especially as, in his view, condoms were an ineffective protection against the virus. When accused of stirring up trouble he claims that it is his duty as a politician to warn the French people of the dangers they face. Again, this contrasts perfectly with mainstream politicians' perceived sense of a responsibility to encourage a more calm and effective approach to such problems. In his handling of the AIDS issue he showed his usual skill of touching on a problem in a way that puts everyone else on the defensive by raising issues they would prefer not to tackle directly. He is clearly an instinctive demagogue who knows full well that the more panic he can create the more chance there is that people will take his views seriously.

Abortion is another issue which arouses passion in public opinion and enables him to blame the establishment for the 'moral decline' of the country. He proposes to stop social security payments for abortions. Le Pen's alliance with Catholic fundamentalists enables him to exploit the ambiguity of popular feeling on this subject. In September 1983, *Present* newspaper wrote of Simone Veil as 'a complete stranger' to Christian morality which was 'the only morality which French political life traditionally accepts'. In the eyes of this morality Mme Veil was, therefore, 'an evildoer of the worst kind, a perpetrator of the most abominable crime' i.e. abortion.[18]

Having examined the FN's ability to plumb the depths of public consciousness, it seems almost facile to examine the manifesto on which Le Pen achieved his electoral advance in 1984. It should not, however, be imagined that the nature of Le Pen's appeal leaves him with a meaningless document for a manifesto. His electoral programme naturally gives prominence to immigration and law and order, but his political strategy does not lack originality.

In a country where the battle to take over the mantle of De Gaulle is going on all the time, the FN distinguishes itself by its apparent enthusiasm for NATO. Unlike the political establishment, Le Pen shows that he is prepared to break with the Gaullist tradition of foreign policy and to reintegrate French forces into the NATO military command structure. Similarly, whereas Giscard and Mitterrand both made attempts to have friendly relations with Moscow, Le Pen appears as the only true anti-communist. He also integrates the pro-European thinking of the new-right into his view of a strong Europe, obviously a white Europe, confronting the Soviet Union. This fits in, as we have seen, with one of the main strands of the post-war ideology of the new right and the neo-fascists. As with other politicians, Le Pen has his coterie of advisers and experts, and whilst his policies are often far from detailed, they are often not very different in substance from those of, for example, some of the right-wing candidates for the Republican nomination for the Presidency of the USA, not to mention Ronald Reagan himself.

Since 1984, the FN's electoral strength has stabilised in spite of a series of attacks on Le Pen. Reports that he had been a torturer in Algeria, suggestions that he had swindled a dying man of millions of francs, photographs of his wife in a pornographic magazine, and his remarks about the holocaust have not destroyed his electoral base, even if it is clear that he has stopped gaining ground. A year after the Euro-elections, the cantonal elections showed that the FN share of the vote had more or less stabilised nationally, with inevitable but not enormously significant regional variations. In March 1986 the FN elected 33 members of the National Assembly following the introduction of a system of proportional representation

President Mitterrand's motives in pushing through this change in the voting system have been criticised. In allowing the FN to take seats in the Assembly he merely recognised a political reality and deprived Le Pen of the argument that he was a victim of a conspiracy to prevent his views being heard. On the other hand, the election for the National Assembly revealed and exacerbated the difficulties which the UDF and RPR have in coming to terms with the extreme right. Their difficulties are no easier for the fact that in practice this means that politicians with twenty or more years of parliamentary or ministerial experience have to take seriously a man who has spent most of his political life in the wilderness of fringe groups, internecine disputes, and lack of funds, and who has been ignored by the media. The depth of the crisis of the French political system is perhaps revealed by the relative ease with which an extremist political activist has moved from the margins to shake up the whole political establishment.

Le Pen's political career

To many international observers of French politics, not to mention most Frenchmen, Le Pen has been virtually unknown throughout his political life. The energetic style and the ability to shake off controversy which he now displays are not, however, something new. Le Pen has had an extremely active career and through many difficulties will inevitably have developed a certain resilience. During the mid-1980s he has lived the dream of all marginal extremists, commanding national and international media attention, a solid electoral base, and the adoration of large crowds in all parts of his country. This is certainly something new, although the fact that he has come with such optimism through periods of apparently total insignificance is perhaps a tribute to the strength of the extreme right in France. This, as we have seen, had begun regrouping, building international contacts, bringing out publications, and setting up various organisations as early as the 1940s. If Le Pen has also survived the internecine strife which characterised these decades, it is a sign not only of his personal strength but also of the strength of support for the kind of ideas with which he is associated.

Observers of contemporary extreme-right politicians make a mistake if they see in each leading figure an attempt to reincarnate Hitler with all his profound personal complexes, precise aims, and clearly developed ideology. Le Pen appears to have no personal complexes as a result of his family background and comes across as a man sure of himself and therefore able to satisfy an electorate crying out for simple believable certainties. His big physical presence, sense of humour, and ability to ride out any attacks have combined to make him a charismatic figure *vis-à-vis* his own supporters. His bluff, simplistic, often crude style is unlikely to take him much beyond his present level of support, let alone make it imaginable that he could become anything remotely resembling a genuine national leader. His adorers, however, see him both as a Celtic hero and as a Reagan for France.[19] To them he is a 'brother to the great Irish orators whose powers of evocation, whose energy and gift of image-making, whose incantatory rhythms' he possesses 'coupled with a combination of French intelligence and Breton genius'. It is interesting to note, however, that a former leader of the far right, Poujade himself, sees him as 'amoral' and 'too intelligent to believe his own speeches'. This may be nearer the mark, especially in the light of Le Pen's carefully calculated provocatory statements and his ability to annoy his enemies.

The possibility that Le Pen, whilst obviously feeding off xenophobia and the traditional ideas of the extreme right, is much more of an opportunist than his less-successful predecessors does not mean that he is any less dangerous. Indeed, it is precisely his ability to appear as a man of the people that makes his influence so strong; Hitler himself always explained his success as a result of his ability to express his ideas through inoffensive and anodyne statements with which it was difficult to disagree, a tactic which inevitably made critics appear to be exaggerating. Moreover, if Le Pen were nothing more than an opportunistic rabble-rouser, he would have become fairly frustrated doing his quarter century in the political wilderness.

Le Pen was born on 20 June 1928, a date which his more starry-eyed followers have pointed out fell exactly midway between the end of the First World War and the beginning of the Second World War.[20] Another sign that the child was born for greatness is, for some, the fact that 20 June is the day of the Celtic mid-summer feast, the day in which Le Pen's ancestors displayed the deep religious faith which supposedly characterises their twentieth-century descendant. Le Pen's youth passed in a modest, patriotic right-wing family of small farmers. With his grandfather Le Pen discovered the sea around Brittany and first heard the heroic legends of his native region. After education in a Jesuit school, he discovered strong political beliefs as an adolescent.

In 1940 at the age of twelve he saw his country defeated. In 1942 his father died at sea when his boat was torpedoed. His body was brought home and was given a public burial in Le Pen's home town of Trinité-Sur-Mer, where he had been the leader of the fishermen, and a local councillor. In 1944 Le Pen, carrying a gun, tried to join the maquis but arrived when the war was over. Whilst he has never pretended to be an admirer of de Gaulle, Le Pen has always claimed to have been in the resistance. His father's name is recorded on a monument in Trinité-sur-Mer as *mort pour la France*. Le Pen's own name is not listed in any of the records of the resistance. It is possible that if the war had lasted longer he would have fought in the resistance. In fact, even to this day, one of his school teachers remembers that he was sent away for lack of discipline and causing trouble. The school teacher does not, however, recall any action that the young Le Pen took against the occupying forces. Perhaps like others, unconvinced experts point out, he joined the resistance on the 35th of August.

At the end of the war his activities showed that he was strongly anti-Gaullist, considering that the General was responsible for the civil war atmosphere which followed the liberation in 1944. He admits that it was then that he became a staunch anti-communist, disgusted by the behaviour of those who took the law into their own hands, executing people they defined as traitors. He proudly recalls having put up handbills denouncing the repression of defenceless citizens by layabouts and failures who merely bore a grudge.

It was in Paris as a student that he first used his political skills, quickly becoming the president of the law students' organisation at a relatively fashionable school, the Institut des Sciences Politiques. His love of action was apparent in his enthusiasm as a rugby player, but politics was clearly his passion. In co-operation with what was left of Action Française he took part in numerous demonstrations, and sold newspapers of the extreme right already regurgitating the ideas of Maurras and Pétain. His aggressive style made him the natural leader of right-wing students at the height of the Cold War, and he was not unknown to the police. In 1951 he felt obliged to give up the leadership of the law students' body. The same year he took part in his first election, on the list of the Unité Nationale des Indépendants Républicains (UNIR), a party which proposed the rehabilitation of Pétain and all those who had suffered for supporting him. The party took advantage of the reports that Pétain was ill in his prison cell. Their public support for him provoked considerable demonstrations from those who had suffered under Nazism and the Vichy regime. To keep order at their leaders' election meetings UNIR called on Le Pen. Their 1950 election score of 280 000 votes disappointed the new party but since the election took place only six years after the end of the war, this result could equally well be interpreted as a sign of the durability of the French extreme right.

In the early 1950s Le Pen took part in demonstrations supporting French control of Vietnam and attacking the communist opposition. At the age of twenty-five he volunteered to fight in Vietnam. Delayed by training, he arrived there after the French defeat at Dien Bien Phu.

He could, however, return to his Parisian political friends with all the prestige of a man in uniform. With another parachutist he decided to take on what he saw as the moribund failures who represented the political class of the Fourth Republic which had just 'lost' Vietnam and was incapable of keeping a firm grip in North Africa. The Poujadist Movement, into which UNIR had merged, reflected both a concern at France's inability to defend its colonies but also a fear of social and economic developments. These concerns were not limited to the extreme right. The decision to join in the attempt with Britain to regain control of the Suez Canal was itself part of an attempt to live in the glory of the past. In spite of the realism of De Gaulle's policy in Algeria, he also symbolised the continuing potency of the myth of French pre-eminence in Europe and domination in much of Africa. Poujadism was a mixture of populism and right-wing extremism, but the circumstances in which it flourished were equally important. The mid-1950s were times of permanent political crisis which went to the heart of France's concepts of itself as a nation. The fear of the future on which Poujade thrived was not something he had artificially created. It was real and understandable.

It was in this context that in 1956 Le Pen became, at twenty-eight, the youngest member of the National Assembly, one of fifty-two Poujadist members elected with a total of 2.5 million votes. He denounced the socialist Prime Minister Guy Mollet for his lack of a coherent policy to hold on to Algeria and made his memorable attack on another socialist Pierre Mendès-France. His prediction that the ruling class then in power in France would eventually be defeated by the Algerian nationalists turned out to be true, and the collapse of the Fourth Republic no doubt confirmed his confidence in his own judgement. It would be more appropriate to see the temporary advance of the extreme right at this time as the revelation of a crisis which partially ended in 1958 when de Gaulle took over and a new constitution was put in place. Le Pen also sensed that Poujade was a natural leader of a protest movement rather than a real contender for power. He therefore chose to abandon his parliamentary activities and returned to the parachutists finally to see active service in Algeria.

His service in this extremely murderous war earned him a medal for bravery. It was a guerrilla war fought in a great city with massive civil casualties on both sides. As with other national liberation movements, the colonialists' intransigence left the FLN (Front de Libération Nationale) with no alternative to terrorism to break France's determination to hold on to Algeria. They were prepared to send women and children on suicide missions and in desperation both sides were sucked into a spiral of violence, terrorism, and torture. Le Pen was part of the 10th Airborne Division charged with breaking up the FLN terrorist network. In 1957 an Algerian complained to French police that he had been tortured by Lieutenant Le Pen in person. At about the same period a drunken Le Pen was also accused with others of an attack on a right-wing member of the staff of a hotel who had refused to serve drinks. Both these police reports became public in 1962. Le Pen took no action. In 1974 the charges were referred to in an extreme–left publication. On this occasion the man who had been secretary-general of the police in Algiers came to court to express his certainty that Le Pen had carried out torture. The newspaper publishing the charge was found guilty of defamation. Le Pen's legal action had been made necessary because he was running for President after Pompidou's death. In fact, in the Assembly in 1957 he had made a speech explaining what an atrocious war was being fought in Algeria. He argued that the violence was caused by the revolutionaries and if tough methods were used in response these should not be attacked by those whose real aim was sabotage, i.e. the left.

In 1984 these accusations again caught public attention and Le Pen expressed a view similar to that which he had expressed over a quarter of a century earlier, namely that war is horrible but men must carry out the obligations placed on them. In putting it this way Le Pen successfully drew attention to the fact that there were socialists, like the young François Mitterrand, who were in the government at the time and therefore committed to winning the war. This is another example of how Le Pen's activities are significant both in what they tell us about France and about his own personal role. Even in 1957 his speech had been widely applauded when, then as now, the centre-right of French politics vacillated between condemnation and an embarrassed tolerance of right-wing extremism. For all these reasons the reminder in the 1980s of Le Pen's past did him no serious damage. The attack merely made him even more important than he was, enabled him to play the victim, and ensured him even stronger support amongst those, especially in the south of France, who still regret the independence of Algeria. When Le Pen took legal action against *Le Monde*, that newspaper was able to argue that it would hardly be a case of libel if the person considered that it is quite defensible to commit the act of which he was accused. Le Pen won the case. Even after the French defeat in Algeria Le Pen did not modify his views as a mere opportunist would have done. He was re-elected to the Assembly in 1958. In 1960 he supported, from Paris, the rebellion against de Gaulle organised by those generals who remained opposed to self-determination for Algeria. He denounced the government for being the first to have ordered the shooting of Frenchmen because they wanted to remain Frenchmen. Even at this time he opposed de Gaulle's policy on withdrawal from NATO and suggested that an alternative to the French nuclear deterrent should be developed in the form of an up-to-date and effective joint European conventional force. Again this is an idea that is heard of in circles other than those of the extreme right.

During the 1960s Le Pen began over two decades in the political desert. He had become totally opposed to de Gaulle, in particular over the referendum which formally sanctioned the independence of Algeria. He had, however, developed the ideas and contacts which have kept him in politics into the 1980s: xenophobia, support for anti-Gaullist soldiers, the hero of the *pied noir*, the critic of the political establishment. The enormous power and popularity of President de Gaulle hid the continuing potency of these issues, but, after 1968, it was clear that the foundations of the regime were much less firm than had appeared. After this date Le Pen could at least breathe more easily in a political atmosphere of economic and social crisis, right/left divisions, and division between the non-socialist parties.

It was in the 1960s, in order to earn a living, that Le Pen helped establish the small record company (SERP) with its records about Hitler and the Nazis. In 1965 he ran the Presidential election campaign of Jean-Louis Tixier-Vignancourt, a lawyer who had been Minister of Information in the Vichy regime and, with Almirante and Blas Pinar, was one of those attempting to keep alive the extreme right as both a national and a European movement. It was during the 1965 Presidential campaign that, as a result of what was written on the sleeves of the records he sold, a legal action started against Le Pen for justification of war crimes. In 1968 he was eventually found guilty of this and fined 10 000 Francs. He also received a two-month suspended prison sentence. Tixier blamed Le Pen when he scored only 5.2 per cent in the first round of the 1965 election. The two extremists completely fell out when the candidate, without consulting his campaign organiser, recommended his voters to vote against de Gaulle (i.e. for Mitterrand) in the second round of voting. Henceforth they were rivals for the remnants of the French extreme right. Ironically, it was Tixier who thought that Le Pen, with his nostalgia for the Nazi era and his racism, was a threat to a movement which he thought should now drop its extremist image and become part of the democratic republican right, accepting, as Le Pen now does, the constitution of the Fifth Republic.

Le Pen remained, however, a focus for various extremist groups linked in particular with the 'European Action' group. On 5 October 1972, the Front National was set up. The roots of this new grouping can be found in disappointment with the old far right of Tixier-Vignancourt, the birth of the new right after 1968, and the development of the 'Ordre Nouveau' (ON). The name itself is a remarkable sign of the continuity of thinking on the extreme right. It built a bridge between those who, like Le Pen, had broken with Tixier and others who had always been out on the fringes such as 'Occident', and the openly neo-Nazi FANE. Many found a renewed sense of purpose in their support for the USA in Vietnam and their calls for a nuclear attack on Hanoi. It is remarkable that in order to escape from the impasse into which Tixier had led his movement, Le Pen should have begun his attempt to build a more successful political policy by moving into the territory of the real hard-liners. This interlude would appear to confirm the image of a man without a clear political strategy. Meetings of the ON were characterised by a spirit of European solidarity, as shown by the presence of people from the Neo-Nazi NPD of West Germany, the Italian MSI, and the Swedish fascists. One of the publications associated with the ON was called *European Elite*. On 13 May 1970 a meeting with 3 000–4 000 people was held in Paris, but in spite of the crowd and the numerous small groups supporting it, ON was too divided and incoherent to form a mass party. Its electoral performance was also poor. In particular, the ON could not shake off the blackshirt rabble-rouser image. In these circumstances co-operation with the FN was necessary and Le Pen seemed to have the best image to present to the public. His rise was not unchallenged, in particular by Georges Bidault who as a 'wise old man' of the OAS and the far right felt he should be leader. Once, however, Le Pen was given the job, he recovered his nerve and succeeded in moulding a movement around him. The ON was itself made illegal in 1973, but reformed as the Parti des Forces Nouvelles (PFN). The PFN and FN fought it out for the leading role. In 1981 the FN still could get only 3 per cent of the vote. In the June parliamentary election of that year Le Pen himself could only get 4.4 per cent in Paris. In another part of Paris the PFN leader got 3.26 per cent and soon more or less dissolved, giving Le Pen his chance in the changed circumstances of 1984.

Following his election to the European Parliament in 1984 Le Pen became chairman of the Group of the European Right. Ironically it had been the PFN which had been the traditional French section of the 'Euroright' and was particularly close to the MSI and the Spanish Falangists. The man to whom events had given the chance to present the extreme right without its hitherto rather outdated image, was a man whose preceding career would appear to suggest that he regretted the failures of the extreme right in Europe in the first half of the twentieth century.

Openly fascist elements remained within the FN into the 1980s. These grouped around the GNR (nationalist-revolutionary-group) whose publication *European Notebooks* quoted Hitler, fascism, and biopolitics as a matter of course. Its editor, François Duprat, carried out some tasks for the FN. Another publication, called *Année Zéro* called for an overthrow of the regime and expressed sympathy with the Italian revolutionary right. It espoused the traditional pro-European nationalism of the post-war extreme right. In 1985 Le Pen's party newspaper contained a photo of him visiting Duprat's tomb.

About this time a controversy broke concerning a particular stroke of luck which enabled Le Pen to inherit millions of francs from one of his supporters who died in mysterious circumstances in 1976. In 1985 Le Pen was accused of having speeded up the death of his alcoholic friend Hubert Lambert. Again, Le Pen's political career was not hurt and by now he could survey the political scene not only from his group chairman's seat in the European Parliament, and his place in the national Assembly, but also from the nobleman's residence at St Cloud which he had inherited from Lambert. This may turn out to have been the high point of his political career.

By the mid-1980s he faced the problem of expanding beyond the 10–20 per cent level of support he had built up. Differences of opinion within his party enabled him to retain a strong grip. On the one hand, Stirbois from Dreux demanded a very tough line on immigration and law and order; and on the other, Arrighi from Marseilles pushed for a more respectable image. Arrighi, as head of the Parliamentary Franco-Israel Friendship Society, faced some problems when, on his return from a trip to Israel, he heard of Le Pen's remarks about the gas-chambers.[21]

The history of Le Pen's early career and his period in the political wilderness illustrate how the extreme right can function on different levels and in different circumstances. The bottom level is that of the underground and activists who have special names for their groups but are sometimes found to be linked to the FN when terrorist attacks or murders are investigated. At a middle level are the militant political groups like FANE, and the think-tanks of GRECE and the new right. They may sometimes, like any group of extremists, disagree with the highest and most visible level of the movement — the FN and Le Pen. The disagreements may be far from insignificant but to imagine that the extreme right in France, with its ideas and its history, does not represent a broad movement with Le Pen as its most successful leader since the war, would be to ignore extremely disturbing political developments.

A crisis revealed

The electoral successes of the extreme-right in the 1980s are best seen as the revelation of a developing crisis for French society and its political system. Whether that crisis will be contained in a permanent fashion remains to be seen. The crisis goes much deeper than Le Pen's ability to grab media attention. The whole feeling of insecurity, which goes beyond the more obvious issues of law and order, rising crime, terrorism, delinquency, and so on, reflects a crisis of political culture. France is a country which has lived through a period of dramatic social and economic change. Between 1950 and 1970 a society which was still generally rural and agricultural was turned into an urban, industrial society. The social unity of a rural society is not easily recreated in an urban society, especially if this is faced with mass immigration and rising unemployment. Just as some Italian writers explain the popularity of neo-fascism as a consequence of the political culture reflected in the films of Clint Eastwood and Charles Bronson, some French analysts consider that a turning point came at the end of the 1970s with the foundation of groups defending the legitimate right of self-defence in a way which these films glorified.[22]

This development came at a time when French Communist mayors were publicly bulldozing temporary dwellings supposedly occupied by illegal immigrants. At the same time, the left was divided and the right was hesitant in face of the wave of neo-liberalism espoused by Thatcher and Reagan. As well as expressing the public's anxieties in face of these phenomena Le Pen tapped the strong vein of right-wing extremism which had for most of the previous century been deeply embedded in France's political culture. It is an extremely mixed, but nonetheless potent, political tradition. Some of the groups find their origins in the reaction to the Revolution and support for monarchy. Others are more directly related to the fascist groups of the inter-war years. To these should be added all those who still resent the loss of French control of Algeria, or remain faithful to Poujadism or even to Nazism. Rabid anti-communism, xenophobia, the cult of strong leadership and nationalism are not the sole property of the extreme right. Indeed, the principal traditional weakness of the extreme right has been an inability to form into a coherent movement able to achieve wider support. In particular, under the charismatic president de Gaulle there was very little opportunity for the extreme right to make an impact. De Gaulle remained a target for the OAS and others who would not forgive him the granting of independence to Algeria. His departure, the 1968 crisis, the 1970s economic crisis, and the absence of an effective successor gave the extreme right a new opportunity. De Gaulle's mixture of nationalism and a strong presidency, coupled with an acceptance of a (non-federal) united Europe, created hopes for the strengthening of France's economic and political status which President Mitterrand has tried to satisfy, combining it with the ideal of a progressive united Europe. As the economic crisis deepened after 1973, the parliamentary conservative parties, however, failed to offer any convincing updated version of de Gaulle's grand vision or an attractive perspective for younger voters.

As a result of its ability to survive through radical changes in circumstances, the philosophy of the extreme right is perhaps best seen as a kind of Loch Ness monster of French politics, remaining under the surface for long periods. During these times, it may be the subject of internecine strife but it survives and for brief periods plays a major part in French life, such as in the period of the Dreyfus case, the Action Française movement, the Vichy regime, and now with the re-emergence of Le Pen. It thrives in periods of economic crisis when the left is in power, and where there has always been a part of the classical right ready to give it some credence.

Bernard Henri-Levy[23] has gone so far as to argue that fascist ideology dressed up in national colours is in fact, the twentieth-century ideology of France. Anti-Semitism, for example, had strong support from the end of the nineteenth century, and for Levy the Vichy regime is far from being an aberration. This seems a somewhat limited view of French political culture and underestimates the importance of anti-Arab feelings. It is, however, clear that Le Pen, as well as benefiting from the economic and social crisis in contemporary France, has also been strengthened by the work of the intellectuals of the *Nouvelle Droite*, whose conscious aim has been to make the ideas of the extreme right dominant in French political life.

The French new right found its opportunity after 1968. In practice almost separate from the political activism of the extreme-right parties, it defined itself as a cultural and ideological movement. This movement is generally considered to be based around the *Groupement de Recherche et d'Etudes pour la Civilisation Européenne* (GRECE). Among its leading figures, Alain de Benoist is linked to various revisionist historians, supporters of sociobiology, as well as prominent journalists and others linked directly with neo-Nazi ideas. Its aim was always nothing less than cultural hegemony. It considers public opinion extremely vulnerable to the acceptance their ideas provided that the message is transmitted in a way which hides its origins and real objectives: 'The political aims may under no circumstances be exposed. We have to present our aim particularly as an intellectual and moral revolution, and must be extremely careful in the political strategy.'[24] In fact, the new right represents, quite consciously, a form of right-wing Gramsciism, in the sense that the concept of cultural hegemony was developed by the Italian communist writer in the 1920s.

This strategy is a lot more sophisticated than the ideas which lie behind it. Its aim being 'the intellectual education of everyone in whose hands the power of decision will come to rest in the coming years', it has built up a network of publications, study groups, and front organisations aiming to ensure that what are really extreme-right ideas enter the very fabric of French intellectual and political life. That such a strategy should be even partially successful is explained by the strong continuing tradition of support for such ideas which Levy has pointed out; that the movement should make such a rapid advance is, however, as Glucksman suggests, more a reflection of a lack of other ideas to talk about, at least on the right of French politics after its defeats in 1981 and 1988.

In the decade after 1968 the new right succeeded in establishing itself with such respectability that when it came under intense attack at the end of the 1970s this merely strengthened its existence as a point of reference in French political culture. The strategy which it had followed in the intervening decade is described by GRECE as a 'metapolitical' struggle, i.e. a cultural war with the aim of taking power through the domination of political culture. Its aim was modestly described as 'a European renaissance'. In this sense the title GRECE (i.e. the French for Greece) is itself significant, given that the aim of the group was the rediscovery of the heritage of ancient Greece as the cradle of scientific ideas as opposed to the alternative Judaeo Christian tradition which had, according to GRECE, undermined the Indo-European tradition with such ideas as equality and–liberalism. These heroic objectives translate in practice as a desire to revive the theoretical basis of Nazism in the sense that the Nazis' aim was also the revival of Europe, the rejection of Jews and of liberal democracy, the abhorrence of the cosmopolitanism of the Jews and of the USA, the desire to challenge communism directly, and indeed the desire to overthrow an existing regime which, in their eyes, was leading to moral and political decline.

GRECE has attempted to update the theories of sociobiology, arguing that there is a fundamental hereditary biological inequality between the races. They see a hierarchy with the 'Indo-European race' as the most superior, above the Semite, African, and Asian races. De Benoist has, for example, argued that musical talent is determined by racial elements. Naturally, GRECE believes that different cultures are destroyed by mutual mingling and considers that it is the destiny of a Europe united from the Atlantic through Eastern Europe to the Ural mountains to bring back this natural order to the world. Modern ideas of equality are rejected as unnatural, and indeed part of the alien Judaeo-Christian tradition. The new right sees the liberal democratic right as nothing better than a watered-down version of egalitarian socialism and American mercantilism. Ironically, GRECE ideology comes across as far more anti-American than Le Pen.

In the context of the extreme-right view of the necessity for a united Europe so eloquently expressed by Oswald Mosley in the 1940s, the European references of the new right are again nothing really new. By attaching themselves to the European idea which is widely supported in France they can hide their real ideology behind banalities.

Similarly, in a country where anti-Americanism is part of the Gaullist heritage, they cause little surprise with their attacks on 'the American cancer', a phrase invented apparently by Raymond Aron. It is perhaps the triumph of Reaganism and his image as a strong leader, aiming to bring about a moral and political revolution, which has led the anti-Americanism of the new right to receive less prominence in recent years than their anti-communism.

Their other ideas have not required refurbishing. In a period of rising xenophobia they find it much easier to express their sophisticated version of racism. Following a period of high immigration, the appeal to ethnic superiority is easier to get across. In a period in which France is perceived as being in a state of moral collapse, symbolised by AIDS, their attacks on the failure of the liberal establishment find a much wider If GRECE and the new right have had some success in permeating French political culture, it is clear that Le Pen has emerged as a populist spokesman who manages to plagiarise eugenics, historical revisionism, and a particular version of Europeanism with unprecedented skill.

The new right is directly connected with the Nazi tradition. De Benoist's articles often quote German professors of eugenics from the inter-war years without mentioning that they were scientific advisers to Hitler. The *Nouvelle Ecole* and *Elements* are the principal publications of the new right. Among those backing the *Nouvelle Ecole* is Roger Pearson, leader of the National Socialist Northern League, which was itself founded in honour of a leading German social biologist. Pearson has also been president of the World Anti-Communist League (WACL).

Alain de Benoist boasts an academic honour from a 'Higher Institute for Psychosomatic, Biological and Race Sciences', which was established by the fascist 'Nouvel Ordre Européen'. New right articles draw on the work of Evola, the intellectual source of Italian neo-fascism, confirming the conscious internationalism of the new right and the fact that we are not dealing with isolated national phenomena.

Given all that has been said about the heterogeneous nature of the extreme right and its propensity for internal splits, it would not be appropriate to view France as being in the grip of some vast conspiracy with everyone from the Catholic fundamentalists, the Nazi streetfighters, the new-right intellectuals, and the FN all lined up behind Le Pen. There are as many differences of opinion as there were within Hitler's National Socialist Party. Le Pen has, however, clearly benefitted from an intellectual climate in which his ideas seem less outlandish than was hitherto the case.

Indeed, the controversy surrounding the rise of Le Pen has, perhaps temporarily, undermined the possibility for the new right to pursue its project for cultural hegemony in a discreet manner. The respectability of GRECE has been openly challenged, leading, for example, to a break with the 'Club de l'Horloge', another right-wing think-tank favoured by he RPR and UDF hierarchy. Part of the crisis of the new-right strategy is reflected in articles and discussions drawing attention to the splits in pre-war Germany between the conservatives and the Nazis. In this sense

GRECE may perceive Le Pen as more of a threat to their plans than a symbol of their success. Whilst it is true that following the clash with the Club de l'Horloge, many Gaullist militants, or even Christian Democrats like d'Ormesson, went over to Le Pen's party, it was precisely this clash between the new right and the classical right that the GRECE strategy was intended to avoid.

GRECE has developed contacts in other countries, including Britain, Italy, and Germany. *Elements* is now a successful European-wide publication. The strength of the new right should not be over-estimated, but it is clearly a cause for concern that they should have been able to contribute to the movement of opinion which has created a wider potential constituency for the political extreme right. They have partially succeeded in creating the elements of a pre-fascist political culture in France and it is the evolution of the political and economic situation which will decide how substantial their impact has really been. The phenomenon which Le Pen represents is clearly so deep-rooted that it would be wrong in the short term to analyse his impact in terms of the ups and downs of opinion polls and election results.

If, moreover, our analysis is correct and, as others have confirmed, what Le Pen reveals is a deep crisis of national identity, it would be short-sighted to limit his long-term political significance to an analysis of election results. It is the continuing fact of his relative electoral success rather than the varying results which confirm the enormity of the social and political impact of the FN and the Le Pen phenomenon. What Le Pen has revealed is a substantial degree of anxiety about the future of France, a disillusionment with the welfare state and a sense of insecurity which together put people in a frame of mind to be impressed by those who would claim to offer panaceas to a supposedly beleaguered Western civilisation. For Le Pen really to go out of political business, others would have to promise and deliver what he demands and what he encourages voters to demand.

Le Pen's Political Impact

When Le Pen had his first electoral successes after 1981 there was a tendency to dismiss his ideas as a re-run of those of the Poujadist movement which had achieved 11.6 per cent of the votes in 1956, but was a social rather than a political movement. It exploited the social discontent of certain sectors of society, in particular small shopkeepers, independent artisans, and others fearing the modernisation of the French economy. The social crisis of the 1970s coupled with the issues of immigration and insecurity, make the Le Pen phenomenon more significant politically and sociologically. Poujade, among whose parliamentarians was Le Pen, did, however, capitalise on nationalism, xenophobia and anti-Semitism, but the movement did not last after de Gaulle came to power in 1958. Le Pen's movement might best be described as 'neo-Poujadist' as it has a similar sociological base. Among Le Pen's supporters has been a well-known admirer of Pétain, Gerard Deuil, who is President of the union of small and medium-sized firms (SNPMI). Although the FN has done well in geographical areas similar to those where the Poujadists had done well, it remains the case that Le Pen's electorate, whilst containing many of the kind of people attracted to Poujadism, has much more heterogeneous support and, indeed, economic circumstances are quite different. In the 1950s Poujade's voters feared the consequences of economic modernisation in a period of growth, now the French fear a period of relative economic decline, and the consequences of 1992.

Precise definitions of Le Pen's policies, cultural heritage, or even his electorate will not, however, fully explain the whole movement or enable a judgement to be made about its likely impact. Voters rarely vote on the basis of precise ideas. If Le Pen has 10–12 per cent of the votes, it does not mean that his ideas and those of the new right do not have wider support. The success the new right was in its links with the established respectable parties. As one new-right writer put it in *Le Figaro* magazine, [25] in 1978, 'in the last analysis it is the cultural climate which determines the sense of values and, in that sense, the direction of society'. When Le Pen, therefore, campaigns for repatriation and a 'national preference'; when he says, as he did during his infamous radio interview, that men are equal only in law and not in reality, he is both speaking for, creating, and representing a political constituency which until the 1980s seemed to have disappeared.

Le Pen may also be perceived as the hero of the city-dweller, the person who feels oppressed by bad housing, immigration, the threat of unemployment, and a general sense that something has gone wrong with his country. Fascism has often been perceived as originating as a radical form of traditional political protest, which is why the extreme right is not insensitive to ecological issues. Urban society enlarges the traditional bases of extremist movements resulting from a sense of rootlessness, failure, isolation, and insecurity. Such feelings are heightened when citizens feel the effects of planners' decisions, or lack of decisions. In this sense one could almost simplify part of the Le Pen phenomenon as a result of mass immigration into areas of already bad housing. Clearly, the assimilation of immigrants into French society will not succeed without adequate housing. The failure on this score leads to discrimination against immigrants precisely because of tough competition for limited housing space. This is an inevitable theme for racist political activists at local level. A situation has been created where a confused mass of people with little interest in politics can easily be roused, especially in a climate of fear and a situation of economic and social crisis. Urbanisation separates individuals from any sense of community; they search for a sense of identity which someone like Le Pen is able to provide. Analyses of developments in Marseilles have confirmed this impression and there Le Pen's support is supplemented by the presence of so many people who left North Africa when the countries became independent of France.

Le Pen's emergence has, therefore, revealed a major challenge to the French political system. It is not a bolt from the blue but neither is there much likelihood that Le Pen himself will sweep to power. The ideas that he has encouraged and the atmosphere from which he has benefited would, however, remain relevant even if eventually one of the scandals around him actually led to his political demise. It is also clear that as the 1980s developed the French political system had not yet proved able to repulse or to come to terms with the rise of the FN. If this rise has revealed a crisis, it is unlikely that the crisis will turn out to be short-lived.

The rise of Le Pen, even if it levels off at around 10 per cent (as it appeared to do in the 1986 and 1988 parliamentary elections) creates enormous difficulties for the other centre and right-wing parties. The extent of these difficulties is such that some commentators consider that the Le Pen phenomenon is nothing more important than an invention of the left developed with the intention of depriving the right of a parliamentary or presidential majority. Even if this were the case, and the introduction of proportional representation was done with this intention, it has not proved an undiluted success. In 1986 the centre-right won back the parliamentary majority which it had lost in 1981, and made no formal deals with FN at national level. It is probably also the case that because of the Gaullist tradition and a large Jewish population deals such as the kind made in Dreux in 1983 cause as many problems as they solve.

The main aim of the centre-right has clearly been to win back voters who have swung from the traditional to the extreme right. The efforts of Charles Pasqua to show how tough the right is on immigration and law and order seem to be intended to suggest that a vote for Le Pen is a wasted vote for those who want tough policies on immigration and law and order. This is part of an attempt to neutralise the far right and to occupy its territory. This is a dangerous choice because it could give respectability to Le Pen's campaign and in the end only strengthen his bargaining position in the negotiation of deals which the strategy of neutralisation is precisely designed to render unnecessary. So far no clear picture of the centre-right strategy has emerged. Even after the defeats of 1988, the right has tried to combine rejection of Le Pen personally with an open appeal to his electors.

The RPR leader Jacques Chirac, like his supporter Pasqua, has adopted some of Le Pen's themes whilst denouncing his movement. Le Pen's remarks about concentration camps led all Presidential candidates into an explicit condemnation, but public memories are short and this issue was clearly not the main preoccupations of voters in 1988. The CNIP, a small grouping representing small businessmen and farmers, has argued that 'there are no enemies on the right' and has served as a bridge between the RPR and the FN. This has been particularly evident in the European Parliament-but there have been direct clashes inside it between Malaud, trying to bring Le Pen in behind the RPR, and Romain Marie, clearly trying to force events in such a way as to maximise Le Pen's strength. The rapidity with which the political scene has shifted since 1981 should not be underestimated. A party which in 1981 had no national or European Parliament Members had thirty-three Members of the National Assembly between 1986 and 1988, ten Members of the European Parliament as well as councillors all over France. It has members, funds, and media attention. The circumstances which permitted its emergence are not about to alter. Since politicians rarely organise campaigns on the basis of inevitable defeat, centre-right candidates cannot ignore the new political reality at local level, even if at national level a more sophisticated response is possible.

In the southern regions of France where the FN is particularly strong there appears to have emerged an anti-immigration consensus. Even some socialists have resorted to blaming the right for the encouragement of immigration. The FN benefitted in 1989 from divisions on the left about the right of Muslim schoolgrils to wear a 'Chadar' or traditional head-dress and this helped the FN to success in local elections and a by-election in Dreux. With such an ability to attract a substantial number of votes it is hardly surprising that the FN is not being treated as any kind of pariah at local level. Even after Le Pen's public espousal of historical revisionism, a leading member of the UDF argued that a statement of this kind was irrelevant to any consensus established at regional level. In fact, these local deals have not led to a recovery by the UDF or the RPR in the south. The UDF was humiliated in Marseilles in the 1986 parliamentary elections when the NF scored 22.5 per cent and came a close second just behind the socialists. In 1983 the FN had not even contested the municipal election, but now it has its eyes on he town hall. The mixture of racial tension, unemployment, and housing problems has made the Marseilles situation peculiar but, as we have seen, not totally different from the rest of France.

The problems on which Le Pen is thriving are unlikely to be the subject of miracle solutions. Attempts to 'unmask' Le Pen by the Communist leader, André Lajoinie, who, like socialist leader Jospin has debated with Le Pen on television, do not appear to have had much effect. Reducing unemployment and dealing with the problems of assimilating immigrants are fairly difficult to overcome in a short period of time. Le Pen's attack on the establishment is only strengthened when parties come to power and then fail to live up to the exaggerated expectations they have created.

On immigration, the centre-right do not really know how to respond. The promises they have made in recent years on such questions as the nationality code have not been acted upon and so Le Pen has been able to throw their promises back in their faces, accusing Chirac of treating public opinion with contempt.

The cohabitation between Mitterrand as President and Chirac as Prime Minister after March 1986 helped Le Pen to argue that there is no real difference between them; when they publicly disagreed they gave an impression of an ineffective political establishment. The French Presidential election of 1988 was a major test of Le Pen's impact.

The 1988 Presidential and parliamentary elections

It was in the Presidential election of May 1988 that Le Pen had the greatest impact and scored his greatest electoral success. It should not be overlooked that at the end of 1987 many commentators felt that the Le Pen phenomenon had run out of steam. In November it was reported that one of his key supporters in the European Parliament, Olivier d'Ormesson, had left the FN as a response to Le Pen's failure to withdraw his remark about the gas-chambers being a mere detail of history. D'Ormesson would apparently have forgiven Le Pen if he had been prepared to admit that he had made a mistake. The defection confirmed the continuing existence of an internal split between the hard-line racists and the more traditional conservatives who had flocked to the FN in the 1980s. The crisis did not, however, have any significant electoral consequences.

The unreliability of opinion polls as a means of understanding the potential of the FN is confirmed by a re-examination of a major *Le Monde* poll published also in November 1987.[26] This poll claimed to show that Le Pen was a declining force, as a growing number of people saw him as a danger to the nation and a man who should never become a Minister: 88 per cent of those polled disapproved of his views on the gas-chambers and the conclusion was drawn that Le Pen was well on his way back to marginality. Whether the poll was accurate is a matter of debate. What is clear is that six months later he achieved an electoral success which belies the analysis of the polls offered in the press. It may be the case that the poll was accurate but that the desperation of mainstream right-wing politicians' attempts to capitalise on his apparently weak hold on his voters backfired spectacularly. Moreover, national polls mask wide local variations. The national leadership of the

Gaullist RPR and the generally more centrist UDF have never looked for a national alliance with Le Pen, particularly because of the violence of many of his supporters. This has, however, never meant that they have stamped hard on all co-operation at local level, even where they had the means to do so.

In the run-up to the 1988 election the Gaullist Prime Minister Chirac did not, however, succeed in hiding from observers that one of the central aims of his campaign was to destroy Le Pen as an electoral force by stealing his votes. As one observer rather graphically expressed it, Chirac had to give Le Pen the 'kiss of death' in order to 'chew him up and spit him out'.[27]

The election campaign was well under way in March 1988 when plans by Charles Pasqua, Minister of the Interior, to parole and then expel thousands of North African prisoners were leaked to the press. With Le Pen's poll rating already back up to 10 per cent Chirac knew that he would need his voters in the inevitable final-run-off against Mitterrand. Pasqua's move was attacked by the anti-racist movements as a clear violation of human rights. Shortly afterwards Chirac took this campaign further, calling for a referendum on a possible reform of the nationality code. He had already stated his view that France could not take any more immigrants, but to put the issue of who is a Frenchman to a referendum was a double assault on Le Pen's terrain. For not only did it respond to the xenophobic mood of parts of the country, it also accepted the traditional extreme-right idea of plebiscites as a form of direct democracy. Chirac had clearly chosen to fight it out with Le Pen in terms of demagogy. Indeed, by March 1988 it was clear that Le Pen had been proved right and that immigration would prove a key election issue. The Gaullists and socialists had staked out their ground, with Chirac saying that although he could not accept racism and xenophobia he could understand it. The socialist leader, Lionel Jospin, responded firmly, insisting that racism did not need to be understood, it had to be combatted. Ironically, this clash hid the fact that the consensus between mainstream parties, revealed in the 1986 television debate between Chirac and Fabius, still existed. The main parties, in practice, agreed that there should be no more immigration, that voluntary repatriation should be encouraged, and that all immigrants staying in France should be helped to integrate. The two main candidates presented very different images to the electorates: Chirac, with his off-the-cuff call for a referendum, differed from Mitterrand; already benefitting from the open support of 'SOS-Racisme' and having himself filmed for television at a school in an area of high immigration.[28] In fact, part of the weakness of Chirac's appeal to xenophobia lay in the fact that in his two years as Prime Minister, he had only partially implemented earlier commitments made in the heat of the 1986 parliamentary election campaign. This did not, however, deprive Raymond Barre, Chirac's centrist rival, of the need to enter the undignified contest with a statement that it was necessary for France to show vigilance in defending its national identity.

Immigration was not the only issue which Chirac used to try to strengthen his standing with voters who might have switched to him from the extreme right. As polling day approached, his government tried a series of spectacular events to try and reinforce the image of the kind of muscular right-wing regime over which Chirac would preside. The highlights of this phase were the breaking of an agreement with New Zealand whereby the French spies implicated in the *Rainbow Warrior* bombing were not to be returned to France and the bloody end of a hostage saga in New Caledonia which left twenty-one people dead. New Caledonia as a colonial remnant had particular symbolic significance and, of course, a lot of Le Pen voters. These dramatic events took place between the two rounds of voting of the Presidential election.

As Chirac shifted desperately and in the end quite unconvincingly towards the extreme right, the socialists presented themselves as the main barrier to Le Pen. Mitterrand's ability to do this naturally outraged the Gaullists even more and they continued to claim that by allowing Le Pen into the National Assembly he had been a pure opportunist whose only aim was to split the right. This argument remains weak so long as the Gaullists are prepared to allow local co-operation with the FN and to campaign nationally on themes which are selected to attract votes from them. The nature of the Chirac campaign itself illustrated how far Le Pen's poison had penetrated French politics. The FN's electoral score was in this sense just a confirmation of a continuing political fact of life.

In the end, of course Le Pen did nothing to help out Chirac in the final run-off which Mitterrand won quite easily. He calculated that he had nothing to gain from a Gaullist President who had promised him nothing directly and expected to have much to gain from a situation where the centre and right would be divided and demoralised. Indeed, even as Chirac shaped up for his final challenge to Mitterrand, Barre suddenly took a new hard line against racism in a pre-emptive operation clearly designed to prevent any direct Chirac-Le Pen deal. Le Pen's endorsement of Chirac was as half-hearted as it could be without undermining his credibility with some traditional conservatives, but his machine did not make any effort to follow this up with electoral mobilisation in favour of Chirac. The electoral strategy of Chirac proved to be both unscrupulous and unsuccessful.

Analysis of the election results confirmed that Le Pen's appeal had been effective beyond the single issue of race. The strength of his showing in the traditional red belt around Paris proved that he had been able to play on workers' feelings of economic insecurity.

International concern greeted the FN candidates' first round election score and for a while Le Pen glowed in his transient importance on the front pages of the world's press. Most observers did look for the social and economic reasons behind his success but as Anthony Lewis wrote in the *New York Times*, 'In the end the fact remains that Mr, Le Pen is a particularly crude and nasty racist. His former wife says he would reminisce about Adolf Hitler and say 'Uncle Dolphie did not do enough.' That four million citizens in the heart of Europe can vote for such a person is not a minor event.[29]

A few weeks later Le Pen's vote had already slipped to below 10 per cent in the elections for the National Assembly, which the re-elected President Mitterrand had dissolved in order to provide an opportunity for the socialists to regain their majority. The election was held on the two-rounds system and not proportional representation as in 1986, and Le Pen lost all but one of his parliamentarians, including his own seat. Only the most superficial observer would, however, see this as the end of the story of the Le Pen phenomenon. Competition for FN votes took place at local level and the election was characterised by the highest level of abstention ever seen in a French parliamentary election. This itself suggests that Mitterrand's re-election may have strengthened some voters' disillusionment with the whole system. The continuing failure of the right could provide Le Pen with the kind of circumstances in which he can exert an impact. More importantly, as at least one journalist noted, if Le Pen's success is indeed a result of the 'crisis' or 'modernisation' of French society the phenomenon will be anything but transitory.[30] France can expect rising unemployment, and structural changes to prepare for 1992 will be painful. The problems of urban decay and social change will not, with the best will in the world, all be overcome by the socialist government. It would be too easy to use the usual academic terms and dismiss Le Pen as the beneficiary of the protest vote. The FN's vote is very heterogeneous and goes well beyond the traditional areas of extreme-right strength. The FN has created a demand for a tough nationalist right wing style of politics and it will only become insignificant when this demand appears to be met. It is this which makes it essential that President Mitterrand and his successors succeed in maintaining a majority for a more optimistic and humanitarian vision of their country.

It should be added that the extreme right has never put all its eggs in the basket of electoral politics, and that if they face electoral decline in a period of socialist rule, then FN activists could well be tempted to put renewed emphasis on extra-parliamentary agitation as other such parties in Western Europe have done in similar circumstances. In this sense Le

Pen could be a bigger menace to French society precisely because he
has virtually lost his parliamentary base.

At the end of 1988 came various signs that fundamentalism was
once again becoming the dominant force on the extreme right as some
moderates withdrew their support and the hoped-for electoral success
that their allegiance appeared to have made possible became all the
more unlikely. On 2 September 1988 Le Pen came up with a particularly
tasteless play on words, calling the Minister of Public Service, Michel
Durafour, 'Durafour-Crématoire'. Again the blunder was revealing as
in French the word 'four' means oven, and 'four-crématoire' is the
French term for the gas-chambers of the Second World War. Stirbois
came to Le Pen's defence with the equally sophisticated explanation
that his leader's play on words was meant to show hat Durafour was
a political corpse. In fact M Durafour is Jewish. Following this incident
Le Pen lost his one remaining member of the National Assembly, Mme
Yann Piat, who denounced him for using 'dormitory humour'. She had
already shown by her individualistic role in the Assembly that she was
not prepared to follow Le Pen's instructions as to how to vote. Again,
opinion polls seemed to show that Le Pen's quip had led directly to
a loss of popular support. Le Pen was prosecuted for his attack on
Durafour and in December 1989 the European Parliament voted to lift
his parliamentary immunity.

As Le Pen lost control of his support and his tongue, there was
evidence that some of his supporters had indeed turned back towards
more traditional forms of extreme right-wing political agitation. At
the end of October 1988 it emerged that FN activists were directly
implicated in incendiary attacks on a cinema in Paris which was
showing the controversial Martin Scorsese film *The Last Temptation
of Christ*. Fifty attacks, using various methods, were reported by
the end of October. Even less surprising was the report that the
inspiration for the violent demonstrations against the film came from
the Christian fundamentalist FN Euro-MP, Romain Marie, who presents
himself also as the leader of the 'Alliance against racism and for the
respect of Christian and French identity' (ACRIF). Amongst other
activities linked to the extreme right was a very effective threat to
boycott all the chemical products of the Roussel-Uclaf company, which
had planned to start marketing an abortion pill. In November, Henri
Charlier, an associate of Romain Marie, was arrested in connection
with investigations of extreme right-wing violence. He is the editor
of *Present*, a magazine which supports Le Pen and the fundamentalist
Catholic priest Monsigneur Lefebvre, who has broken with the Vatican
because of his opposition to the reforms of the early 1960s. Hundreds
of thousands of French Catholics support him in spite of the Vatican's
condemnation.

In January 1989, the mayor of Dreux, who five years earlier had come to power with FN support, announced that whilst he was campaigning for re-election he would not under any circumstances seek an alliance with the FN. He claimed that this approach followed a hardening of Le Pen's views. By this time the deputy-mayor of Dreux, another FN Euro-MP, Jean-Pierre Stirbois, had been killed in a car accident, but his widow claimed that the FN could till count on the good will of many of the members of the RPR/UDF list for the March 1989 municipal elections. Her prediction proved correct, when the FN, under her leadership, picked up 22.2 per cent in the first round of municipal voting in Dreux on 14 March 1989, and later in the year she won a seat in a National Assembly by-election in Dreux. These were even better than the 'shock' results of September 1983. Moreover, given the relative lack of central control of all local politics in France, this could very well remain a political reality in many parts of France. For this reason one has to remain sceptical as one reads yet another opinion poll [31] which appears to show a continuing decline in Le Pen's electoral support and a growing realisation that he represents a danger to democracy, a view still held by only 67 per cent of those questioned. Such figures are not very different from those in a similar poll before the 1988 elections referred to above. In fact, in the 1988 elections Le Pen did much better than the press had expected. It should also be noted that in analysing the FN's impact, we are talking about the views of a substantial minority, whether it be of the electorate as a whole or of the supporters of the RPR and UDF in particular or the voters who float between them and the FN. The levelling off or even the decline in voters' support for the FN will be significant only if and when it becomes clear that racism is no longer a major political issue or, as has been emphasised, the left looks like providing a credible alternative capable of attracting the firm support of those who have turned to Le Pen. This is clearly not the situation at the beginning of the 1990s, with the socialists back in power and with the opposition lacking a single leader, a set of policies, or a disciplined electoral machine to face the municipal and European elections. Having held its ground in 1989 in various municipal elections, it is clear that the FN under Le Pen has developed into a force in French politics of a kind that no other extreme-right leader has achieved in France since the Second World War.

Not only has the party a hard core of support too big to be ignored, it is also associated with certain issues which will definitely remain significant. The FN cannot be dismissed as an ephemeral single-issue movement which will disappear as circumstances change. The saliency of the main issue, immigration, on which it has thrived is not about to evaporate and the historical circumstances in which the FN has grown will not change quickly.

Perhaps the most significant new development in early 1989 was the clear rejection, in a positive manner, of Le Pen's views by the French government. In his New Year address, President Mitterrand put his personal authority behind government plans to revise the Pasqua Law on immigration which had been enacted under Chirac's premiership and which made it almost impossible for immigrants to use judicial methods to resist expulsion from France. Human rights organisations in France welcomed the government's new policy, whilst the RPR and UDF accused Mitterrand of a deliberate attempt to revive immigration as an electoral issue and therefore of being Le Pen's best election agent.[32] This seems rather an overstatement, as Mitterand has always been the most outspoken of all socialists on the race issue, in particular through his strong support for 'SOS-Racisme'. It is also important to note that Mitterrand expressed views on immigration in a speech dominated by the importance of 1992 and France's role in uniting Europe. The 1989 elections for local councils and the European Parliament provided an important test of the trends, but if the confusion on the centre and right helps Le Pen, it should be added that if the socialists face new economic difficulties, as occurred in the 1980s, there will be further potential for Le Pen to recruit more disillusioned voters from the left.

In the spring of 1989 Le Pen expressed the hope that in the Euro-elections he would improve on his score in the Presidential elections. In fact he only got 11 per cent but this confirmed that under his leadership the FN had achieved a firm electoral base. The slogans he used in 1989 were little different from those of 1984, but the fact that all the media exposure he had received and his near total isolation from mainstream parties in France and inside the European Parliament had not removed this base confirms a disturbing reality.

After the June 1989 Euro-elections Le Pen continued as chairman of the European Right Group but the new composition of this Group appeared to confirm a shift towards extreme-right fundamentalism on his part. The REP refused to sit in the same group as the MSI. The latter argued that they could not accept Schönhuber's support for German reunification and the two parties clashed over the South Tyrol question. The MSI also continued to support the political objective of European union, whilst the REP played on some Germans' negative attitudes to the 1992 objective and its political implications. The exclusion of the MSI from Le Pen's group will leave him free to take an even more nationalist approach to European affairs and to reject the apparent consensus of the socialists, Gaullists, and Centrists in favour of European union. When the European Parliament reconvened in July 1989 Schönhuber and Karel Dillen of the Flemish Vlaamse Block became vice-chairmen of the European Right Group, which, perhaps confirming Le Pen's problems, had changed its name to the

'Groupe Technique des Droites Européennes'. This is translated as the Technical Group of the European Right. The word technical suggests a failure to agree a political programme. The fact that this coup should have survived and reconstituted itself in 1989, despite various internal crises, is, however, a further confirmation that we are not dealing with a temporary electoral phenomenon in one particular country.

At the end of this book we reproduce an extract from a work of political fiction by Peter Jay, in which in 1994 a Le Pen-type figure uses his platform in the European parliament to mobilise a pro-European Fascist movement on the issues of immigration and unemployment. This would not appear likely to be repeated in reality. It is the case, however, that the economic situation, which is clearly the key to political developments, is such as to provide the kind of atmosphere of insecurity in which the extreme right thrives. Condemnations by the establishment, highly publicised gaffes and defections, court decisions, and statements by church leaders have not so far seriously weakened Le Pen's electoral strength, and it is unlikely that they would be any more effective in even more difficult circumstances. The condemnations of racism, and implicitly of Le Pen, by the European Parliament have also clearly not turned the tide.

If Jean-Marie Le Pen's political past is ambiguous, if its current success is indubitable, what will happen in the future remains extremely and disconcertingly unpredictable. What is certain is that what he represents cannot be wished away or dismissed as a passing fashion. As Michel Rocard, the French Prime Minister, said in May 1988: 'Le Pen's voters suffer no more and no less than the same troubles of other French people, they just react more badly.'[33] Even if expressed rather flippantly, Rocard's view is accurate: Le Pen is responding to a national crisis. As Rocard's fellow socialist Jean-Pierre Chevenement put it: 'He represents the feeling of a relative decline, unfortunately all too real.'[34] He went on to argue that France looks anxiously at Germany's renewed economic strength and as a country whose history has been dominated by great political ideals it now lacks any great national sense of purpose. The unification of Europe is seen as a threatening inevitability, and in a period of great uncertainty people feel a need for order and security. Chevenement concluded that for France to contribute best to Europe it had to recover its national self-confidence and avoid confusing patriotism with nationalism. Such observations could be applied to other European countries, but it is certainly encouraging to see that the Le Pen phenomenon has led those at present in power in France to think lucidly and deeply about their country and not to fall into either of the traps of complacency or despair.

Notes

1. RTL, *Le Monde: Grand Jury*, 13 September 1987. The quotations used here are the author's translation of the full text made available by the press service of SCP-RTL.
2. The *Independent*, 20 September, 1987.
3. *L'Evenement du Jeudi*, 24 September 1987.
4. *Le Monde*, 17 September 1987.
5. The *Guardian*, 27 October 1987.
6. Evidence presented to the EP Committee of Inquiry, Annexe G, pp. 3–4.
7. Ibid, Annexe, p. 11.
8. *Le Monde*, 20 June 1984.
9. Quoted in *The Extreme Right in Europe and the United States*, Anne Frank Foundation, 1985, p. 57.
10. *Evrigenis Report* p. 35.
11. *New Statesman*, 2 October 1987, p. 11.
12. *Le Nouvel Observateur*, 15 June 1984.
13. *Present*, February 1984.
14. Evidence presented to the EP Committee of Inquiry (by G. Pau-Langevin) Annexe, p. 6.
15. *Evrigenis Report*, p. 34.
16. Nelly Gutman, Institute of Jewish Affairs, *Research Report No. 13*, November 1984, p. 10.
17. Interviewed on 'Fréquence Gay', 11 June 1984.
18. Quoted in E. Plenel and A. Rollat, 'The revival of the Far right in France', *Patterns of Prejudice*, 1984, pp. 18, 2.
19. Alain Rollat, *Les Hommes de l'Extreme Droite* pp. 14ff. Calmann-Levy, Paris, 1985.
20. *New Statesman* 2 October 1987, p. 11.
21. Edwy Plenel, *Le Monde*, 19 June 1984
22. *L'Ideologie Française*, Paris, 1981.
23. Quoted in *The Extreme Right in Europe and the United States*, Anne Frank Foundation, 1984, p. 53.
24. Subrata Mita, 'The National Front in France – a Single issue issue movement?, *West European European Politics*, II, 2 April 1988.
25. *Le Figaro* magazine, 27 May 1978.
26. *SOFRES* poll analysed in *Le Monde* 4 November 1987.
27. Jean D'Ormesson quoted in *Agence Europe* 5 May 1987.
28. Robert Solé, 'Immigration: Consensus et dérapages', *Le* Monde 16 March 1988.
29. Anthony Lewis, 'A river of racism flows through Europe: Le Pen proves it', *New York Times* reprinted in the *International Herald Tribune*, 29 April 1988.
30. 'Le Pen et l'Avenir', *Libération* 21 May 1988.
31. *SOFRES* opinion poll analysed in *Le Monde*, 6 January 1989.
32. *Libération* 3 January 1989.
33. *Le Monde* 3 August 1988.
34. ibid.

Four

Terrorism

Extreme right-wing politics cannot be understood in terms of single strategies, or simple conspiracies. Nor should any activity by a particular group be automatically considered as part of a vast conspiracy with clearly thought-out aims and objectives. Intimidation of minorities, spreading fear amongst the general public, disseminating propaganda, participating in elections are all political tactics to be used in the appropriate circumstances by the appropriate people.

Whilst the terrorist outrages for which the extreme right has openly claimed responsibility have caused far more deaths than Arab or left-wing terrorism, there remains a tendency among commentators to assume that terrorism is most naturally associated with the ultra-left. In fact, whilst no form of mass murder can be defined as rational, it is much easier to understand the political motives which lie behind the assassinations, hijackings, kidnappings, and terrorist attacks carried out by the IRA, the Red Brigades, or particular Arab groups. The targets are precise and carefully selected. The murder of tourists in a busy railway station has another purpose altogether: that is, to create panic. What is also striking about many of the extreme-right terrorist attacks is not that they target the innocent and are not preceded by the slightest warning but that they are not followed up by the issuing of demands or attempts to justify their action to the public at large. It is perhaps also the spasmodic, unpredictable, and apparently unplanned nature of so many of these attacks that has caused so many difficulties both for investigating magistrates and for professional analysts. The problems of analysis are compounded by the fact that random murders are combined with assassinations of policemen, journalists, immigrants, and other 'enemies'. These murders are themselves only part of a general campaign of arson, beatings, and attacks on property which all serve to augment social tensions and demoralise political opponents.

Right-wing terrorism in Europe is also a particular cause of concern because of what it tells us about the functioning of the institutions of some European countries. It is the political background to right-wing terrorism which makes it wrong to ignore what has been a very real and direct threat to democracy. For it would appear that the lack of interest in the media is accompanied by a relative lack of interest or concern among security services in dealing with the problem as effectively and drastically as they have tried to deal with left-wing, Irish, or Arab terrorism. This widespread complacency becomes all the more cause for concern if one recalls that the most successful indigenous terrorists in Western Europe are those from the extreme right. It is these people who kill in the largest numbers. It is these people who find it is easiest to make use of 'friends' in the security services or havens in countries where fascists are actually in power. The extraordinary lack of discussion of this in the media and elsewhere cannot be justified or explained by any particular difficulty of analysis or lack of information.

Since the 1960s our societies have faced growing problems of public disorder. Whether or not society has become more violent is a matter of endless sociological speculation. It is certainly clear that the media and the security services felt it appropriate to concentrate on the threats coming from the 'left', in particular from the IRA, the Baader–Meinhof Group in Germany, and the Red Brigades in Italy. As a result, it would appear that this menace has been met head on and, in some cases, virtually defeated. It is, however, the case that the activities of these groups also provide an alibi for those who wanted to strengthen the role of the police and the state in general. They provided encouragement for the kind of authoritarianism that the extreme right wanted to put in place of liberal democracy. As Paul Wilkinson has pointed out: 'the track record of terrorism as a weapon for winning political power is pretty abysmal'.[1] He expresses with irony his view that the only occasion in which terrorism succeeded in destroying a liberal democracy was in Uruguay in 1972. This was precisely because the Tupamaros' campaign provided the occasion for the overthrow of a democratic regime by a ruthless right-wing authoritarian government.

In spite of this, it would have been remarkably naive to have imagined that in the crisis years of the 1960s and 1970s the threat of violence from the extreme right could be discounted. We have already seen how many leading lights of fascist regimes took up new roles in post-war Europe or departed to the tranquillity of one or other fascist country outside Europe. On the borders of democratic Europe three countries continued to be ruled by fascists. Italy faced a series of attempted coups. In Spain democracy, which had been re-established in 1977, survived only because of the role of the king during a coup attempt in 1981. In Turkey fascist violence reached a horrible crescendo before its purpose was achieved by the overthrow of democracy in 1981. In Greece fascist violence continued even after the overthrow of the colonels regime in 1974. These events were only the confirmation of what was obvious in the 1950s and the 1960s, namely that the fascist tradition and the violence associated with it had not been eradicated.

It might be argued that it is a distortion to overstate the significance of right-wing terrorism when, in practice, almost all the victims have been in Italy. In fact, the terrorists who committed these outrages were all very active in the international movements of the extreme right and it is this which provides their strength and their historical significance. Moreover, their primary advantage in avoiding detection was their co-operation with various security agencies in Italy and elsewhere. This also makes them part of a much wider phenomenon apparent in many European countries where police and security services sometimes seem to act outside the law, turning a blind eye to racist and fascist acts of violence. There are those who argue that the Italian fascist group 'Ordine Nuovo' was nothing less than the armed wing of the P2 lodge which conspired to concentrate power in the hands of its members in the military, in politics, finance or the judiciary. In France the FANE boasted of the numerous policemen in its ranks. In Belgium the leaders of an underground right-wing group, the 'Westland New Post' (WNP), openly claimed to have infiltrated Belgian state security. In Spain it is clear that the same army officers and policemen who worked for the Franco regime have continued their careers in the same era. The enormity of abuse of the very purpose of a democratic law enforcement agency is perhaps too much to grasps but what makes Italy so much less of a special case is, unfortunately, the fact that in other countries there is considerable evidence of fascists being protected by sympathetic people in influential positions and therefore avoiding detection. It is this general cause for concern which must be borne in mind as we look at events first in Italy and then elsewhere.

Italy

The events in Italy over the last twenty years surpass the imagination even of a public opinion used to a daily diet of violent entertainment and spy stories. The reality is far stranger than anything any novelist has yet imagined. The presence of double agents has been discovered in many countries, but what is more extraordinary in the case of Italy is that events have exposed the existence of a parallel secret service capable of perpetrating murders, planning coups, and diverting the course of legal action. In a country which in the 1940s saw the ignominious collapse of a fascist dictatorship and a spontaneous and heroic rebellion by partisans, it appears that there were many who got on very well in post-war society whilst maintaining their fascist beliefs. Indeed, the strong anti-communist emphasis of defence and internal security policy assisted them, in same cases, to get on a lot better than others who had risked their lives fighting dictatorship. We have already looked at the career of Licio Gelli. His life, extraordinary as it is, would be of far less interest if it was merely a question of helping old Nazis find a peaceful retirement home in South America, or even of setting up 'masonic' arrangements to ensure 'jobs for the boys'. In reality what we are talking about is much more serious. For the investigations of right-wing terrorism in Italy have revealed that many of those involved were, in fact, secret service agents, with influential positions in Italian society working with political activists and manipulators enjoying massive finance and world-wide backing.

During the decades after the Second World War the MSI had long tried to establish a respectable image and to acquire legitimacy as an anti-communist ally of the dominant Christian Democrats. Having been marginalised in the 1960s, the movement saw by the end of the decade new opportunities arising with the crisis of the centre-left regime and the wider economic crisis in Europe. During the 1960s the failure of the alliance with the Christian Democrats had led to a return to fundamentals by many activists with Almirante at the time a critic of the MSI leadership. He allied himself with the proponents of extremist agitation and when he became leader in 1969 he adopted a double strategy combining the toleration and stirring-up of violence in the streets at the same time as seeking respectability under the slogans of law and order. This was referred to at the time as the politics of 'the cudgel and double-breasted suit'. As we shall see, this image could fit certain other right-wing political leaders in Europe. The failure of the MSI to get back into any kind of alliance with those in power naturally strengthened the arguments of the extremists, and on the fringes of the party and outside it terrorism seemed a more likely path to political success. In the 1960s various new-right movements sprung up, such as the 'Ordine Nuovo'and 'Avanguardia Nazionale'. These groups rejected parliamentary democracy and adopted a strategy aimed at justifying dictatorship. The MSI as a party did not, of course, officially adopt this strategy, but the links of so many of its key figures with various terrorist outrages make their ritual denunciations of terrorism sound very hollow and unconvincing.

On 12 December 1969, seventeen people were killed in an attack on the Banca dell'Agricoltura in the Piazza Fontana in Milan; eighty-eight people were injured. The truth about the origin of this attack would not have come out without the bravery of magistrates such as Alessandrini and Stitz. Their main achievement was to get the investigators to leave off following the anarchist connection and to look at the more obvious right-wing connection. This itself required two years' work. The various trials which have taken place into this attack revealed the role of the secret service in interfering with the investigation, including the setting up of false evidence in order to divert inquiries to the 'red' connection.

One of the accused, Guido Giannettini, was a secret service agent closely connected with the 'Ordine Nuovo'. The full truth behind this attack has still not been unearthed.

On 22 July 1970 sabotage led to the derailment of the Treno del Sole at Gioia Tauro (Reggio Calabria). This attack killed six people.

Late at night in the town of Peteano near Venice on 31 May 1972, three policemen were killed when their Fiat 500 was blown up as they went to answer an anonymous telephone call. Fifteen years later yet another trial of those accused began in Venice in 1987. The investigating magistrate, Felice Carson, stated after three years of inquiries that the secret services had frequently attempted to prevent the murderers being brought to justice and in practice only a handful of officials had really tried to serve the cause of democracy.[2] The truth is now coming out because, for once, the author of the attack, thirty-seven year old Vincenzo Vinciguerra from Udine, has admitted responsibility. A member of 'Ordine Nuovo' he is reported as having told investigators: 'this was an act of total war against the state'

This confession makes the role of the police in trying to divert the course of inquiries all the more reprehensible. Officials and secret agents tried, immediately after the Peteano murders, to put the responsibility on to the extreme left. They tried to explain it as an act of purely criminal violence. The six accused were completely acquitted only after four trials, and have themselves now decided to sue the police whose trickery resulted in their years of suffering in jail. One of the people who should have been in the defendants box with Vinciguerra, Carlo Ciccuttini, has escaped to Spain. Two extradition requests have been turned down and he now, apparently, is in the arms and the uranium business on behalf of South Africa and some Latin American governments. Whilst Ciccutini and Vinciguerra had been together in Spain they received thousands of dollars of assistance from MSI. This was after they got in touch with Stefano delle Chiaie. At one phase Almirante also risked standing trial in connection with the Peteano murders because of his help in obstructing justice, but he benefitted from an amnesty. Vinciguerra still has some distinguished company in the defendant's box: army General Tino Mingarelli and police Colonel Antonio Chirico, both accused of having destroyed evidence. Two former secret service agents are also on trial in connection with this particular fascist outrage. Together, their aim had been to divert investigators away from those responsible for the crime, namely the neo-fascist 'Ordine Nuovo' in Trieste. This group had, in fact, been responsible for a series of attacks in this part of Italy and thirty-four people involved have now been sent for trial.

In a magazine interview[3] Vinciguerra speculated on the motives of his more prestigious co-defendants. He considered that it would have been very easy to convict him if anyone had really tried, e.g. through phone-tapping. The decision to cover up fascist involvement was, he considers, a strategic one, taken at a high level; it was not simply an act of solidarity with a friend in trouble. Vinciguerra added that 'Ordine Nuovo' in his view, was a group invented by the secret service.

On 17 May 1974 four policemen were murdered at Milan police headquarters. Police are considered a legitimate target because they are voluntary defenders of the state which the neo-fascists, with their protectors in key positions within the same state, aim to destroy.

Eleven days later, on 28 May 1974, in the Piazza della Loggia in Brescia, eight people were indiscriminately murdered; seventy-nine people were injured, thirty-six seriously. This attack, which represents the peak of the first major wave of post-war Italian fascist terrorism, was aimed at a political meeting organised jointly by socialist, communist, and Christian Democrat trade unions. The rally was the high point of a four-hour general strike called as a demonstration against the rise of neo-fascist violence in the Brescia region. The bomb was placed in a rubbish bin in an arcade and was timed to murder workers as they arrived to take part in a demonstration. Police and newspapers received a message from the 'Ordine Nuovo', admitting responsiility for the attack and listing other people and places on a 'hit list'.

The preliminary inquiries into this attack were inevitably the subject of manipulation and the sabotaging of evidence. In this case, an apparently repentant fascist, Ermano Buzzi, started acting as a witness for the prosecution. He was assassinated in prison, strangled with his own shoe-laces. The assassin was another fascist terrorist prisoner, Mario Tuti, who regained prominence in 1987 during an abortive attempt to escape from prison on the island of Elba. The manipulation and covering up of evidence meant that in the end it was judicially impossible to produce convictions in court, even though there was massive evidence against well-known neo-fascists, who were also members of the 'Ordine Nuovo'.

On 4 August 1974, a bomb exploded on an express train as it passed through a tunnel outside Bologna. This was the *Italicus* train on a journey from Bologna to Florence. Twelve people were killed and forty-eight injured. The only apparent motive of this and other even more horrific attacks in Bologna is that Bologna is a communist electoral stronghold. Inquiries following this attack immediately turned to the subversive Tuscan groups led by Mario Tuti of 'Ordine Nuovo' and to MSI circles in Arezzo. On 20 July 1983 the Assise Court in Bologna decided to grant an acquittal because of lack of evidence.

According to an Italian Parliamentary Committee of Inquiry, chaired by Tina Anselmi, a Christian Democrat, it remains highly probable that the attack was, in fact, organised by a group of Tuscan terrorists and their accomplices from the Emilia region. According to the judge in this case: 'In the opinion of the parties claiming damages, the accused members of "Ordine Nuovo" were inspired, armed and financed to carry out the attack by the masonic movement, which took advantage of right-wing subversives and terrorists, within the context of the so-called "strategy of tension", in an attempt to halt the country's gradual drift to the left and set up the necessary basis for a future *coup d'état*.' This theory was alarmingly confirmed during the trial, particularly in relation to the famous P2 masonic lodge, although the evidence gathered was somewhat insufficient it was proved that freemasons had ordered and financed the right-wing terrorist attacks and that some of the funds were allocated to the Arezzo branch of 'Ordine Nuovo'.

Licio Gelli's P2 masonic lodge also included among its members the examining magistrate, the public prosecutor Mario Marsili (Gelli's son-in-law), Arezzo's head of police Antonio Amato, and head of the Carabinieri, Lt Col Tumminello, and, as is well known, many of the national leaders of the internal security police (SID), including General Miceli. It is, therefore, not surprising that, as the Anselmi report states, 'some fascists in the group of terrorists in question worked for the Carabinieri, that others had contacts with the army or the police and that they received valuable and timely information on the progress of investigations into their activities'.[4] In December 1986 Mario Tuti and Luciano Franci were given life sentences for the *Italicus* bombing.

In the period 1974–80 there was no single outrage of the kind dealt with above. It is clear, however, that such attacks represent only the tip of the iceberg, and that fascist violence covers the whole spectrum from street brawls to mass murder. The sources of such violence had hardly dried up in this period. For example, on 24 January 1975 Mario Tuti shot and killed two policemen who had come to his flat in Empoli following up inquiries into the *Italicus* bomb.

Other investigations and crises were causing difficulties for those in control of the dark side of Italian public life. In particular, the investigations into Roberto Calvi were beginning. He was being investigated because of an almost incredible swindle in which his bank, the 'Ambrosiano', was involved. He was also well connected with many dictatorial regimes in Latin America, and one of his pillars of support was the Vatican financial adviser Archbishop Marcinkus, an American, whom Italy has tried, without success, to extradite from the Vatican State to face charges of financial misdealings. Among the magistrates investigating Calvi was Emilio Alessandrini, the same magistrate who had dealt with the Piazza Fontana bombing. On 29 January 1979 he was shot dead just after he had driven his children to school. In this case a left-wing group, Prima Linea, was apparently responsible.

On 23 June 1980 Judge Mario Amato was murdered. He had become an obvious target since having initiated a vigorous examination of extreme right-wing activity in Rome. He was denied police protection despite repeated requests. This murder took place in a period of crisis for extreme-right activists. Successful investigations and arrests had led to accusations of betrayal and internal tensions. There was, however, also a rising spiral of violence and murder which came to its climax in August of the same year. Given that many fascists consider violence itself as having purifying or even glorifying qualities, there were perhaps concerns coming from some elements in the Italian establishment that the terrorist antics would not help them strengthen their power through manipulation or election. A further reason for not seeing every act of violence as part of some well thought-out plot is that many of the activists considered 'spontaneismo' (spontaneous violence aimed at the state) as more effective than overt or even covert political activity. Mario Tuti was a proponent of this approach, and it is perhaps ironic that he was sent for trial on the morning of 1 Augusta 1980 for involvement in the 1974 train bombing referred to earlier. Whatever may be said of the Bologna massacre, it was not an isolated spontaneous gesture by mindless fanatics.

On 1 August 1980 the worst single outrage was perpetrated in the attack on a second-class waiting room at Bologna railway station. The intention of those who placed the bomb was to kill or hurt as many people as possible: eighty-five were killed and two hundred injured. The explosion took place on one of the busiest days of the year, namely the first Saturday in August, the peak of the holiday season. It was also the eve of the anniversary of the *Italicus* bomb. Investigators directly implicated Licio Gelli, Stefano delle Chiaie, and Francesco Pazienza (an associate of Calvi) in this mass murder. Direct responsibility was claimed by the Armed Revolutionary Nuclei (NAR) but investigations show that it was part of a much wider plot, the objectives of which are by no means clear. Pazienza and Gelli were both charged with subversive association in connection with the Bologna massacre. Also charged in connection with this is Stefano delle Chiaie. All these three are far more experienced and sophisticated operators than the younger generation of militants obsessed only with violence and attacks on the state, rather than its manipulation, or overthrow through a *coup d'état*.

Any idea that the Bologna bombing was an isolated incident is ruled out by an examination of the career of Stefano delle Chiaie. Like Gelli, he is significant not just through his own activities but through his worldwide associations. Given the importance in the world of some of his friends it, is hardly surprising that he cried out 'I am not a terrorist', when he was arrested in Venezuela on 27 March 1987. Delle Chiaie was known as the 'black pimpernel' or 'shorty'. He was born in 1936 into a very poor but fascist family. In 1960 he and some friends were recruited by the Italian Interior Ministry to help break up left-wing student demonstrations. These gangs were moulded by delle Chiaie into the 'Avanguardia Nazionale'. They helped in the attempted coup organised by the Head of the secret service, General Giuseppe de Lorenzo, in 1964 and by the end of the decade delle Chiaie had established widespread contacts in Europe and elsewhere, and it was then that the concerted bombing campaign began in Italy, with the most probable aim of creating the circumstances to justify another coup attempt. Indeed, a year after the Piazza Fontana bomb, fascist war hero Valerio Borghese did attempt another coup. Delle Chiaie did, in fact, briefly take part in an occupation of the Ministry of the Interior, but the coup failed and the plotters fled to Spain, which was still then under Franco's rule. In Spain delle Chiaie met Otto Skorzeny and Yves Guerin-Sac, a leader of the French OAS. From Spain mercenary groups were organised to help 'friends' in Southern Africa and Latin America. Delle Chiaie worked for Skorzeny, who was perhaps under contract to the Spanish government, delle Chiaie's job being to murder opponents of Spanish fascism in Spain and outside. He has been charged in connection with the *Italicus* murder. The gun which killed Alessandrini during the Calvi investigation has been traced to him.

When Franco died in 1975, delle Chiaie moved to Argentina, where he was employed by the internal security police (DINA). He specialised in murdering the regime's opponents abroad. He had contacts throughout Latin America, and it seems inconceivable that the CIA was unaware of his activities. One of his most powerful contacts was Klaus Barbie, the former Nazi torturer in Lyons, who had close links with the fascist regimes in Bolivia. Barbie and delle Chiaie also worked on behalf of the drug barons in Bolivia and Colombia. It was Barbie who provided the links between the extreme-right activists and the drug baron Suarez, who employed them as mercenaries. They established a sanctuary which became known in Europe and delle Chiaie joined them from Argentina. Delle Chiaie was among the leaders of the so-called 'fiancés of death' which was based in a police barracks in the centre of La Paz, next door to the West German embassy. In practice, they were under contract to Roberto Suarez, a leading light in the multinational cocaine trade. Suarez, aided by brutal fascist torturers and murderers, more or less bought himself a government in 1980. The 'fiancés of death' then became highly paid government security advisers. This was the high point in delle Chiaie's career. He had achieved this prestige through his connection with Klaus Barbie.

Barbie had escaped an initial French extradition demand with the help of President Banzer in 1973 and had repaid this debt by acting as a security adviser to the Bolivian dictator. Again, it is hard to imagine that the CIA was unaware of what was going on and it has been claimed that Barbie actually compiled an intelligence report on a liaison meeting between right-wing organisations.[5] Barbie apparently also acted as an adviser to the government on torture methods and helped in attempts to encourage immigration from South Africa.

In the late 1970s delle Chiaie could, therefore, boast of his worldwide connections (Portugal, Chile, Argentina, Costa Rica, Spain, Bolivia, and El Salvador). He visited London and Rome. He was reported to be in contact with the Libyan regime. It has also been reported that the Bologna bombing was planned at a meeting in the Buenos Aires Sheraton Hotel between Licio Gelli and Stefano delle Chiaie. Their motives may never be known. It may have been that although they realised that a coup was no longer possible, they felt it appropriate to show their power to those people in the establishment in Italy who had aided them during the previous decade, and perhaps had benefited from their help. Before his arrest delle Chiaie was spotted in Spain where he was working with the GAL, a group of hit men who attack Basque separatists. Accusations have been made of connections between GAL and the Spanish secret service.

When, in 1982, the puppet fascist government collapsed in Bolivia a new centre-left President agreed to a joint operation by the CIA, the Italian secret police, and the American Drugs Enforcement Agency. Although one of his associates died, delle Chiaie apparently benefitted from a tip-off and escaped. In 1984 the Italian Parliament was told by the Italian secret service that the Americans had not given adequate assistance in tracking down delle Chiaie. Francesco Pazienza told journalists in 1985 that delle Chiaie could travel without problems to and from the USA.

Delle Chiaie himself has said little during the trials for the *Italicus* and Bologna bombings. His luck may have run out because of his involvement in the cocaine trade which is causing such concern to the American government. If this is the case it is sadly rather late in the day. The involvement of the USA in giving encouragement to fascist coups in Chile and Greece, their employment of Barbie as an agent, and the role of the CIA in encouraging an excessive fear of the communist menace are all part of the context within which delle Chiaie operated. Naturally, he resents the charge that he was nothing more than a terrorist. He was part of the worldwide war against communism in which the US has always seemed to act as if anyone who is anti-communist is a friend.

Between 1980 and 1984 fascist terrorism continued in Italy even though there was no single massive outrage of the Bologna type. There were murders resulting from internecine disputes within fascist groups. Murders of policemen, sometimes as revenge for arrests in connection with fascist terrorism continued. The wierdest elements were at work at this time, inspired by the anarcho-maoist-fascist ideas of Franco Freda. Christian Democrat offices were attacked, and in Vicenza in

July 1982 two priests were murdered. In the same period an apparently anti-Semitic attack took place in Milan. This was a period when the truth about P2 and the manipulation of fascist terrorism began to come to light. Delle Chiaie narrowly escaped arrest. Fascist suspects were interviewed by the police in London following information received from Interpol.

On 13 September 1982 Gelli was arrested in Geneva. It is, however, important to note that the truth about the political nature and role of P2 began to be suspected only as a result of inquiries into the Banco Ambrosiano affair and the 'Sicilian connection' with the international drugs trade. The scandal had already brought down one Italian government in May 1981. Not surprisingly, Calvi's Latin American subsidiaries were generally based in countries with fascist regimes where Gelli was well connected: Peru, Nicaragua, Paraguay, Uruguay, and Argentina.[6] Once again, however, a period of crisis for the various occult or fascist groups was the occasion for another attempt at mass murder.

On 23 December 1984 another bomb exploded, this time on the Naples-Milan express in the same tunnel in which the *Italicus* bomb had exploded ten years earlier. Again, the aim was to cause maximum suffering, this time during the Christmas period. Much worse carnage was only just avoided because the bomb went off near enough to the tunnel exit for many potential victims to escape. The President of Italy, Sandro Pertini immediately denounced the fascists for this horrible attack, although the head of the government, another socialist, Bettino Craxi, was more circumspect. The precise motives of the attack may have been similar to those in Bologna to show the continuing power of the fascist network. In practice the pre-Christmas massacre of 1984 put pressure on the police to be seen to be doing something. Pertini and others drew attention to the lack of prosecutions of fascist bombers compared with the relative success of the authorities in dealing with the Red Brigades. During 1988 a former MSI parliamentarian, Massimo Abbatangelo, was arrested in connection with this bombing. The security police (DIGOS) had found arms hidden in his home in Naples and investigating magistrates saw him as providing the material for those who planted the bomb on the train. Abbatangelo holds the distinction of being the only Italian member of Parliament to have been imprisoned during his term of office. In 1984 he had been sentenced to two years imprisonment for having, in 1970, thrown an incendiary device at a Communist Party office. As a member of the Naples municipal council from 1975–1983, he was remembered as often interrupting debates with physical confrontations with his opponents. The other main suspect in the Christmas train bomb case is a former member of the MSI. Alongside the fascists it appears that the Camorra and Mafia also gave support to the terrorist operation.

Another confirmation of the direct involvement of fascist and P2
figures in murderous terrorism came with the trial of the Bologna
station murderers. The full truth behind the Bologna bombing has
still not emerged. In court the prosecution succeeded only in getting
Gelli and delle Chiaie sentenced to ten years each on the charge of
aggravated perjury in connection with their role in trying to cover up
the truth. The charges of mass murder and membership of an armed
gang were not considered to have been proven. The prosecution actually
considered Gelli to be the prime mover behind the attack. After the trial,
delle Chiaie claimed he had been set up and that he was an idealistic
revolutionary who opposed terrorism. One of the four sentenced to life
imprisonment for this mass murder was, however, a long-time associate
of his. The prosecution claimed that the trial had substantially confirmed
the role of P2 and sectors of the secret service, certainly with regard
to the protection which they extended to the bombers. In a sense the
Bologna sentences of July 1988 were a point of departure for further
investigations and prosecutions, especially as the direct links between
the P2 and terrorism had been established, even if, for legal reasons, not
all the prosecutions proved successful. This may be partly explained by
the links revealed in 1989 between Gelli and the lawyer acting on behalf
of the victims' families.

Having looked at these events, it is important to remember that the
terrorist outrages referred to did not come out of the blue. There were
other attempted train bombings, attacks on political parties, attempts
at recruitment in schools and football grounds. In some regions of
Italy almost every street has symbols from one or other fascist group.
Similarly, what has come out concerning secret service involvement
can only be a very small part of the truth. The fascist sympathisers
in the secret service are not an isolated handful. As Aldo Aniasi,
Vice-President of the Italian Parliament, told the European Parliament
Committee of Inquiry, the post-1945 purge of fascists was perfunctory;
'the widespread surge of popular democratic and anti-fascist feeling
was not matched by similar convictions in the administration. On many
occasions personalities who had been compromised with the fascist
regime were called upon because they were felt to be compliant and
useful to the Government.'[7] Within the administrative hierarchy fascist
sympathisers did not die, but the 1950s were relatively stable and the
left had been totally defeated. It was from 1960 onwards that the whole
atmosphere changed when the Prime Minister Tambroni worked openly
with the MSI, and fascist sympathisers reverted to type. Aniasi quoted
a fascist, Galore, who referred to neo-fascism precisely as the classic
example of the tip of the iceberg. There may be only a few armed
activists but they can do much if they have the support of members of
the extra-parliamentary groups and the younger elements of the MSI. It

is this which makes it difficult to produce precise measurements of the extent to which the extreme right is really a threat.

In November 1988, the Italian Prime Minister, De Mita, told a parliamentary investigation that sixty wanted extreme right-wing terrorists were still on the run and that most of them had found refuge in Central and South America. He referred to attempts by the neo-fascists to regroup and feared that their main success had been in establishing forms of co-operation with the organised underworld, itself a powerful political force in Italy anyway. He considered that right-wing terrorism remained dangerous. As in an earlier phase, the extreme right had fanned the flames of regional conflict during the Reggio Calabria riots, now its hand could be seen behind regionalist terrorism in the German–speaking Alto Adige region. The continuing efficiency of the extreme right's international operation was dramatically illustrated in January 1989. Judge Alba Dora of Tuscany issued sixty-two warrants for arrest after uncovering a gun-running and drugs operation which seemed to confirm not only the close contacts between the Mafia, the drug salesmen and the terrorists of the extreme right but also their wide-ranging international links. The arrest followed the discovery in the port of Bari of a boat arriving from Beirut, carrying not only an American-made missile, Soviet grenade throwers, an anti-tank bazooka, Kalashnikov rifles, and so on, but also 25Kg of hashish and 0.5Kg of heroin. Judge Dora's investigation led him to describe the 'Ordine Nuovo' as an international terrorist organisation of the extreme right financed by illegal drug dealing. Among the people for whom warrants were issued, were many from South America and an Italian right-wing extremist already under arrest in France. This discovery confirms De Mita's view that although there have been no recent right-wing terrorist attacks their capacity to cause enormous damage remains substantial.

The enormity of the crimes of the Italian extreme right should not lead to an underestimation of its relevance to other countries. This would be a serious error. We have already seen the vast network of *ad hoc* co-operation within which delle Chiaie operated. It should also be noted that when their activities reached their climax in Italy in 1980, they coincided with other outrages in other European countries.

West Germany

On 26 September 1980 a 24lb bomb exploded at the entrance of the Munich beer festival, the Oktoberfest. Thirteen people were killed and 312 injured. The main group suspected of this attack was the Military Sports Group (Wehrsportgruppe) led by Karl-Heinz Hoffman. This attack took German police by surprise, not because neo-Nazi violence was something unknown in West Germany, far from it, but because in July 1980 the Federal Office for the Protection of the Constitution

(BFV), produced figures suggesting a decline in such activity. In fact, during the spring of 1980 the DeutscheAktionsgruppe bombed three targets associated with giving help to migrant workers. In one such attack two Vietnamese refugees were killed. Among those killed at the Oktoberfest was a member of Hoffman's group, and it is assumed that he was planting the bomb when it exploded. The Wehrsportgruppe had, in fact, been banned in January 1980.

Right-wing terrorism had only really begun in Germany in 1979. Until then activities had been limited to nostalgic reunions, street brawls, and collecting weapons. From 1979 they turned to bombing and arson aimed at Jewish and immigrant targets. The BFV estimated that in 1979 1400 neo-Nazis had been responsible for 1483 criminal acts, 117 of them innvolving violence. The upsurge of violence was preceded in 1978 by a robbery of machine guns from a NATO training ground in Lower Saxony. The group involved was suspected of involvement in a bank raid in Hamburg. It was at this time that neo-fascist violence was becoming a significant issue again in Italy.

Professor Franz Gress of the University of Frankfurt[8] has perceived a constant trend rising from 1974 onwards. At the end of 1978 six neo-Nazis were charged with forming a terrorist organisation. This was the first prosecution of its kind. Including the Oktoberfest, at least twenty people were killed during the years 1980–82. After that, statistics show a decline in such violence, although it is inappropriate to give too much weight to statistical trends when there is an obvious mixture between opportunist violence and planned outrages as well as continuing muggings, threats, recruitment, and propaganda activities. The main target of extreme right-wing violence remains the immigrants, but it appears that by 1983 the police had got the growth of organised terrorist activity under control.

The Oktoberfest bomb was not, therefore, an isolated example of the spillover of international right-wing terrorism into West Germany. After the short-lived electoral success of the NPD in the 1960s, and in particular the 1980 Federal Administrative Court ruling that the party pursues unconstitutional objectives, many militant former NPD members took the alternative road and prepared themselves for a kind of civil war. Since the early 1980s the police have unearthed various secrets organisations explicitly inspired by Nazism such as the Nationalsocialistische Deutsche Arbeiter Partei (NSDAP), with its leadership based in Lincoln, USA. In 1971, Friedhelm Busse of the Partei der Arbeit (PdA), a former NDP member, was convicted of weapons offences. This party later merged into the Volksocialistische Bewegung (VSB/PdA) and specialised in political violence, robberies, and storing arms. Another grouping, led by former NPD activists in the Nationalistische Front (NF), which, according to Searchlight has thrived on funds provided by the security police in exchange for information about right-wing extremist activities and the possibility that they actually help the police to spy on left-wing groups has been mentioned. Perhaps more important are those groups which concentrate on racial terrorism with attacks on immigrants, reflecting the xenophobic atmosphere in certain cities, particularly when, as occurs all too often in other countries, the police sympathise with the prejudices of the extremists and do not put much effort into bringing them to justice.

There has also been more concrete confirmation that the bombing of the Oktoberfest, coming so soon after the Bologna massacre, was not perhaps an isolated event or merely the culmination of a period of right-wing terrorist activity in West Germany. A Channel 4 television programme, *The Other Face of Terror*, revealed that the Bologna and Munich bombings were to be followed up by an attack on the Notting Hill Carnival at the end of the summer of 1981. This was an obvious anti-immigrant target. The programme was based on evidence from Ray Hill, who had infiltrated the British and European extreme right and tipped off the Special Branch so that the Notting Hill plot failed.[9] Hill's contacts, which were secretly filmed for television, revealed Europe-wide links between the French FANE, Italian facist terrorists, German neo-Nazi terrorists, and bank robbers. His information reveals that behind the apparently insignificant Euro-Nazi gatherings in Diksmunde and elsewhere lies an extraordinary matrix of mercenaries, terrorists, and gun-runners. They also co-operate to help each other escape from the police or to find safehouses in Paris or London. Ray Hill had got to know all these people following his involvement in establishing a South African National Front. In South Africa the Italian expatriate community included Italian terrorists linked to the New European Order network. Ray Hill had confidential meetings with members of the European Parliament's Committee of Inquiry.

Britain

It would be wrong to see the planned attack at Notting Hill in 1981 as a purely isolated incident. Paul Wilkinson has frequently warned British readers of his books not to take a complacent, parochial, or unhistorical view of Nazi violence in Britain. The electoral weakness of the National Front and other groupings should not be misunderstood. The rise of Thatcherism has deprived them of many possible voters who were put off by Edward Heath's more emollient Conservative style. Since the late 1970s, as in West Germany, there has been a conscious change of tactics away from activities aimed at electoral success. As with Hitler, the public veneer of respectability is of no significance.

The Notting Hill attack would have been a spectacularly horrific example of the racial violence which has now become endemic in

British society. Anti-Semitic attacks on immigrants, arson, propaganda in schools and football grounds, are not rare events in Britain, and they are the type of activities associated with extreme-right terrorist groups in other countries. Violence in British football grounds, often openly fomented by neo-Nazi activists, is by no means a purely British phenomenon. The British Movement has taken part in paramilitary training exercises in Germany. Camps for this purpose have also been organised in Britain by 'Column 88' and the 'Edelweiss Group'.

Britain has also seen the establishment of various paramilitary groups who have taken seriously what they read in sections of the press about the menace from socialism and the collapse of Britain. In the 1960s and 1970s, when, as in other European countries, the democratic left was enjoying a period of relative electoral success and major demonstrations took place against apartheid and the Vietnam War, the inspiration for these paramilitary activities was naturally somewhat greater than in post-Falklands Britain, where Mrs Thatcher appears to be electorally impregnable. In the 1970s Major Ian Souter Clarence emerged from a group known as 'Column 88' from where the British Movement 'Leader Guard' had also developed. Clarence, a former schoolmaster, helped provide a 'safehouse' for West German neo-Nazi terrorists. In 1975 the British press reported joint training exercises between some members of the the Territorial Army and 'Column 88'. These groups do not pose a serious threat to the state but their links to European terrorists and the fact that the police and security services have tended to turn a blind eye to their existence may be a cause for concern if they become more active in any future period of change or crisis in Britain.

During the last 'crisis' period it has emerged that the security service appeared to consider it a particular priority to check whether the British Prime Minister Harold Wilson, was a KGB agent. One cannot avoid some doubts as to whether priorities will have changed if such a period ever arrives again. There is no evidence of any P2 type clique in British society, but the virulent anti-communism and fear of democracy which provided the justification for the Italian Secret Service links with the extreme right are certainly present in the British establishment and security service. Peter Wright's book *Spycatcher* confirms that this is not an imaginary concern.

Given that violence and terrorism are an easier tactic when an organisation lacks personal and financial resources for anything else, rising violence does not mean that the various right-wing extremist groups are growing significantly stronger. Richard Thurlow[10] has referred to a veritable 'guerrilla war' against Asians and West Indians in Britain mounted by the NF and the British Movement. Racism in the police has undoubtedly in some cases given the racist terrorists a sense of political legitimacy. Certainly, surveillance of the kind used by the security services to keep an eye on anti-nuclear weapons activists could have been better to put to use to deal with the much more real threat to law and order coming from the extreme right. Whilst the NF's attempts to import the 'strategy of tension' into Britain have remained laughable, their activities against immigrant communities and in football grounds represent a serious social and political problem.

With regard to racial violence, it clearly cannot all be blamed on, or explained away by reference to, extreme right-wing political activists, even if they are very often involved in such incidents. The European Parliament's Committee of Inquiry referred to a growth of xenophobia and racial attacks and it is in such a climate of violence that the extreme right might hope to make progress. What is going on in Britain is most aptly described as a form of racial terrorism. Such terrorism involves petrol bomb attacks on cars and homes, graffiti, and racial attacks. This is an easier and more effective way of making an impact on society than organising political meetings. As we have seen, random attacks on the innocent, are a hallmark of fascist terrorism aimed at heightening a climate of violence and intimidating particular sections of the community. Reports from the Commission for Racial Equality confirm what is going on. Attacks on Jewish targets are also a common event in Britain and there appears to hare been an increase in such attacks in recent years.

Britain is also important in the analysis of European fascism today because of the people who find it appropriate to live in this country. Italian terrorists, in particular, have over the past decade found London a very congenial place both from the point of view of finding friends and benefiting from the way the legal system operates. Recent publications of the NF have included fulsome praise of the theoreticians and practitioners of fascist terrorism in Italy such as Francesco Freda, who was involved in the Piazza Fontana bombing of 1969. Nearly twenty years later the British NF finds his ideas relevant as they try to breed a new generation of political soldiers. Freda drew his inspiration directly from such groups as the Iron Guard of Romania in the 1930s.

The presence in London of various Italian fascists, many of whom have been tried and found guilty in Italy, is not just a matter of coincidence. Roberto Fiore, perhaps the most notorious of those involved is quoted as saying: 'It was a deliberate choice, I would never have gone to Lebanon because in England they still have some kind of political system and right-wing Italians can wangle their way into the top echelons of the National Front, the British party of the extreme-right.'[11] The facts of this case caused concern in the House of Commons. Italian Ministers have raised it with the Prime Minister and others. Fiore successfully fought extradition proceedings through the courts. He won his case because as Leon Brittan, then Home Secretary, told

the House of Commons, the Government has to be able to prove that
he represents a threat to society. Having been convicted of forming an
armed gang (*banda armata*) in the Italian courts, it is clear that he is
not, as his NF friends claim, a political refugee of some kind. European
community law, which permits deportations only for reasons of 'public
policy, public security or public health', is being interpreted in a very
restrictive way.[12]

Equally unfortunate is the fact that whilst in London Fiore and others
have not been politically inactive. They have been hosted by various
figures from the British extreme right and have taken an active role
in the internal life of the NF. British newspapers have revealed that
they have helped organise secret training sessions and camps for young
militants. Fiore is also linked to the Hancock family, which has been
prominent over the years in the international neo-Nazi movement, in
particular as publishers of such works as *Did Six Million Really Die?* and
the periodicals of various groupings. It was in the company of Hancock
that Ray Hill first received intimation of the plan to bomb the Notting
Hill Carnival. *Searchlight* has even referred to an Italian takeover of
the NF. Fiore was involved with NF fundraising and in internal faction
fighting against Martin Webster. A sign of the Italian influence is the
extent to which the NF now urges its members to become 'political
soldiers'.

In 1987 a German neo-Nazi, Gerhard Topfer, came to Britain to
escape the German courts, knowing that the offences he is charged
with are not covered by the Anglo-German extradition treaty. Two of
his associates had been killed by police during a Munich bank raid in
1981. He has also been given hospitality by the FANE in France. The NF
in its efforts to justify political violence, is reported also to be trying to
get involved in national liberation struggles. Through connections with
American black ultra-nationalist movements, they have sought backing
from Libya and Iran and have also tried to get close to the PLO. It was
presumably with this objective that the NF set up its own Campaign
for Palestinian Rights. The PLO representative in Britain stated in 1988
that it would have nothing to do with any organisation linked to racism,
mentioning the NF campaign specifically. *Searchlight* has also linked
the NF to underground ultra-nationalist groups from Scotland, Wales,
and in particular Northern Ireland. Violent attacks on the homes and
property of anti-fascist activists and racial terrorism are all too frequent
in Britain in the 1980s. In April 1988 there was also a suggestion that
racist activists planted bombs in the Midlands hiding behind the name
of the 'Black Liberation Fronts', an organisation completely unknown
to community leaders in the region. The aim of all this effort is clearly
to fan racial tension and school extremist activist in underground violent
political activity. A Channel Four television programme described the

modern NF as 'the disciples of chaos' and explained their international
links and training facilities in Britain. The party leadership claimed a
'special relationship with Libya' and admitted that their most important
influence in recent years had been Roberto Fiore.

The model of the Italian terrorists may be appealing to the NF but for
the time being, at least, it is unlikely to have the same dramatic impact
in Britain as the followers of Freda and delle Chiaie have had in Italy.
Not only do they lack the vast resources available to their would-be
counterparts, they cannot expect the undercover assistance of sections
of the security services or the political establishment that someone like
Licio Gelli was able to provide.

As well as being a favourite 'safehouse' for terrorists, it should be
recalled that London was also the scene of the murder of Roberto Calvi,
and the press has frequently referred to the role of London as an obvious
place for the laundering of Mafia money. Given the relative modesty
in which the terrorists live and the fact that connections between the
extreme right and the drug trade have not been reported in Britain, one
can for once conclude that it is unlikely that this is anything more than
coincidence.

France

Analysis of the extreme right in France has become more serious since
the electoral success of the Front National (FN), but this country has
also been the scene of terrorist outrages and is a crossroads at which
many of the key figures meet. As in Britain, the target of political and
terrorist activity is primarily the immigrant and Jewish communities. In
both cases propaganda activity is accompanied by terrorism involving
attacks on individuals, bombing and arson. In early 1978 a group known
as 'the Charles Martel Group' attacked a camp of foreign guest-workers
in Nice. In May of the same year they carried out attacks in Paris against
the North African Moslem Students Association and the Algerian con-
sulate. An attack in June 1978, by the French National Liberation Front
on the headquarters of Club Méditerranée, a large tourist organisation,
was justified as an act of 'resistance to the Jewish occupation of France'.
Nothing was heard of these groups afterwards and so the timing of these
attacks remains unexplained.

As in Germany and Italy a climax of a kind was reached in 1980. On
4 October, in between the Bologna and Munich bombs, the synagogue
in the Rue Copernic, Paris was bombed and four people were killed.
The FANE claimed responsibility, but this has not been proved and
it seems more likely that an Arab group was responsible. This attack
was not an isolated event. In the week before 4 October, five Jewish
institutions were sprayed with machine-gun fire. In the nine months
before October the French police recorded 122 incidents of violence and

arson perpetrated by neo-fascist groups. During the summer of 1980 the FANE sent death threats to prominent Jews. An anti-racist group was attacked, as was a Jewish-owned clothing shop. In September 1980 the FANE was banned and regrouped as the FNE, under the leadership of the former director of the Vichy regime's 'Centre for the Study of Jewish Questions'. Ray Hill, who had infiltrated the British NF, came, on several occasions, into direct contact with Marc Friedriksen, the leader of the FANE, who explained to him the system of cross-membership between his movement and the FN in France. The FANE still claims to assist in security measures at FN meetings, in the way Le Pen himself did at the beginning of his own political career. Given the traditional dispute between the terrorist and parliamentary elements of the extreme right, it is hardly surprising that it is difficult to identify the dividing line between the FN and FANE. Whether or not the FANE directly helped in the Rue Copernic attack is a matter yet to be cleared up. Experience in the other countries like Britain and West Germany has revealed occasional collaboration between neo-Nazi and certain Arab groups linked by their common anti-Jewish objectives.

As in Italy, serious questions have been raised about the role of the police in following up investigations into fascist terrorism. The secretary general of the French detectives union claimed that the Minister of the Interior knew of 150 policemen who were active in right-wing groups. The FANE newsletter of the time boasted of its successful infiltration of the police force. Among contributors to this newsletter is Paul Louis Durand, a former Nice police inspector who has been linked with Italian neo-fascists and who was reported to have visited Italy just before the Bologna bombing. There is no evidence of his having been directly involved in the Bologna massacre, but he had been made responsible by the FANE for liaison with Italian neo-fascist groups. His contributions to the FANE newsletter make clear his admiration for Hitler.

Racial terrorism continued in France throughout the 1980s. In 1982 a mosque was burnt down in Paris. In the summer of 1984 a Turk was murdered by an unemployed man who suddenly shouted 'Heil Hitler' and started shooting. A young Nazi murdered his landlady because she was Jewish. The FANE also helped a German neo-Nazi, Michael Kuhnen, to evade justice for some time. Their literature can be bought at FN meetings and some of their members have been on FN electoral lists.

Whilst Le Pen has not been associated directly with racial violence, it is quite clear that he has contributed to creating the political atmosphere in which violence is likely. As always, the extreme right combines different tactics and FN members have been involved, as individuals, in various outrages. Le Pen has used the opportunity created by Arab terrorism to suggest that the immigrant community is a hotbed of terrorism.

In August 1986 four people died when their car was blown up by the bomb they were carrying in an area of Toulouse heavily populated by immigrants. The police found racist leaflets at the scene. As a response to the anti-racist movement 'SOS-Racisme', the members used the title 'SOS France'. Among those dead was Claude Noblia, the founder of 'SOS France', who had been an FN candidate in the 1984 municipal elections. He fell out with Le Pen's deputy Jean-Pierre Stirbois, but stood in another election in 1985, publicly maintaining his fidelity to the ideas of Le Pen. The FN naturally condemned the bombers, but about 500 people turned out for their funeral, where a tribute was paid by the local secretary of 'SOS France'. He referred to those who had blown themselves up by accident as 'soldiers' and tried to suggest that they had in fact been murdered. The mayor of the town where the funeral was held was present at the funeral, as was a policeman who was immediately suspended. His suspension does not, however, adequately counter the fears that many policemen may, in fact, be overtly or covertly sympathetic to racist and fascist terrorism. This incident also confirms that whilst many of these movements have few members, they can make a major contribution to creating a climate of violence and insecurity.

In October 1988 Glyn Ford, MEP, presented to the European Parliament details of a number of events linking the FN to political violence. He referred to various FN election candidates who had faced charges in this connection and to the brutal attack on Armand Klarsfeld, the son of the distinguished Nazi-hunters Serge and Beate Klarsfeld, who had dared, in 1987, to open his mouth in protest during an FN rally in Paris. He mentioned the murder in 1986 of a socialist election worker by an FN member. The fact is that whilst precise cases of violence by FN officials may be rare, the violent hatred which their campaigns are designed to encourage, the atmosphere of violence at their meetings, and the support the party receives from violent organisations like the FANE link Le Pen and his movement inextricably to the same strategy of tension practised in other countries. It should be added that there are also those who, having left the FN because they find it too moderate, join parties like the Parti Nationaliste Français Européen (PNFE), a typical small group specialising in the terrorising of immigrants in the South of France, with the objective of encouraging their voluntary repatriation.

Belgium

Belgium is another country with a large immigrant population frequently the object of abuse and violence, with synagogues that have been attacked and where many streets are covered with fascist slogans and symbols. It is the scene of the annual Diksmuide rally of extreme-right groups from all over Europe, and has been the headquarters for many

European contact groups of the extreme right. It is also important to note that here also the problem of police involvement in extremist activity has been evident.[13] In 1980 a group known as 'Westland New Post' (WNP) was founded by some members of the 'Front de la Jeunesse', an extreme-right group. A police investigation following a street fighting incident came across a house containing an arsenal of weapons, secret NATO documents, blank identity cards from the Belgian Ministry of Defence, and of the West German Police. The WNP had a police section, which had received training from a senior officer of the state security service. Its leader, Latinus, who was later murdered by other members of the WNP, claimed that he had, in fact, infiltrated the WNP on behalf of the Security Service. During the trial of his murderers in 1987 serious doubt was thrown onto this claim. The murder of Latinus has been linked to the fire in 1981 at the offices of a left-wing newspaper, 'Pour', which had exposed the WNP. Those responsible for the fire apparently escaped through Spain to Chile and Paraguay. WNP documents seized showed that terrorist outrages were being planned. The Belgian press made the obvious comparisons with the corruption and abuse of power which characterised the P2 lodge in Italy, pointing out that at least, in Italy, the truth had finally come out, whilst in Belgium the mystery remained. In September 1987 it was reported that Belgian police wanted to interview a former senior government official, associated with the extreme right, in connection with a series of robberies and indiscriminate attacks on supermarkets in the Brabant region which left twenty-eight dead. Once again, Paraguay was referred to as the country in which this man had found refuge.

During the trial in January 1988 of six people charged in connection with the Brabant killings, it emerged that a gun linked to the attacks was found in the home of a former policeman. This individual had himself made extraordinary claims concerning a plot by extreme right-wingers within the gendarmerie apparently angry at inadequate support from the Belgian Government for the forces of law and order.

Spain

The death of Franco deprived European fascists of one of their main areas of safety within Europe. Whilst Franco himself never openly encouraged fascist activities elsewhere and did not help Hitler in the Second World War, his security services were well connected with both the older and newer generations of European Nazis. Of the various groupings in Spain, one of the most interesting is the CEDADE, based in Barcelona. Their full title is Circulo Espanõl De Amigos de Europa (the Spanish Circle of the Friends of Europe). Their name could be found on specially printed posters saluting Rudolf Hess following his suicide in Spandau prison in August 1987. Earlier that same summer the Spanish newspaper *El Pais*[14] revealed that Barbie's son had lived, under a secret identity, in Barcelona from 1965 to 1978, during which time he had maintained close contacts with CEDADE. While he was studying law, he also acted as representative of his father's shipping company. Barbie's trial in Lyons was told by the former Bolivian deputy Interior Minister that the shipping company had also acted as a cover for co-operation with former SS colleagues and to help organise fascist groupings.

Groupings in Spain have also received direct help and encouragement from General Pinochet of Chile and as their electoral prospects have faded they have turned to violence and terrorism, attacking left-wingers, lawyers, newspapers, and even threatening the Prime Minister. Their activities and the continuing left-wing terrorism naturally encourage those who would like a return to dictatorship. In 1981 and 1982 such attempted coups did take place. Apart from isolated terrorist acts the main danger for Spain is the continuing presence of Franco sympathisers in the army and secret service. Italian terrorists have turned up in the Spanish and French parts of the Basque country, and have made claims to be working in close co-operation with parts of the Spanish secret service. The GAL (Groupe Anti-Terroriste de Libération) is, they claim, an organisation manipulated by the secret police. This co-operation was apparently initiated in the early 1970s, i.e. before the death of Franco. Stefano delle Chiaie lived in Spain during the mid-1970s even as the transition to democracy was getting under way. Various reports haved linked him to the 'dirty war' against Basque terrorism.

Some of those referred to in the press are Italian neo-fascists on the run from the police who have successfully fought extradition proceedings. The main advantage for the Spanish secret police in using the Italians would be to undertake action against the ETA on French territory. In fact, scepticism was expressed in the French and Spanish press when Prime Minister Gonzales of Spain strongly denied that the Spanish secret service had been involved in anything of the kind claimed by the Italians. The number of Italian terrorists who managed to stay in Spain after the death of Franco remains, however, remarkable, and it has even been reported that a gun used to kill an Italian magistrate was, in fact, a Spanish police weapon. The explosive used in Bologna is reported to have been brought to Italy from Barcelona, although delle Chiaie's personal friend Alberto Royuela denied any personal involvement. Royuela was taken by Italian magistrates to Bologna to confront those facing charges for the August 1980 bombing who had accused him of financing extreme-right terrorist attacks in Italy. In the early 1970s he had offered hospitality to various Italian fascists who were on the run. At the time Royuela was a leading fascist in Barcelona and said that giving help to Italian and, indeed, Cuban friends with similar political views is not a crime; in this sense he admits that he has helped finance Italian fascists.

The story of the GAL remains obscure, combining the usual elements of fascist activities, criminal funds, hired killers, and policemen and secret service bodies playing an extremely ambivalent role. By February 1986 the GAL had become the most murderous right-wing group in France since the OAS, with twenty-five people killed between December 1983 and February 1986. In March 1986, when Chirac and Pasqua came to power in France, the killing suddenly stopped and there has been press speculation that this resulted from a political deal between the Spanish and the French governments. Over the next two years 250 suspected Basque Terrorists (ETA) were expelled from France under emergency powers.

International Links

With such examples of how rapidly security agencies can act against perceived threats to the state and public order, it is sometimes hard to accept the slowness which results from the fact that in a democracy the law must take its course. It is an unfortunate reality that terrorism of all kinds places enormous difficulties on security services. The opportunities for manipulation are vast. In spite of the extraordinary series of events in 1980, the conspiracy theory of post-war fascist terrorism can be discounted. In such a developing integrated political entity as Western Europe, co-operation between groups of all kinds remains inevitable. The fact that groups with similar historical and ideological origins and objectives should co-operate, hold meetings, exchange information, and even organise training camps is not itself particularly surprising. Indeed, international contacts give tiny fringe groups a sense of importance which their marginal social and political role denies them. It is precisely this marginality which provides the pressure to turn towards terrorism.

As we have seen, these international links find their origins in the post-war period, but in the 1960s these *ad hoc* contacts could be built upon in a more organised manner. It was in 1965 that CEDADE was founded. With Franco's agreement, its headquarters was set up in 1966 in Spain, where contacts with Latin America were particularly easy. CEDADE appears to have provided a meeting place, information point, and publishing house. Identical pages are to be found in the pages of CEDADE publications and Italian extreme-right publications. It is interesting to note that CEDADE had, in fact, been founded in West Germany by former Nazis in co-operation with younger Spanish and Italian sympathisers, including those who had fought in the Division Azul, the pro-Franco international volunteer force of the 1930s.

The FNE, originally FANE, had more ambitious objectives to establish a European-wide network. Its newspaper contains news on everything from fascist football hooligans to terrorism. Given the role of Barbie and his son referred to earlier, it becomes less of a surprise to learn that in its June 1985 edition, the FANE newspaper published an interview with Maître Verges, who, in 1987, defended Barbie in court. In this interview he gave credence to revisionist historical theories. The title of this newsletter, *Our Europe*, sets it precisely in the framework of an ideological form of neo-fascism as initiated in the post-war period.

There are, equally inevitably, bilateral links. During the 1970s, particularly before the fall of the colonels' regime in Greece, there was close co-operation between the Greek and Italian 'New Order' groups. Similar contacts have existed between the FANE and NAR, either to organise political activities or to help in escapes from the police. These loose contacts are sometimes continued with more formal gatherings either on the margin of such events as the annual Diksmuide rallies in Belgium, or World Anti-Communist league (WACL) meetings. In summer 1978 a major meeting took place in Brazil, where 480 groups were represented, and in 1979 a follow-up meeting took place in Barcelona.

There is no doubt that some *ad hoc* co-operation between left- and right-wing terrorism has taken place. According to an Italian press report,[15] the meeting in Barcelona in 1979 decided to 'intensify collaboration with groups of the extreme left who have identified their points of view with the major part of the programmes established by the Black International'. A bizarre trade in weapons for cash has apparently sometimes taken place. In Germany, on one occasion at least, guns used by the Baader-Meinhof gang were obtained from the paramilitary wing of the neo-Nazi NPD. Another area of overlap is apparent from the fact that both left and right groups have significant contacts with Arab terrorists. Even British National Front leaders have turned up in Libya.

Since Arab terrorists often attack Jewish targets and one of their main objectives is to undermine European support for Israel, it is likely that left and right terrorists have benefited from the training facilities put at their disposal in Lebanon. The Lebanese Falange used members of the Hoffman Military Sports Group, who, in 1981 were reported in Beirut as having switched their allegiance to the PLO. Just before the Oktoberfest bombing, a PLO official told a Beirut newspaper that at the end of 1979 the PLO had captured several Hoffman group members who boasted of a series of attacks which would begin with an attack on Bologna because it has a left-wing administration.[16] Italian terrorists are also known to have stayed in Falange military camps in the Lebanon, although, as Roberto Fiore pointed out, the atmosphere is somewhat less tranquil than in London.

Letters have also been discovered showing that delle Chiaie hoped to receive help from Colonel Gadaffi of Libya. Sympathy for the

Libyan regime has also been expressed by other Italian fascists who are impressed by the renaissance of Islam precisely because they seem to share with the fundamentalists a rejection of the modern world. Belgian neo-fascists claimed that links with Al Fatah had been set up in Madrid in 1969 under the auspices of former Nazi leaders. In 1970 a trial of PFLP terrorists heard evidence of close links between the Swiss Nazi Party and Al Fatah. German neo-Nazi publications have included adverts for the PLO At least one neo-Nazi has actually been arrested with a PLO membership card. During recent years, however, no more substantial evidence has been reported on this aspect. The PLO is anyway a very fissiparous body and, therefore, any particular activity cannot implicate the whole organisation. As anti-Arab racial terrorism has become fashionable, any Arab extremist tempted to co-operate with European racist agitators might find such *ad hoc* co-operation all the more problematic. It remains remarkable, however, that Maître Verges, Barbie's lawyer, also represented Georges Ibrahim Abdullah, a Lebanese whose arrest had been the occasion of an unprecedented series of bombings, apparently by his associates, killing many people indiscriminately in Paris in 1987. Again, this suggests nothing other than the overlap of objectives between various groups; it does not suggest any carefully prepared plot.

If one looks at the direct and indirect help received by right-wing terrorists, it is clear that there is co-operation on a much grander scale, involving the active involvement of governments, businesses, the underworld, and the security services. Fascist dictatorships in Nicaragua or Bolivia facing directly a threat from left-wing guerrilla movements have found a natural affinity with contemporary fascist terrorists as they did with the older generation of Nazis in the 1940s and the 1950s. People such as Licio Gelli have served as a bridge between continents and between generations. Latin America has seen numerous fascist coups, often with the connivance of the American CIA. Death squads have been a typical weapon of intimidation and destabilisation, with some businessmen and participants in the drug trade often ready to provide finance. The role of people such as delle Chiaie and Barbie has been referred to above and it remains to be seen whether their arrests will lead to the drying up of help from South America to European neo-fascists. During his escape from custody it was widely assumed that Licio Gelli was in hiding in Uruguay or Argentina, where his friends were highly placed. In November 1986 a Spanish magazine[17] reported that Chile is financing new extreme-right groups in Spain. On 30 September 1986, President Pinochet received a figure from the Spanish extreme right, Jaime Alonso, on an official visit. Although this received little publicity in Spain, it was widely reported in Chile. Alonso is only thirty-five years old and learnt politics alongside Blas Pinar, who would like to be Spain's Le Pen, but as in Italy a younger generation cannot live on old memories and tends to sneer at electoralism. At the end of 1989 Le Pen's Euro-Parliament Group met in Madrid and advised their Spanish allies to 'modernise'.

The involvement of the Chilean and South African regimes draws attention to the completely ambivalent position taken up by the USA towards fascist regimes, and the unwillingness of the CIA to help break up fascist networks. The USA has now, for example, formally apologised to France over the concealment of Barbie after the Second World War. However, it still seems hard to believe that they were unaware of his more recent activities in Bolivia, or that they were unaware of the activities of the Italian secret service and the comings and goings in the USA of delle Chiaie. When the Greek Colonels were in power, the USA was openly friendly with a regime which was not only brutal towards its own subjects but provided shelter for those who were hoping to establish a similar regime in Italy. It is, however, all too likely that as with Noriega in Panama and the Contras in Nicaragua, the USA has on occasions been prepared to turn a blind eye to criminal activities when undertaken by rabid anti-communists. Whether or not the USA actually gave its blessing to coup attempts in Italy, it is hard to imagine that the organisers of such a coup would not have made plans without an assumption of CIA understanding. The experience of Chile suggests that had the Italian communists ever seriously looked like getting to power, a coup in Italy could not by any means have been discounted. Indeed, this reality has sharply influenced the style and evolution of the Italian Communist Party. The USA is also the home of various neo-Nazi and racist groups which have had contacts with European extremists. Again, it is more likely that there have been *ad hoc* contacts rather than a co-ordinated plot or campaign. Vast sectors of the American extreme right have been subsumed into Reaganism but their tactics might change if President Bush turns out to be a less conservative President and unlike Reagan willing to pretend that he does not know what his officials are doing.

South Africa is another country where terrorists have found a haven among like minded people, obsessed with racism and the communist menace. Delle Chiaie is reputed to have acted as an adviser to Jonathan Savimbi in Angola and various fascist organisations have been involved in recruiting mercenaries for black dictators. Mercenary activity is an obvious way for a neo-fascist to gain the necessary experience to become a fully fledged 'political soldier'.

Turkey

Finally, it is important to look at a European country where the 'strategy of tension' actually succeeded. For, while Franco was dying and the

Greek colonels were getting themselves into trouble in Cyprus, tension rose to such an extent that a coup took place in Turkey in 1980. As *The Times* put it on 13 September, a message of loyalty to NATO from General Evren was 'well received by the Allies who had become increasingly worried by the chaotic political situation in this exposed but vital area on NATO's South Eastern flanks'. Again, it is likely that the USA was well aware of plans for the coup and did not discourage it. The coup had been preceded by continuous murder and intimidation by the 'Grey Wolves'. For example, thirty-four people died in Istanbul at disturbances following a May Day rally. *Agents provocateurs* and plain clothes snipers appear to have been at work on this occasion, and within the government and army there was obvious connivance and sympathy for these attacks. Bulent Ecevit, the Social Democratic former Prime Minister, who was present on that occasion, actually called on the security services to intervene to restore order. It was clear then and on other occasions that the agencies for the protection of the state were not doing their normal duty of protecting citizens from violence. The violence occurred as elections showed a continuing shift to the left. In January 1978 Ecevit became Prime Minister. In February members of his Republican People's Party claimed that, as a response to the growing strength of the left, 'counter-guerrilla' centres had been established by an army general, apparently at the suggestion of the CIA. They claimed that these centres had been providing arms to the 'Grey Wolves' and to members of the neo-fascist MHP or Nationalist Action Party (whose vote had increased from 1.3 per cent in 1973 to 6.73 per cent in 1977). In spirit of compromise Ecevit refuted these rumors and paid his respects to the armed forces. Others accused the left of provocative actions and right-wing figures were the object of bomb attacks. This led to a wave of fascist attacks, murders, and propaganda activities, clearly aimed at provoking civil war; attacks were even carried out against left- wingers abroad. Franz-Josef Strauss of the Bavarian CSU was criticised for a meeting, at this time, with the MHP leader.

Ecevit continued his efforts to make peace with the establishment, agreeing to re-open military facilities for the USA and to establish martial law in thirteen provinces. Trade unionists, journalists, lawyers, magistrates, and innocent civilians continued to be the targets of terrorist murderers. The MHP did its best to maintain a clean image, and the 'Grey Wolves' who were identified as being involved in terrorism, were helped to leave, in particular for West Germany. In spite of all his concessions, including banning May Day demonstrations and introducing economic austerity measures, Ecevit still felt he was being 'stabbed in the back' by business circles who continued openly to encourage the overthrow of his government. It is estimated that during Ecevit's period of rule over 1000 people were killed by fascist terrorists.[18]

It is important to be clear that this is not just a matter of speculation, or of the inevitable results of mob violence. The leader of the MHP at this time was an extremely experienced military figure, Alparslan Turkes, who had already participated in a coup attempt in 1960, during the time he was serving as head of the NATO Department of the Armed Forces Headquarters. Turkes's political experience did, however, go back much further. During the Second World War, he had been a leader of the Pan-Turkish movement which backed Hitler in exchange for financial support from Berlin and in the hope that a victorious Reich would allow Turkey to annex those parts of the Soviet Union inhabited by people of Turkish origin. Arrested at the end of the war, Turkes, like others in Germany and Italy, made his way back into the army during the period of Cold War tension and, in due course, got the job of liaising with NATO within the Turkish general staff. MHP members received training in military camps, arms were found in their offices, and party officials were arrested in connection with political assassinations. This party was the most pro-American of the Turkish political parties. It worked very closely with the 'Grey Wolves'. The title refers to the symbol of the Turkish race and the MHP encourages the liberation of peoples of Turkish origin within the Soviet Union. In 1979 MHP members were openly campaigning for an army takeover. It was at this time that the Pope's would-be assassin, Mehmet Ali Agca, was arrested for the murder of a newspaper editor. Resistance to closing down the MHP came from friends in the legal establishment and from Ecevit, who feared that the votes of the MHP would ago to strengthen his main opposition, the Justice Party. Leftist and Kurdish terrorism continued, on a smaller scale, but still objectively serving the interests of the fascists. In October 1979 Ecevit lost a general election, and under his successor Demirel, anti-terrorist measures were taken specifically aimed at the left. Political murders continued at the rate of eight per day in the early weeks of the new government. The government was actually aware at this time that an MHP death list existed.

During late 1979 and early 1980 strong economic measures and an extension of co-operation with NATO sparked off demonstrations. In spite of this atmosphere, a NATO meeting was held in Ankara in June 1980. In July massive strikes and demonstrations were held in protest against continuing fascist violence. On 12 September a coup took place. This is not the place to analyse the precise motives of General Evren, but it is hard to deny that with this coup the objectives of various groups had been achieved; NATO, business circles, and the fascists had got what they wanted. Even Demirel later expressed suspicion as to the remarkable rapidity with which peace was restored. Evren clearly aimed his law and order measures at the left, whom he considered to be under Soviet control. His regime has been heavily criticised by the Council of

Europe and Amnesty International for its human rights record. Turkes was imprisoned with other party leaders, but in practice the 'Grey Wolves' were able to join in their great fight against communism. The head of state radio and television was a former MHP leader as were other officials of the regime. Turkes openly claimed that Evren was doing wham he had campaigned for. After serving two years of an eleven-year sentence, Turkes was released from prison and the 'Grey Wolves' began to reorganise within the Nationalist Labour Party (MCP).

Even before the coup the MHP and the 'Grey Wolves' had established a network in Germany for terrorists on the run to find safe-houses. The secret services apparently let some of the killers escape and in West Germany extreme right-wing lawyers helped them with legal proceedings. During the 1970s Turkes had established close relations with the NDP, and indeed with Franz-Josef Strauss of the Bavarian CSU. At this time Turkes served as a senior Minister in centre-right coalitions and *Der Spiegel* alleged that Strauss helped the MHP with financial support. In the mid-1980s the 'Grey Wolves' resumed their attacks on other Turks in European countries, in particular trade union activists. Fifty members got into Ali Agca's courtroom in Rome and shouted their solidarity with him and his fellow defendant Serdar Celebi, chief of the 'Grey Wolves' organisation in Europe.

The plot to kill the Pope remains an extraordinary event, the motives of which remain a mystery. CIA sources accused the KGB of manipulating Agca, whilst in the Soviet Union the real instigators of the plot were accused of having invented the so-called Bulgarian connection. As in other, cases, there seems to have been a close connection between the 'Grey Wolves' network, the smuggling of drugs and arms, and the Turkish mafia. During his trial, Agca confirmed the view that the P2 had an interest in getting rid of the Pope because of his desire to solve the Banco Ambrosiano scandal. Agca claimed links with Pazienza, a key P2 figure, close to Roberto Calvi and at present in jail in connection with Italian terrorism.

This is not the point to wander further into the realms of what may be pure invention of criminals trying to escape conviction or cover up the truth. It remains the case that the tactics of those who hoped to justify and organise a *coup d'état* failed in Italy, but succeeded in Turkey. The evolution of the Evren regime does not undermine this thesis. The fascists were the catalysts of a military takeover which suited important economic and military interests. They escaped serious condemnation for their crimes before the coup and many were able to escape abroad to intimidate the regime's opponents. In 1981 their leader, Abdullah Catli, attended a WACL meeting in Buenos Aires. During that year he is also reported to have met delle Chiaie. It was Catli who gave Agca the gun with which he shot the Pope. The precise relationship between individuals, security agencies, military and business circles, and acts of terrorism is a matter for much more careful consideration as more information becomes available. It cannot be seriously denied, however, that in the case of Turkey it was perceived by NATO that Western interests would be better served by the overthrow of democracy than by the defeat of all kinds of extremism. The military took power rather than the fascist party, but the positive attitude of NATO in general suggests that in the defence of a major strategic area co-operation with dictatorship to defeat a perceived communist threat is acceptable. Indeed, as the report of the European Parliament put it, the fact that Turkey in 1985 was still under 'authoritarian rule' is itself 'a confirmation of the survival of extreme-right tendencies in contemporary Europe'.[19]

As Turkey has been attempting to re-establish a semblance of democracy, Turkes has become a more marginal figure. The MCP won only 2.9 per cent of the votes in the 1987 elections. In fact, many of the 'Grey Wolves' had posts in the army or within the governing ANAP (Motherland) Party of Prime Minister Ozal. The secretary-general of ANAP when it was founded in 1983 was a former MHP sympathiser. In the light of the fascist sympathies of many Ozal supporters, it is hardly credible for the Turkish government to refuse to take seriously the continuing reports of repression and torture being carried out under a regime which is pretending to be ready to join with other pluralist democracies in the European Community. Behind the image Ozal presents to the West as a modern conservative is an uneasy alliance between neo-fascists and Islamic fundamentalists, whose domination of ANAP at the expense of more liberal elements was strengthened at the 1988 party congress. These complicated realities are, however, probably overlooked by the new right and conservative admirers of Ozal in the West.

If Turkey in 1985 did confirm the continuing relevance of extreme-right political ideas and the power of fascist violence, the acceptance in the 1990s of a semi-democratic authoritarian regime, into the European Community would represent perhaps their greatest triumph.

The extraordinary extent of fascist violence in Europe, particularly in the late 1970s and early 1980s, is a matter of historic importance which has not yet been fully analysed. There are too many mysteries to draw firm conclusions. Throughout this bloody phase there are, however, continuing themes: anti-communist agitation, racism, protection for murderers through connivance or, more often, inaction by the main Western security agencies, direct assistance from openly fascist regimes, co-operation with the underworld, and a combination of targetted and indiscriminate murders or acts of intimidation. This was a period of

enormous terrorist activity by left-wing and Arab terrorists. The latter
have continued with sporadic but equally murderous attacks. Right-wing
terrorism was, at its height, however, only the tip of an iceberg, and
under the surface, society has not changed so fundamentally for it to
be possible to argue that the circumstances which provided the impetus
for the events we have examined no longer apply.

The apparently indiscriminate nature of some extreme right-wing
violence and psychological analyses have led some observers to the
conclusion that the right-wing terrorist has more personal problems
than those of the left. Their yearning for an authoritarian state, intense
nationalism, and obsession with racial purity could suggest a lack of
social integration. Left-wingers at least have a clearer set of ideas
and find in universities and elsewhere many ideological sympathisers
as a source of psychological and sometimes practical support. Such
theories should not be given too much importance since the main aim
of the neo-fascist strategy is to root out communists and reformists,
immigrants, or refugees and with these objectives they find many
sympathisers both in the establishment and in society in general.

Those who manipulated the terrorists perhaps are more of a continuing danger than the terrorists themselves. Few of these have yet been
punished. General Miceli, head of the Italian secret service, for example,
who planned a coup in 1974 went on to become an MSI parliamentarian.
Licio Gelli, although convicted in connection with terrorism, is allowed
to live at home and be interviewed by the press, since the authorities
consider it unfair for the ailing 'venerabile' to live in jail. The activities
of Colonel North suggest that American adventurism could still be a
threat to democracy in Western Europe, as it is clear that the CIA in
the 1980s again escaped political control and took up co-operation with
arms and drugs smugglers in order to continue the campaign against the
Sandinista regime in Nicaragua. The Irangate affair, the revelations of
Peter Wright, and the P2 scandal all give a picture of parallel or invisible
authorities operating alongside the governments for which people have
voted, and motivated by a sense of mission and importance which leads
them to ignore the law, which their positions of power enable them to
overcome or manipulate.

The sense of insecurity which encouraged the activities of MI5 in the
1970s or the Italian secret service at about the same time may have been
reduced through the re-establishment of right-wing dominance in most
European countries and the USA. The crisis which began in the 1960s
could be seen to have ended for the time being with the general defeat of
social democratic parties, the weakening of trade unions, and the arrest
of so many left-wing terrorists. In a period of right-wing political and
cultural dominance, manipulation is no longer necessary. Giorgio Galli,
an Italian writer, [20] argues that right-wing violence found its opportunity

when reformist parties appeared to have run out of steam. The case of Turkey under Ecevit would fit the pattern. The failure of reformism means that social tensions develop of the kind which led in France to the 1968 crisis, and in Greece to the 1967 *coup d'etat*. Galli quotes no less of an authority than Giulio Andreotti, Defence Minister in the early 1970s and Prime Minister on a number of occasions, as arguing that whilst finance and execution of terrorist acts is a major problem in Italy, its origins lie elsewhere.[21] Andreotti referred to Paris, from where a wanted terrorist told a newspaper that it was British, American, German, and Israeli intelligence who were manipulating events in Italy. We are talking about a period when socialists like Willy Brandt and Harold Wilson were in power in countries whose intelligence services did not trust them or many of their colleagues and collaborators. The threat of PCI participation in government in Italy and instability in Turkey were, therefore, not isolated problems. The 'invisible government' of certain European countries encouraged by the CIA therefore came to see the extreme right as part of a possible solution. In this context the terrorists themselves were only tools in a bigger enterprise. In Turkey few directly involved in terrorism took up positions of power, but they helped others to achieve their political objectives.

It remains to be seen whether right-wing terrorism will re-emerge. The lesson of this episode, however, is that forty years after the Second World War, the mentality which led to the rehabilitation of Klaus Barbie as a Western agent still motivated important areas of the establishment who found it possible to co-operate with rabid racists and fascists in order to face up to a perceived communist menace. Fascism not only remains a major element of the political culture of Western Europe but also continues to be a living and deadly force.

Notes

1. Paul Wilkinson, *Terrorism and the Liberal State*, Macmillan, 1986 p. 111
2. *La Repubblica*, 22 March 1987.
3. *Panorama*, 29 March 1987, p. 6.
4. Marco Revelii, University of Turin, Evidence presented to the EP Committee of Inquiry, Annexe R, p. 5.
5. Tom Bower *Klaus Barbie* Corgi, 1984, p. 259.
6. Rupert Cornwell, *Gods Bankers* Counterpoint, 1984, p. 133.
7. Aldo Aniasi, Evidence presented to the EP Committee of Inquiry, Annexe A, p. 1.
8. Franz Gress, University of Frankfurt, Evidence presented to the EP Committee of Inquiry, Annexe H, p. 8.
9. *Searchlight* 107–9, May-June-July 1984.'The Ray Hill story'.
10. Richard Thurlow, *Fascism in Britain 1918–1985*, Blackwell, 1987, pp. 287–8.
11. EP Committee of Inquiry Report, Annexe A p. 11.

12. EEC Treaty Article 48.
13. René Haquin, *Le Soir*, 11 May 1987.
14. *El Pais*, 13 May 1987.
15. *L'Europeo*, 18 January 1987, pp. 14–7.
16. Quoted in Bruce Hoffman, 'Right-wing terrorism in Europe', *Conflict*, Vol. 5, Part 3, pp. 185–210.
17. *Cambio 16*, 24 November 1986, pp. 52–59.
18. For a detailed account of this period in Turkish history see D. Ozguden, *Extreme Right in Turkey*, Info-Turk, Brussels, 1988.
19. *Evrigenis Report*, para. 184.
20. G. Galli, *La Destra in Italia*, Gamma Libri, 1983.
21. Galli, op. cit. p. 68.

Five

Europe Looks at Itself

The problem of how democratic institutions and movements should respond to the activities of fascist movements is as old as the idea of fascism itself. Since the early part of the twentieth century fascist leaders have combined a contempt for parliamentary democracy with a deep understanding of the potential of the techniques of mass mobilisation. Since elections provide an obvious opportunity to raise tension, get recruits and votes, and win legitimacy, major fascist parties have rarely missed the chance that they provide. Hitler was one of the most energetic and efficient modern election campaigners. The extreme left has, by way of contrast, rarely shown the ability of the extreme right to dress itself up with sufficient respectability to mount even a modest election campaign.

All elections, and particularly elections where the election of a government is not the issue, can provide surprises for even the most experienced politicians. The elections for the European Parliament provide an obvious chance for maverick or extreme elements, as the public has little idea of the role or function of the institution for which they are required to elect members. The relative demobilisation of the major parties may also provide a clue to the success of the French Front National in the European Parliament elections of June 1984.

In those elections the party of Le Pen won 2 million votes. The leader of the FN, in spite of decades of activity in politics, was almost unknown. As we have seen, his appeal to xenophobia had provided the key to his success. His slogan '2 million unemployed equals 2 million immigrants too many' was a direct repetition of a slogan used by the Nazis in the 1920s. In a significant local election held nine months earlier in Dreux just outside Paris the FN had already made a major breakthrough, but it had been explained away as a result of the local importance of the immigration issue. In Dreux the socialist mayor had opted for a high-profile stand confronting racism head on. The European elections showed that immigration had become a national issue. This was confirmed in the 1986 elections for the French National Assembly. Following Dreux, the FN's success could no longer

be considered a real surprise. It does, however, appear that in spite of
rising racism and xenophobia, any electoral success by the extreme right
is still considered by commentators as a surprise. In fact, election results
do not come out of nowhere, and, as we have seen, electoral successes
in Berlin, Denmark, or Flanders have been far from isolated events.

One of the first consequences of Le Pen's electoral success was,
however, that he became not only a celebrity and regular television
performer but also a subject of numerous articles and publications. The
simple respectable image which he had sought to portray was designed
to hide his ambiguous political record. He had benefitted from the lifting
of the taboos which had influenced the whole style and content of
post-war French politics. The decline of the consensus introduced by
de Gaulle, the emergence of a new generation of voters, the loss of the
memory of the 1930s and 1940s all helped provide Le Pen's chance.
The advance of the ideological right and historical revisionism about
the holocaust had obviously opened the way to a new political appeal
to old ideas deeply rooted in French society. Le Pen's attacks on Jewish
political figures, and on the Jewish-born Cardinal Monsignor Lustiger
were, in fact, a direct echo of the attacks on Dreyfus and Leon Blum.

Having burst on the scene, Le Pen could not expect any less media
exposure, in the full sense of the word, than any other modern politician.
His past, his family, and his ideas were inevitably subject to close
attention and it is both interesting and encouraging to note that Le Pen's
success also awakened great concern in other countries and within the
European Parliament about a possible resurgence of racism and fascism.
For Le Pen, this Parliament and the preceding election campaign were
meant to be nothing more than a platform and an opportunity to try
to achieve political respectability. The formation of an extreme-right-
wing political group was to be part of this process. The old dream of
Almirante of a Euroright was finally to take a concrete form; but with
ten out of the sixteen members, it was Le Pen who provided the novelty
and the leadership.

The issue for everyone concerned by this development was to consider the appropriate response. This debate was not limited to the
corridors of Strasbourg. The electoral success of Le Pen and the
formation of an extreme-right group in the European Parliament were
the subject of widespread press comment. By the time the newly elected
Parliament came to meet in Strasbourg in the last week of July 1984
the only consensus to have emerged was about what should not be
done. Parliamentarians had by then carefully studied the Treaties and
the rule books to see if there was some way in which Le Pen could be
prevented from speaking, or taking his seat. The possibility of hanging
the rules to prevent the sixteen extreme-right MEPs forming a group was
considered, but, as the *Guardian* stated in an editorial on 25 July 1984:

The new fascist group conforms to the rules by consisting of more than ten members from not less than three countries. Ten are from France, led by the formidable Mr Jean-Marie Le Pen, five from the Italian Social Movement, and one from the Greek Epen party. All of them were democratically elected in June by the proportional representation systems of their respective countries. In other words, voters with a free choice put them where they are. In a democratic system the will of the voter is supposed to be paramount. It may be depressing, even disgusting, that only 40 years after the fall of Mussolini and Hitler (and only ten after that of the Greek colonels) there are free Europeans ready to vote for neo-fascists. But that is a matter of opinion, regardless of whether the vast majority of Europeans share it.

The arrival of Le Pen on the European scene touched many very sore points. In many political groups both right and left there were people who had taken part in the resistance movement, been held in concentration camps or lost members of their families in the holocaust. There were also others who, certainly not fascist sympathisers, had made a political career without ever having to face in public the problem of having parents who had fought in the war on the side of the Reich. Throughout the work of the European Parliament's Committee of Inquiry deep emotional feelings were inevitably at the root of certain political actions. Some members reacted spontaneously with gestures of little political meaning. Somewhat unfairly, the *Guardian* sneered at those who announced a policy of social ostracism towards the extreme right. For example, Alf Lomas, Labour MEP for a part of London with great racial problems as well as decades of history of fascist political activism, announced that he would never sit at the same restaurant table as Le Pen.

On the day the extreme-right group was formed nearly 200 MEPs took part in a symbolic silent protest. They each carried a white rose, the symbol of the German resistance to Nazism. This action was initiated by the Socialist Group but was widely supported. This support was, however, not universal. Otto von Habsburg, a member of the Christian Democratic Group from Strauss's Bavarian Social Christian Party (CSU) stated that the white rose demonstration was deplorable and that it showed the absence of a balanced view of democracy. The white roses were a symbol of resistance to all totalitarianism and he considered that people who worked continuously with totalitarian communist parties had no moral right to appoint themselves as the judges of others or to deny the parliamentary rights of members who were certainly no worse democrats than the agents of an oriental superpower. Otto van Habsburg later served as a member of the European Parliament's Committee of Inquiry, but this outburst showed that at this stage he was not prepared to join in any condemnation of Le Pen.

It was already obvious that symbolic protests could not be kept up for the five-year term of office of the European Parliament. Attempts to change the rules in some way would only weaken the credibility of the Parliament and provide an opportunity for the extreme right to attack the whole idea of parliamentary democracy. The initial spontaneous reactions did, however, serve one purpose. They showed that Le Pen and the group of which he became the first chairman would not find it quite so easy to get political respectability and, more importantly, they could not expect to draw without difficulty a veil over the historical origins and political objectives to which they subscribed. Perhaps most disturbing in those first days was the way Le Pen tried to join in normal parliamentary activity. He gave his group's support to a centrist Christian democrat, Pierre Pflimlin, in the elections for the presidency of the Parliament. When he himself stood for the position of Vice President he received a few dozen votes, showing that he had friends outside his own sixteen-strong group.

The idea of establishing some kind of Committee of Inquiry was a response to the decision not to take any action to prevent Le Pen and his fellow MEPs receiving all the rights, privileges, and financial back-up available to all Members of the European Parliament. Since democratic methods were to be used another approach was needed. It was also clear that the majority of the European Parliament would not spontaneously have taken any action whatsoever. The rules of procedure of the European Parliament provided a way to overcome this initial obstacle even if it was already clear that any meaningful action to isolate the extreme right could not be conceived without wide-ranging support beyond the ranks of the left, which had no majority in the European Parliament.

The need for full exposure of the nature of the French Front National (FN) had already been illustrated by a minor incident in Maidstone at the end of June 1984. On 21 June the *Daily Telegraph* reported Le Pen as saying that the only similarity between his party and the British National Front was the coincidence of the name. There were no contacts or ideological affinity. On 26 June the *Guardian* reported that a Mr Paul Johnson, regional organiser of the NF had sent a congratulatory message to Le Pen following his electoral success and had invited him to a rally in Maidstone. Le Pen was reported as having accepted the invitation although he did not in fact turn up. Paul Johnson told the *Guardian* 'we've nothing in common really, apart from our immigration and repatriation policies. Our economic policies are quite different. It was a courtesy invitation.' Mr Johnson's statement may have been made with a sense of irony; the incident, however, showed Le Pen's intention to play down his links with the kind of marginal groupings within which he had hitherto spent most of his political life. In fact, international links between such groupings have, as we have illustrated earlier, been in existence since the 1940s.

Initially the Committee of Inquiry idea was part of the emotional reaction to the appearance of an extreme right group in the European Parliament. Under the rules of the European Parliament it is possible for one-quarter of the members to initiate the procedure to establish an inquiry.[1] Once the idea had been agreed within the Socialist Group, it was necessary to collect signatures from at least 109 MEPs. This took a little time as even within the Socialist Group there were some members who did not consider this a worthwhile initiative which would achieve its intended objectives. At the end of September 1984 the Bureau, which deals with the day-to-day management of the European Parliament, accepted that the inquiry should go ahead. In theory, this was a formality, but some Christian Democratic representatives expressed opposition, partly for procedural reasons and partly for political reasons. Significantly, however, the President of the European Parliament, Pierre Pflimlin (a French Christian Democrat), gave a firm ruling stating that the request to establish the enquiry was absolutely in order and that it could not be argued that the issues of fascism and racism were beyond the competence of the European Parliament. Once this ruling had been given it remained only to name the members of the inquiry. Before looking at the people who were named and the way they set about their task, it would be appropriate to look at the objectives and terms of reference of this inquiry.

The political objective was clear. It was to bring to public attention the real nature of the political parties which had formed the Group of the European Right under the chairmanship of Jean-Marie Le Pen, and the political and social context from which they drew their strength. It was a democratic approach to the problem of denying the political respectability which the group was formed to achieve. It was also intended to look more closely at the relationship between extreme-right political activity and the major social issue of racism. Whilst these objectives were quite straightforward, it soon turned out that the inquiry had been set a mammoth task. The request for the inquiry asked for an urgent report on:

1. the growth and size of fascist, racialist, and related groups within Europe, both inside and outside the European Community;
2. the inter-connection and links between these groups;
3. the relationship between their activities and racism in member states.

4. the relationship between the growth of fascism and racism and the worsening economic and social conditions, for example, poverty, unemployment, etc.;
5. an examination of the machinery already used by member states' governments to respond to these organisations;
6. ways of combatting them.

There was within these terms of reference a threat to the effectiveness of the whole exercise. The danger was that a massive report would be produced in which all these issues were confused and, therefore, no political impact or lesson would be forthcoming. Almost every word in these terms of reference could be interpreted in a variety of ways and in particular the problems of definition of fascist and racist groups could be used as a way of confusing the issues. Only work on the basis of consensus between MEPs with different democratic political outlooks would enable progress towards the success of the inquiry, both in terms of the collection of facts and of achieving the political objectives which underlay the establishment of the inquiry. It was also important to bear in mind from the outset that the inquiry, under the Parliament's rules, would last for one year. This placed a premium on filibustering.

This was already apparent at the first meeting which took place in Strasbourg on 25 October 1984. The meeting lasted only half an hour, but given that only twelve months would be available for the whole task it was vital to set the inquiry procedure in motion. Some hesitation had been expressed about holding the first meeting at all, but under the rules this could not be prevented. The chairmen of the political groups had met beforehand and agreed that the chairmanship of the inquiry would be undertaken by a member of the Socialist Group. The vice-chairman would be nominated by the Communist Group. The key position of rapporteur would be held by a Christian Democrat. Following consultation within the Socialist Group, Glyn Ford was chosen as the candidate for chairman and he was duly elected at the constituent meeting. During this first meeting the chair made no political statement whatsoever, as it was clear from the tense atmosphere of the meeting that a number of very experienced parliamentarians were just waiting for an opportunity to attack the chair and block the inquiry.

A Conservative member and M. d'Ormesson, at that time a member of Le Pen's Group, spoke in favour of there being a second vice-chairman. For practical reasons the left accepted this proposal, and this meant that the vice-chairman would, in fact, be a British Conservative. In spite of the group chairmen's decision, Derek Prag was elected vice-chairman, with a French communist and former resistance leader, Robert Chambeiron, being elected only as second vice-chairman. Both carried out their tasks with equal honesty and impartiality.

After this, the only substantive point to be dealt with was the holding of the next meeting. Here it was clear that, apart from the left, there was no enthusiasm for holding a meeting before the end of 1984. Some members argued that there was no time for meetings and that they already had other pressing engagements. Some provocative statements were made, but a clash was avoided, and by a majority of one, the Committee of Inquiry voted to meet again a month later in Brussels. In retrospect this was a significant political victory. The meeting then closed without any of the enormous underlying tension coming out into an open clash. It was clear that there was sufficient bad will on both sides of the traditional political divide to make the inquiry extremely difficult to carry forward.

The presence of d'Ormesson was itself significant. Under the rules of the European Parliament, each group nominated its proportional share of the fifteen member inquiry. Nothing could stop a member of the extreme-right group from taking his place as a full member of the Committee. No statements were made by the left, either to the meeting or to the press. D'Ormesson was, unlike Le Pen, not a new member of the European Parliament. He had previously sat as a member of the Christian Democratic Group before defecting and being elected on the Front National list. This itself showed that Le Pen had had success in France in widening his support beyond the ranks of the extremist elements he had traditionally frequented.

It was, however, quite obvious that d'Ormesson did not want the inquiry to work properly. His presence was something of a surprise, not because he had no right to be there but because Le Pen was quite aware that he was part of the target of the inquiry and had lost no time in pouring ridicule upon it. It seems that his first intention had been to play no part in the exercise. This would have been the most appropriate tactic on his part. His problem was that some of his friends and allies were far more sensitive to the charge of being fascist than he was. Perhaps out of ignorance, perhaps out of naivety, perhaps out of an expectation that the left would lack the necessary self-discipline of consensus politics and destroy its own initiative, they wanted to give the impression of being genuine opponents of fascism and racism at the same time as seeking an alliance with politicians who had never hidden their support for such ideas. The contradictions of this position soon led them into greater difficulty and, as we shall see, Le Pen reverted to his original approach of ridiculing, boycotting, and attempting to close down the inquiry.

In these early meetings d'Ormesson's blocking tactics were backed up by Philippe Malaud. He is a leading figure in the National Centre of Independents and Peasants (CNIP), a French Poujadist grouping. Although he had been elected in 1984 on the list led by Simone Veil, his main aim was to see the French right combine forces with the a Front

National. Whilst this has often occurred at local level, most notably in Dreux, it is not part of the national strategy of the Gaullist RPR or the centre-right UDF. In the run-up to the March 1986 French parliamentary elections Malaud's strategy was formally rejected by Jacques Chirac. Then, in the aftermath of the 1984 Euro-elections, Malaud still had reason to be hopeful of convincing at least the RPR and part of the UDF of adopting his approach. Any effective attack on the democratic respectability of the Front National was of great importance for French domestic politics.

Otto von Habsburg, another active member of the Committee, had opposed Hitler in the 1930s and 1940s and is now a member of Franz-Josef Strauss's CSU. As the inquiry got under way it was interesting to note that von Habsburg, who had openly been friendly with Le Pen in the corridors of Strasbourg, and had denounced the left's white rose demonstration, now intended to play a very positive part on the committee. D'Ormesson (also a CNIP member) had, of course, previously been a member of his Christian Democratic Group. Another West German Christian Democrat who, although not a full member of the inquiry, was active from its very first meeting, was Graf von Stauffenberg. His father had been a leading general until 1944 when he took part in the attempt to overthrow Hitler. He had been planning to assassinate Hitler himself.[2] The assassination would have taken place after the Normandy landings but was consciously intended to show the world that there was resistance to Hitler inside Germany. Throughout the inquiry Stauffenberg concentrated almost entirely on questions of wording rather than those of substance, and whilst clearly he had no sympathy with Nazi ideas, he seemed to get angry only when suggestions came from the left that denazification in Germany and Austria had been quite insufficient – indeed, if Hitler had won the war in the early 1940s his father would have been one of the top generals of the victorious Reich.

The ambivalence of the role that the Christian Democrats planned to play in the inquiry became a subject of controversy within hours of the first meeting having been held. Rumours circulated in Strasbourg that the Christian Democratic Group intended to nominate as rapporteur Gustavo Selva, an Italian member of their group. Having been for many years a very prominent figure in the presentation of Italian television news, he had lost his job after his name was published among many others as a member of the secret, supposedly masonic, lodge, the P2. Ironically, this fact had been exposed in a Committee of Inquiry into the P2 set up by the Italian Parliament. An Italian socialist went as far as writing to the President of the European Parliament insisting that since the P2 had itself been accused of being involved in fascist terrorism, the nomination of Selva as rapporteur would bring ridicule upon the whole exercise of the Committee of Inquiry. This information was of great concern to socialist members, but there was equal concern that any attack on Selva would lead to such a row that the inquiry would be blocked. After careful consideration the left decided not to raise the issue within the committee itself. This was for the same reason as that which led to there being no challenge to d'Ormesson's presence on the Committee. It would play into the hands of Le Pen by distracting attention from his own group and would create deep conflict between the mainstream political parties of right and left. It is probable, however, that although Selva responded robustly to the attack on his good faith, he and his group could see dangers in pressing ahead with his nomination as rapporteur. Even if the left had then been put in a minority and isolated, many Christian Democrats would have faced with concern a situation in which they were all being accused of refusing to allow a properly constituted inquiry into genuine problems from producing a report. Habsburg, Stauffenberg, and Selva could not in this sense be seen as completely representative of European Christian Democracy in general, even if their attitudes and activism in this inquiry pointed to deep ambiguities in their parties' role in post-war West Germany. Selva was replaced as the Christian Democrats' nomination for rapporteur by Evrigenis.

Dimitrios Evrigenis was a Greek whose party leader Konstantin Karamanlis was known throughout Europe as having opposed the Colonels' regime. As a democratic conservative party, New Democracy in Greece had no problems with fascism. They had always totally opposed it and, indeed, Evrigenis had himself been imprisoned by the colonels' regime. Perhaps as a Greek he was also more sensitive to the problems of racism which are directly felt by millions of migrant workers in Western Europe. In retrospect, it is clear that his nomination as rapporteur was a much bigger political success than it appeared at the time. Evrigenis was already familiar with many of the issues, both as a Greek and as a member of the Council of Europe's Commission of Human Rights. As an anti-fascist democrat and as a judge his qualifications to be rapporteur were outstanding and a great deal of the value of the work of the inquiry is a direct result of his own enormous personal contribution.

He was appointed rapporteur at the inquiry's second meeting. This was held in November 1984 in the usual private fashion in which all European parliament committee meetings are normally held. It would not be overstating the case to say that it took place with the usual indifference of the press to meetings within the European Parliament. Like any committee it had to decide how it would work. The decisions made at that meeting might seem to an outside observer to be pure routine. In fact, each one was the subject of great controversy in what was another tense meeting.

As well as doing all that was possible to maintain a consensus approach, the left was also aware of the value of publicity. There was a feeling that the filibustering tactics of the first constituent meeting would not have been used by the right if the meeting had been open to the press and public. Habsburg, d'Ormesson, and Selva spoke out against holding meetings in public. An official from the Parliament's security service had to be called in to guarantee that there was no security risk attached to holding meetings in public. It was then decided that meetings could be held in public even if formally speaking a decision would have to be taken at the end of each meeting as to whether the next meeting would be in public. After this decision had been taken the meeting was then opened to the public. As a symbolic gesture on this first occasion, the public consisted of only one person. She was Mme Yvonne Jospa, President of the Belgian 'Movement against Racism and Xenophobia' (MRAX). Hers was the first of a number of outside groups of activists to take a close interest in the work of the inquiry and in doing so to bring it to the attention of a far wider public than would normally be expected to follow any activity within the European Parliament. As we shall see, this interest was soon to take on a very substantial size. The records of the inquiry show that the decision to hold that particular meeting in public was made by only eight votes to five, whereas the procedure with regard to future meetings was agreed by nine votes to two.

The decision to meet in public was an important victory for the left since one of the main problems with racism is the refusal of some people in authority to recognise that there is a problem. Having been defeated on this issue, d'Ormesson and his friends from the German Christian Democratic Party continued their blocking tactics with long semantic discussions as to whether the title of the inquiry should refer specifically to the rise of racism and fascism in Europe. Having lost on that point they moved on with long statements arguing that Nazism and fascism were two quite distinct phenomena. These procedural wrangles soon proved counter-productive and it emerged that only a minority of the non-left members of the Committee really wanted to block its work. Habsburg, d'Ormesson, Stauffenberg, and Malaud were not only, to varying degrees, provocative, they were also perhaps short-sighted. In particular, it should be noted that the two conservative members Derek Prag and Christopher Prout did not join in any of the blocking manoeuvres. They certainly did not take up firm positions in backing up the left's procedural proposals but when forced to choose they respected fairly the need to carry out the mandate which the inquiry had received. They were unclear as to what they themselves wanted the inquiry to achieve but they were not prepared to align themselves with those who wanted to stop it functioning properly, let alone achieving any political results.

The main weakness of the blocking tactics was that there was no way they could be dressed up in a positive fashion. Everyone was prepared to agree that the terms of reference of the inquiry could have been worded better, and Evrigenis himself went on record in a personal statement in which, whilst not questioning the legitimacy of the committee, he questioned the procedure under which it had been established. Like the British conservatives, however, he took no part in the blocking manoeuvres referred to earlier.

The absence of a positive approach on the right meant that they had very few ideas to contribute as to how the inquiry should go about studying the issues within its remit. The left was convinced that the calling of experts would confirm, as a vast literature had already done, that there was a problem of increased racist and fascist political activity in Western Europe. This was already apparent from numerous books, official reports, and impressions gleaned from the press. Whatever the inquiry eventually reported, it was clear that publicity about these problems would itself help to raise consciousness of the need for an effective response. Almost all experts on these issues tended to look at them in a national rather than a European context, and just bringing them together would contribute to developing a European response. The committee had, therefore, less difficulty in accepting the proposal for a series of public hearings in Brussels at which a couple of dozen experts would be called in to give their views and answer questions. The committee met again on 17–18 December 1984 to agree how these experts should be chosen.

The left was prepared to agree that the experts be chosen on a consensus basis. This approach was taken up in order to show that the left was not expecting that the committee would only hear left-wing experts. Ironically, the Christian Democrats preferred a system whereby experts would be chosen proportionately according to the numerical strength of the different political groups. An arrangement was also agreed by which the groups could also name experts from whom written evidence would be requested. A detailed questionnaire setting out at greater length than the terms of reference of the inquiry, the subjects on which evidence was required was agreed without much difficulty. The scene was, therefore, set for the committee to be inundated with evidence. In fact, the left was convinced that the quantity of evidence which would be received would make it even more difficult to ignore the issues at stake.

An early example of the kind of problem which would have to be overcome was provided by Ivor Richard, who, at the time the outgoing Labour member of the Commission, was invited to appear before the committee on 17 December 1984. He made a general statement about the way in which rising unemployment was putting strains on the social fabric of Western Europe. He agreed that at local level there was enormous evidence of increased racism. He was, however, extremely modest in what he thought the Commission could propose for action at Community level. He was so modest on this point that even Stauffenberg as well as Evrigenis challenged him, arguing that since the European Convention on Human Rights had been effectively integrated into European Community law there would be a basis for European Community action against racism. Since this was one of the first times the Conmission had been pressed on the issue of racism, the modesty of Ivor Richard's approach was quite understandable, but it did suggest that even if the committee produced a constructive report a long battle would then ensue in order to get any effective action by the institutions of the Community.

It is, perhaps, somewhat unfortunate to have to recall that the only person who really appreciated Ivor Richard's approach was Le Pen, who used the outgoing Commissioner's statement as evidence of the illegitimacy of the whole Committee of Inquiry exercise. In a letter referred to below, which Le Pen addressed to the chairman of the inquiry, he quoted the doubts that had been expressed about Community competence in this field and expressed an identity of views between his group and the former Commissioner on this issue.

By the end of 1984 the scene was set for the committee to get down to its real task of collecting facts on the issues at stake. Written evidence was already being received, sometimes from grassroots organisations. This was an encouraging sign that the existence of the committee was becoming known outside Brussels and Strasbourg, and was raising expectations amongst people and organisations dealing with these problems on a day-to-day basis. D'Ormesson continued to attend these meetings but was less outspoken. At the end of 1984 Le Pen, on behalf of his group, wrote to President Pflimlin with a further challenge to the committee's legitimacy. This was itself a confirmation that there was now a chance that the left would achieve some of its political objectives. Le Pen's letter was a carefully worded attempt to argue that the inquiry should never have been set up. He claimed that inquiries should deal only with very specific issues and appealed to European parliamentary traditions in the member states as confirmation that this was normal practice. He also claimed that the issues under discussion went beyond the bounds of the competences of the European Community. He attacked the questionnaire sent out to experts as being tendentious, and asked that the inquiry be told to stop work immediately. Whilst the letter was clearly carefully drafted, the political result was zero. For the President or the Bureau of the European Parliament to have responded favourably to Le Pen's demand was quite unthinkable. In this sense Le Pen's move was quite maladroit. It drew attention to his own isolation within the parliament and highlighted the confusion within his own group. While the chairman of the group of the European Right called for the inquiry to be disbanded forthwith one of the members of his group, d'Ormesson, continued to participate in the work of the inquiry. He even nominated experts from which evidence should be sought, as he was quite entitled to do.

This contradiction had finally become apparent to Le Pen himself early in 1985. On 16 January, just before the first public hearing, he wrote to the chairman of the Committee of Inquiry to announce that d'Ormesson would no longer sit on the committee. He also announced that he would contest by all means (he underlined these words in his letter) the validity of the committee, adding, rather strangely, he would deny it all authority. He reserved the possibility of taking legal action. The letter, which followed the failure of his appeal to President Pflimlin, contained a hint of menace combined with quotes from Ivor Richard. It also contained a bald statement claiming that everyone knows that there is no rise of 'so-called' fascism or racism in Europe. He went on to state that it is in Eastern Europe under Soviet hegemony that minorities are being persecuted. Le Pen even had the extraordinary hypocrisy to refer to the persecution of Jews in this region. Le Pen used a press quotation from a Belgian socialist, Ernest Glinne, to support his claim that the whole Committee of Inquiry was aimed at him and his group. In this he was obviously correct. Glinne had made this statement following a riot in the Brussels suburb of Schaerbeek, which had taken place just after Le Pen had addressed a rally with the mayor, Roger Nols, who had been elected to the European Parliament on the Liberal list. Le Pen's letter was proof that the Committee of Inquiry was likely to do more damage to his image as an ordinary democratic politician than the violent demonstrations which occurred during his frequent appearances in different parts of Europe.

Le Pen's fears as to the likely impact of the inquiry were confirmed when the first public hearing took place in Brussels on 30 January 1985. The meeting room was packed with observers from the public. This itself was quite unprecedented in the life of the European Parliament. The attendance was maintained during the other two hearings in February and March 1985. The evidence provided is now a public document[3] of great academic and political interest. What is of greater interest for our purpose is to observe how different experts approached the issues and what tactics lay behind the different groups' choice of experts.

The strength of the left's approach was that it concentrated on what was the primary task of the Committee of Inquiry: getting the facts. None of the experts nominated was particularly well-known outside their own countries or their own academic or political fields. For example, Aldo Aniasi, an Italian socialist parliamentarian and vice-president of the Italian Parliament, referred to the rather perfunctory ways in which fascism had been purged from the Italian state hierarchy after the liberation of 1945. He showed the continuity between the P2, attempted coups in Italy, and various people who had held important positions in the fascist police and military in the 1930s. He referred to the wave of fascist terrorism that hit Italy from the late 1960s and the links between terrorism and the secret service. He quoted in support of his argument Italian politicians, like the former Prime Minister Fanfani (Christian Democrat) and Spadolini (Liberal), who had pointed out links between terrorism, drug trafficking, secret service corruption, and extreme-right political activism. He quoted the Italian Parliament's own inquiry into the P2 lodge. His evidence was confirmed by a Turin University Professor, Marco Revelli, who was nominated to give evidence by the Communist Group. To many Italians a lot of the evidence given, and the incidents referred to, would be quite familiar. It was, however, one of the rare occasions it had been brought to wider European attention. In spite of the fact that Italy is one of the main areas of activity of contemporary fascists, only the socialist and communist groups thought it appropriate to seek evidence from an Italian expert. This in itself shows the lack of a keen interest in really getting at the facts which characterised other groups' approach.

One of the high points of the inquiry was when the Italian Christian Democrat Minister of the Interior, Eugenio Scalfaro, addressed the committee. He paid tribute to the establishment of the inquiry. As a Minister, speaking in his capacity as President in office of the Council of Ministers of the European Community at that time, he was obviously much more circumspect than other Italian speakers and was prepared to state only that it was 'highly likely' that Italian train bombings were the work of fascists. In particular, he argued for European co-operation in the fight against terrorism, referring to the enormous difficulty of extraditing terrorists to stand trial in Italy once they had found 'safe-houses' in Paris or London. The fact that the President of the Council had been prepared to address the inquiry confirmed that his was a matter of genuine interest to the European Community. The fact that a senior Christian Democrat politician was prepared to praise publicly the establishment of the enquiry totally destroyed the possibilities for blocking tactics by Christian Democrat MEPs. The fact that they had not, in the first instance, thought it appropriate to call for evidence from Italian experts spoke for itself.

Amongst the non-political experts nominated by the left, most were experts in the problems of racism and the use of racism as an element for mobilisation by the extreme-right. Mrs Anne Dummett[4] gave details of racism and anti-racist laws and activity in Britain. She referred to the problem of racial attacks, and of racism within the police and immigration services. Whilst the conservative members did not like some of what she said about the racist aspect of immigration control, she was appreciated as a sincere and objective observer.

A number of experts talked about racism in France. Marie-Jo Chombart de Lauwe, a leading French researcher and anti-racist activist, provided evidence about racism and xenophobia. Emphasising that this was a constant element in French politics, she illustrated with documents the continuity between Le Pen and the pre-war fascist movements. Her colleague from the French Movement against Racism (MRAP), Mme Georges Pau-Langevin, provided documentation showing the identity between Le Pen and Hitler's racist election slogans. She emphasised the importance of the economic situation in encouraging racism and xenophobia, and the whole scapegoat syndrome, which was also apparent in the 1930s. She referred, like Mrs Dummett, to increasing attacks on immigrants, sometimes by extreme-right political activists. She emphasised, however, that racism was a much wider problem than just dealing with fascist trouble-makers.

This point was made with great emphasis by a Dutch expert, Philomena Essed, who concentrated on the everyday racism which characterises the lives of ethnic minorities.[5] She argued that for ethnic groups racism is not just an occasional problem, it is a constant component of everyday life and must be combatted accordingly. This phenomenon is apparent in housing services, employment, education, shops, and on public transport, where, even in Holland, there are unspoken assumptions that black passengers have less right to a seat than white passengers. She illustrated how racism can be encouraged by stereotyped figures in school books. Another Dutch expert, Joke Kniesmeyer of the Anne Frank Foundation, referred to the extreme-right Centrum Partij in Holland whose electoral success refuels the growing social problem of racism to which it directly appeals. Mrs Kniesmeyer effectively put the Dutch problem in the European context of links between extreme-right groups and historical continuity in fascist politics.[6] This point was also brought out in the evidence from Professor Stephen Rose of the Open University. He illustrated the phenomenon of historical revisionism and the re-emergence of the scientific racism which had been a key element of Nazi ideology. He made it clear that this was a European phenomenon carried forward by such publications as *Elements*, which started in France but is now published in several European countries. He also pointed out that whilst these ideas had been around for decades something has happened to make the political climate more receptive to them.

Perhaps the most controversial expert nominated by the left was Ernest Mandel, a Belgian university professor and well-known left-wing political activist. He linked the contemporary situation in Europe with that of the late 1920s, in which mass unemployment was undermining parliamentary democracy. He showed how big business had at the time helped the fascist parties work hand in glove with the fascist regimes. He emphasised the historical continuity in business circles, where, in the post-war period, industrialists like Flick and Krupp who had worked with the Nazis were able to continue business as usual. Looking at Europe today, he argued that we could be at the initial stage of processes of the kind which operated at the end of the 1920s and he used the P2 lodge as an example of links between the establishment, big business, and right-wing extremism. In spite of his controversial background, Mandel effectively showed that even if many could not share his political view, the dangers of the present situation could not be easily denied.

The strength of the evidence produced by the left was also apparent in submissions concerning Germany and Austria. Professor Franz Gress of the University of Frankfurt analysed in detail evidence contained in the annual reports of the German government's 'Office for the Protection of the Constitution'. He emphasised that this material showed quite clearly that right-wing extremism in Germany is something more than a remnant of the fascist era. This was particularly clear from details of activity amongst young people, and in particular football fans. In the mid-1980s there had been, for the first time since 1970, an increase in membership of certain extreme-right groups. He also emphasised that statistics could not give any firm idea of the dimensions of the problem, especially as many of the racist terrorist attacks are carried out by unknown individuals or groups.

Brigitte Galanda of the Documentation Archive of Austrian Resistance in Vienna referred to the more than fifty organisations which could be classified as extreme-right wing in Austria. She pointed out how a law against National Socialism, which had been adopted in 1947, had been very little used. She also referred to an economic situation which was leading to increased hostility to foreign workers.

Austria and its President, Kurt Waldheim, have since been the object of enormous press coverage and heated debate. Even during the work of the inquiry the issue of the release of Walter Reder, an Austrian Nazi who had ordered the mass murder of Italian resistance fighters, and his reception in January 1985 by an Austrian Minister, caused controversy and embarrassment among right-wing members. What was most remarkable was the evidence given to the committee by Simon Wiesenthal of the Jewish Documentation Centre in Vienna, who had been asked to give evidence by the Christian Democrats. He is not known as an expert on contemporary racism or fascism, having gained celebrity for his tenacity in finding Nazis in hiding in different parts of the world. He is certainly no socialist and is particularly critical of anti-Semitism in the Soviet Union. What the Christian Democrats hoped to achieve by inviting him to give evidence is by no means clear.

German Christian Democrats had already shown their concern about the whole nature of the inquiry months earlier, in particular their fear that it would be used as a platform by the left to attack them.

In fact, Simon Wiesenthal spoke with devastating clarity in a way which totally undermined any further attempt to prevent the inquiry getting to grips with fundamental issues. Unlike those who had pressed for him to be invited, Wiesenthal made it clear that he welcomed the establishment of the inquiry and he hoped it would have an impact on public opinion. He emphasised both that anti-Semitism did not begin and end with Hitler and that the spirit of Nazism was not dead. He argued that it was present at all levels of society in Germany and Austria. This was because the process of denazification had been stopped by the West when it was felt that it had to concentrate on the perceived threat from an expansionist Soviet Union. He denounced Soviet anti-Semitism, but he also made points which would have been denounced as left-wing propaganda if they had come from any other source, pointing out, for example, the strong positions in Austrian society occupied by people who had been Nazis. He denounced the role of the Italian Catholic Church in helping Nazis escape to Latin America. Although he is no sociologist, Wiesenthal confirmed what the academic experts had said about not attempting to judge the strength of right-wing extremism by looking only at election results. To prove his point, he stated that immediately after the war there were 10.5 million people who had been Nazi party members in Germany and Austria. Others had been indoctrinated. With the disbanding of the Nazi parties, these people's ideas did not change overnight. Precisely because it was a totalitarian system, Nazism had penetrated all aspects of life and, therefore, a kind of 'everyday fascism' survived the collapse of the regime. The Waldheim affair served as a dramatic and disturbing reminder of what Wiesenthal told the European Parliament on that occasion. During questions from members, Habsburg revealed the confusion of his own position when he asked whether Wiesenthal agreed that an antidote to neo-Nazism might be a very wide distribution of Hitler's *Mein Kampf*, presumably to show everyone how atrocious are its contents. Wiesenthal did not think this would have a positive salutory effect, particularly in the face of the necessity to maintain legislation to prevent denial of the holocaust. In fact, the Christian Democratic majority in West Germany is against such legislation. Wiesenthal also spoke of neo-Nazi activity among younger generations since they are the priority target for recruitment. He concluded his evidence with the following statement:

> The new Fascism and racism is taking slow, small steps to test people's reactions, so that later it can take further steps. For of course, National Socialism did not begin with gas-chambers and crematoriums; but because we or our fathers ignored the

beginnings, later, when the crisis had come, it was too late. It is not yet too late to react to all this and the existence of this Committee makes me confident that there are politicians and people in Europe who will not ignore it.'

Wiesenthal's evidence was not only valuable in its own right. It weakened the impact of the interventions by other experts put forward from the non-left groups. Few of the experts whom they put forward were really experts on the subject. Erwin Scheuch, a sociology professor from the University of Cologne, tried to get the inquiry to look at extremism in general and argued that the only real threat to democracy came from left-wing terrorism. He argued that there were more left-wing extremists around. For example, he stated that the neo-Nazi Hoffman group was linked to the PLO and involved only 400 people, whereas he estimated that the Red Army Fraktion involved about 40 000. These facts may perhaps be accurate, but what Scheuch was being encouraged to do was to change the subject. He compared anti-Semitism and xenophobia with anti-Americanism, and claimed that the Greens were comparable to the Nazis in their opposition to democracy. He made good debating points but he had actually provided little useful evidence which could be used in the committee's report.

A similar attempt to change the subject explained the choice of Professor Michael Volensky of the University of Munich, another expert called in by the right. He is an expert on the Soviet *nomenklatura*, or elite, and put emphasis on the similarities between the Nazi and Soviet systems. He drew attention to the Socialist element in Nazi ideology and questioned whether there is any difference between right-wing and left-wing extremism. From an academic point of view-there is no doubt that such an analysis is quite defensible. Unfortunately, Professor Volensky was not addressing himself to the issues which the Inquiry had been set up to establish. He did not even mention racism.

A similar obsession with terminology was shown by the well-known French journalist Jean-François Revel. He expressed the view first set out in his book on the crisis of Western democracy[7] that the threat of fascism had been invented by the left to distract attention from the communist threat. There was, he claimed, a decline of fascism, not a rise. He pointed to the recent defeats of fascism in Greece, Spain, and Portugal, and denied that there was any clear evidence of direct involvement of the extreme right in terrorism. He denied that the ideology of the 'New Right' contained any serious threat to democracy, or that it was particularly influential anyway. He did, however, accept that racism was a social problem which could and should be combatted through education.

André Glucksman, the French philosopher, also came along at the invitation of the right. He suggested that there was too much discussion of the Le Pen phenomenon in France and that this was because French politicians did not have very much else to talk about. He also felt that there was a danger of crying wolf too often but he concluded by pointing out that racism and fascism were only academic issues if people insisted, quite wrongly, in treating them as historical phenomena. As an active founder member of the French anti-racist group 'SOS-Racisme' Glucksman was probably not aware that his terminological ramble over the whole question of totalitarianism gave pleasure to right-wing MEPs as it distracted attention from the object of the inquiry. Since he provided no evidence or proposals on this his evidence had little impact on the final outcome of the inquiry.

Another former student revolutionary, Dr Gunther Muller, now a West German parliamentarian from Strauss's CSU, took a similar line about totalitarianism. He even argued that some apparent neo-Nazi activity was manufactured by agents of the Soviet and Czechoslovak secret services in order to back up Eastern European radio propaganda beamed into West Germany. The credibility of this view was strengthened by the way in which the collapsing Communist Party in East Germany attempted at the beginning of 1990 to justify its role by exaggerating the extent of the neo-Nazi threat.

A Parisian professor, Olivier Passelecq, who is also a member of Malaud's CNIP, attempted to prove that Le Pen was neither a fascist nor anti-democratic. He could not deny Le Pen's appeal to racism and he denounced semantic manipulation before going on to emphasise the socialist nature of fascism. He also argued that racism was part of left-wing ideology. By taking a historical, and therefore highly academic, view he could not influence the results of the inquiry. He did, however, accept that there was a rise of racism, but this was not due to political agitation, it was due to a coincidence in Europe between demographic decline and increased immigration. Very similar views were expressed by Professor Raoul Girardet of the Parisian 'Institut des Etudes Politiques' from where Passelecq also came. Whilst his intervention angered many left-wing members of the inquiry, it in fact contained little of substance.

A more substantial argument urged by the right concerned the overlap between anti-zionism and anti-Semitism. Experts from the Jewish community were naturally and genuinely concerned about this issue, which is dealt with in the Committee's report. Research by Jewish groups, in particular the Institute of Jewish Affairs in London, from where Dr Michael May came to give evidence, was very useful in providing documentary support for the kind of arguments put forward by Wiesenthal. Jewish representatives, such as Martin Savitt, vice-president of the Board of Deputies of British Jews, emphasised their support for the development of a multi-racial society in Western

Europe, but he insisted that anti-Semitism was not only apparent in right-wing circles. Dr May provided evidence of the use of terrorism by extreme-right groups. Both denounced the West German government's legislation on the 'Auschwitz lie' and the laxity shown with regard to reunions of SS members.

The lack of clarity in the approach of the British Conservatives was apparent right at the start of the hearings, when Profesor Parekh of Hull University spoke. He had been invited at the suggestion of the British Conservatives, but proceeded to denounce Mrs Thatcher for appealing to xenophobia among the British electorate. He traced the electoral decline of Britain's National Front to her rise to the Conservative leadership in the second half of the 1970s. He was critical of her anti-immigration policies, pointing out that of all deportees from Britain, over 80 per cent were black. He referred to racist attacks as a sign of increased racism in British society. A former Conservative Party official, Mervyn Kohler, claimed that the National Front had been 'beaten back' in the 1970s. He argued that there were many positive developments in race relations in Britain and went on to denounce 'militant anti-racism' as a negative influence, denying that state or institutional racism was a serious problem.

So much of the 'evidence' which the right produced either defeated its own initial starting point or failed to address the issues which the inquiry was set up to establish. Events taking place during the short lifetime of the enquiry confirmed the serious issues at stake. Racial murders in France led to the spontaneous mass mobilisation of 'SOS-Racisme', whose leader, Harlem Desir, spoke to the inquiry. The horrific bombing of the Milan–Naples express train on 23 December 1984 aroused concern about continuing fascist terrorism. The release of Walter Reder and the fortieth anniversary of 1945 reminded people of the problem of historical continuity. Race riots and fascist football violence gave the lie to any complacent view of race relations in Britain.

Early in 1985 the European Parliament held a wide-ranging debate on the problems of migrant workers and adopted a resolution which referred in passing to the problems of racism and xenophobia. Le Pen had fought hard against this resolution. The Commission had also begun to take the issue of racism more seriously. Ivor Richard's successor, an Irish Christian Democrat, Peter Sutherland, spoke openly of xenophobia as part of the crisis of change taking place in the economy of Western Europe, where a multiracial society had to be developed.

As the evidence mounted of the rise of racism and fascism in Europe, Otto von Habsburg and others appeared to have abandoned their attempt to block the work of the inquiry. In April 1985 Le Pen appealed on behalf of his political group to the Court of Justice of the European

Community based in Luxembourg. He asked the court to annul the decision by the European Parliament's Bureau under which the inquiry had been established in the first place. The appeal was based on similar arguments referred to earlier. In fact, since the court works slowly, there was no way this action could have prevented the inquiry from completing its work. The court did not rule on this appeal until June 1986, when, refusing to comment on the details of Le Pen's appeal, it decided that it was not receivable anyway. Le Pen was ordered to pay the costs.[8]

By early summer 1985 the inquiry had gathered a mass of material and had seen the failure of attempts by both the extreme and the more traditional right either to prevent it working at all or to distract its attention from the real issues at stake. During most of the hearings Evrigenis had been remarkably quiet, limiting himself to very specific questions and avoiding all polemics. He was perhaps helped by the fact that very little mention was made of his own country. The most tense moments in the committee's work arose out of clashes between left and right-wing members of the same nationality, For example, between Rothley, a German Social Democrat, and Stauffenberg.

The great public interest in the hearings led many groups to contact the committee spontaneously. Vast quantities of extremely provocative racist material were received. Journalists from as far afield as Latin America and South Africa reported on the work of the inquiry. A special hearing was held with anti-racist and immigrants' organisations from Belgium. Evrigenis also received evidence from international organisations like the United Nations and the Council of Europe which had done a great deal of work on the subject of racism. Organisations of former members of the resistance in France and Italy sent in evidence, as did numerous church organisations. A great deal of material was also collected from national parliaments and local authorities. Searchlight and Amnesty International also provided evidence. Socialist members organised a fact-finding mission to London and Manchester, where evidence of everyday racism, fascist agitation, and racial attacks was collected. All this outside interest also created a certain level of expectation about the content of the European Parliament's report which was again quite unprecedented in the life of the institution.

An incident in the early summer of 1985 showed that the concerns which had led some members to challenge the very basis of the inquiry had not been completely overcome. On 29 May 1985 a catastrophe occurred at the Heysel Stadium in Brussels just before the European Cup Final between Liverpool and Juventus. The whole of Europe watched with horror as dozens of people were trampled to death. Evidence was quoted from Liverpool Football Club and the mayor of Brussels about fascist agitation having contributed to the disaster. The chairman of the inquiry was interviewed on BBC television news and promised to collect evidence on this issue. He collected a dossier of information for presentation to Evrigenis and held a press conference in Strasbourg, where the European Cup Final disaster was the subject of an urgent debate. The evidence named fascist agitators who had been arrested in Brussels. It pointed out that neo-fascist symbols had been carried into the stadium by British and Italian 'fans'. It quoted the mayor of Brussels, who had been informed of fraternisation between fascist agitators from Italy and England in the hours before the disaster. Searchlight in London and Professor Revelli from Turin (home of Juventus) confirmed that supporters of the British Movement and the Italian 'Ordine Nuovo' were present and active at the match. The inquiries into the Heysel disaster have shown that the causes were extremely complex, but there was no doubt that the issue of fascist agitation in football grounds was one of genuine public concern. There was no reason for the chairman of an inquiry into racism and fascism in Europe to keep quiet about the issue.

The fact that he did not was used by Habsburg and others in the final attempt to try to push the inquiry off the rails. In a letter to the inquiry chairman on 13 June he expressed 'genuine shock' at the holding of a press conference on fascist agitation in football grounds and stated that this action had created a 'genuine crisis of confidence in the Committee'. The letter spoke of the failure of the Chair to respect the trust which had been placed in him. They asked him to explain himself before the Inquiry and ended their letter threateningly, stating that 'it is from your statement that the form of our future collaboration in the Committee under your presidency will depend'. This somewhat excess- ive response to a minor incident was undermined by the fact that the Chair's concern on this issue had been publicly shared by Mrs Jessica Larive-Groenendaal, a Dutch Liberal member who was doing a more general report on violence at football grounds. The excited response of Habsburg, Prag, Stauffenberg, and others is rather odd in retrospect, as the Evrigenis report confirmed the concern expressed by the chairman as have numerous other documents. It was odd that a minor procedural confusion about a press conference should have created a 'genuine crisis' for the committee. Indeed, the only crisis was that at the end of the evidence-gathering stage of the inquiry, the right wing had been totally out-manoeuvred. Their blocking tactics had apparently failed. The report, drafted by Dimitrios Evrigenis, confirmed the seriousness of the problems and made numerous proposals for action. The left succeeded in strengthening its content during the voting on amendments. The report was adopted by the Committee unanimously, with only one abstention (a French Gaullist, Mme Anglade) in November 1985, and was widely welcomed by all organisations in Europe concerned with resisting the resurgence of racism and fascism in Europe. The extreme right denounced it. The rest of the right could do no more than join in the consensus of praise and hope that the inquiry and its report would be quickly forgotten.

The main proposals contained in the Evrigenis report are considered in the following chapters. Before looking at them it is worth reflecting on why there was so much resistance from the democratic right to the establishment of the committee, and whether it was justified. None of the questions raised here about the role of Habsburg or Stauffenberg, for example, is intended to suggest that they are, or ever have been Nazi sympathisers. Certainly no such charge could be made against the British Conservatives. They feared from the outset that the inquiry would be no more than a left-wing stunt. Like Revel, they presumably felt that the left was prepared to attack only Nazi racism and not racism in the Soviet Union. Given the national compartmentalisation of most of political life in Western Europe, in spite of the existence of the European Community, they perhaps genuinely considered that the problems of racism were not substantial. Some moderate Conservatives no doubt sincerely felt this, and Glucksman was quite right to insist that nothing is gained by exaggerating the problem.

Others beyond the FN's own ranks seemed not to want Le Pen's true nature to be exposed. Habsburg had been a public friend of many in Le Pen's group. Luc Beyer de Reyke, a Belgian Liberal who was often present at the hearings, was shown on Belgian television to have worked with Le Pen at the time of his visit to Schaerbeek. Selva had been denounced in the P2 scandal. Many French politicians were prepared to denounce fascism while at the same time playing up to public opinion on immigration in order to get back some of the million votes Le Pen had attracted in the 1984 Euro-elections.

Ironically, there were some on the left who refused to have anything to do with the inquiry. Among Labour MEPs some argued that it was pointless to have an inquiry into racism and fascism in which supporters of Le Pen could play a full part. A. Sivanandan of the Institute of Race Relations in London refused an invitation to take part in the public hearings because he was not prepared to sit in a room with fascist sympathisers. In retrospect, all have agreed that the inquiry was a useful political exercise.

The purpose in reviewing the work of this inquiry and the evidence it received is to underline just how difficult it is to get democratic politicians to work together on this subject, and to get Europeans to look at what is really happening in their society. The attempt by some conservative politicians to pretend that there was no substantial problem even to be studied was not part some complicated plot. It was their natural instinct to ignore inconvenient problems or even signs of sickness in society. Since it is true that Soviet propaganda used to concentrate enormous effort on denouncing a mythical revival of Nazism in Germany in the 1950s, a certain concern that the left was over-reacting to Le Pen was understandable. It is, however, equally clear that for many members of democratic conservative parties, looking at what is really happening in Europe was seen instinctively as a painful exercise to be avoided if at all possible. The fatalistic hyperbole of a few people on the Left, who may see some political advantage in presenting an exaggerated impression of what is at stake now, is equally deplorable. It is not a question of whether racism and fascism represent a big or a small problem. It is a question of accepting the obvious historical reality that Nazism and fascism did not die out with Hitler and Mussolini and that the deep crisis of political and economic adjustment to Europe's reduced status in the world to which they offered a response is a continuing process. The fact that whilst the Committee of Inquiry was at work the whole Community structure was gearing up for further structural change in advance of the 1992 deadline merely confirms that Europeans still face the necessity to modernise and reform social and economic structures. The new right and the racist extremists, as we have seen, had been aware of what was at stake from the 1940s onwards. If the Committee of Inquiry has any lasting value it will be in convincing democratic politicians to provide an alternative vision of the positive potential for a united and open Europe rather than a Europe based on nationalism and racism. In retrospect, it may be that Le Pen's arrival in the heart of the European Community's institutional structure itself drew attention to the need for a positive acceptance of Europe's multiracial destiny.

The very fact that Le Pen had been forced to publicly try and stop the inquiry from working was a kind of victory. The massive endorsement given to the report by 286 votes to 1 in the European Parliament in January 1986 was more valuable than the social ostracism and silent demonstrations which were originally the only response to Le Pen's arrival on the European scene. Even before the inquiry reported, Le Pen had become quite isolated and could only concentrate his efforts on trying to ridicule the whole institution. This showed that his original plan to play the role of a constructive democratic parliamentarian had failed.

This may have contributed in part to his readoption of a more nationalistic anti-European integration style in the Euro-elections of 1989. During his first term as leader of the European Right Group he had failed to establish genuine working relationships with other political groups. His right to participate in meetings of group chairmen was accepted and some of his members were elected to minor posts in accordance with the system under which appointments are made within the Parliament, but none of this amounted to the achievement of the political respectability to which Le Pen initially aspired after his 1984 breakthrough.

Even when one of his members, Claude Autant-Lara, a retired film director, was allowed, as the oldest member, to preside over the opening of the Constituent session of the European Parliament in Strasbourg on 25 July 1989, the protests and walk-outs this provoked only served to underline this party's isolation. Autant-Lara had become notorious for explicitly anti-Semitic remarks. Whatever success he might have felt as his presence in the Chair provided him with a brief opportunity to reach a wider public must have soon evaporated as the Spanish socialist Enrique Baron Crespo was easily elected as President of the European Parliament. As it happened this election had its own significance as President Baron had begun political life as a lawyer defending trade unionists in Spain during the Franco era. His total opposition to fascism had resulted in his having been jailed by an extreme right-wing regime. Moreover, the consensus between socialists and Christian Democrats which Baron's election symbolised resulted not only from their rejection of extremism but also their common commitment to build a democratic European union of the kind Le Pen would deplore.

Notes

1. See *Evrigenis Report*, p. 6.
2. See Allan Bullock, *Hitler*, Penguin, 1962 p .738.
3. *Evrigenis Report*, Annexe 4.
4. See Anne Dummett, *A Portrait of English Racism*, CARAF Publications, 1984.
5. See Philomena Essed, *Alledaaqs Racism*, (*Everyday Racism*), Sara, Amsterdam, 1984.
6. See Anne Frank Foundation, *The Extreme Right in Europe and the United States*, Amsterdam, 1985.
7. J-F. Revel, *How Democracies Perish*, London, 1985.
8. Decision of the Court of Justice of the European Communities, 4.6.86, Case No. 78/85.

Six

Nineteen Ninety-Two and Beyond

Democracy in Western Europe is not about to be overthrown by the extreme right any more than the prevailing order has been seriously imperilled by the terrorist revolutionaries of the extreme left. An electoral breakthrough to government by any overtly racist or fascist party is not about to occur. Hardly any support for a *coup d'état* exists in any Western European country, even in military or secret service circles. Yet European society faces a widespread social malaise of which the trends and events referred to in this book are a disturbing illustration. There has been some remarkable new growth from the old roots of fascism which were cut down but not torn out of the ground in the 1940s. As Europe prepares for greater integration after 1992 new opportunities for the extreme right are clearly apparent.

Racism in Europe is nothing new nor is it about to disappear. Since the end of the nineteenth century writers like Gobineau in France and Chamberlain in England opposed multiracialism and glorified what they saw as the Aryan race. Their ideas form the dark side of Europe, of its political culture and of its society. This is a political and historical reality which cannot and should not be ignored. Europe has other more noble and more popular ideals to work for, but in so doing, Europeans cannot ignore their present social problems any more than they can ignore their history or the common future which their political leaders boldly talk about. Even in the decades of European integration, with the burial of historic enmity between France and Germany, with the increasingly rapid development of a supranational Europe some things have not changed.

Contemporary events confirm that the ideas of fascist and racist politicians were not just the product of a particular historical period or something which appealed only to certain parts of Europe. Neo-nazi activity amongst young people in Britain shows that a generation and a country living in circumstances quite different from those pertaining in Germany in the 1920s and 1930s contains many who find the ideas of Hitler appealing. In the face of this unpleasant reality, it is no more appropriate to deny or ignore the threat posed by right-wing extremists than it is to over-react to their activities. A carefully considered response is needed which is based on a defence of the ideas of human rights and democracy which represent the strongest element of Europe's political culture. Most certainly Europeans can ignore exaggerated propaganda of the kind which, until recently, came from Moscow about the threats of a fascist revival combined with German revanchism. Similarly, the fascist threat cannot be effectively met by those on the extreme left who refer to it just as a slogan for mobilising support and yet do not themselves have any commitment to pluralism and parliamentary democracy. At a very minimum an optimistic approach based on the belief that Europe is capable of overcoming these problems is certainly more appropriate than one based on the view that our society is so sick that history somehow could repeat itself.

Apart from the interest shown in this subject by the European Parliament, the Commission of the European Communities also considered the phenomenon of the extreme right as significant enough to merit a special study in 1985 in the framework of Eurobarometer, a series of EC-wide opinion poll surveys. Analysis of the results[1] shows that in spite of widely varying electoral results between different countries and different dates there is, in virtually all West European countries, a permanent potential for right-wing extremism. Success in the ballot-box depends on various factors, such as the absence of an attractive alternative for right-wing voters and external circumstances (economic or political crises). Moreover, sympathy for the extreme right emerges from this study as an almost ubiquitous phenomenon, apparent not only in social structure and the problems of modern society but also in a particular kind of personality structure. Even voters who define themselves as sympathetic to the extreme right do not automatically vote in elections for such parties. Electoral success depends, as we have seen, on the ability of extreme-right parties to mobilise potential support, on the relative attractiveness of other right-wing parties, on the propaganda skills of the leadership, and on the economic and political circumstances in which any particular election takes place. It is because of these unpredictable elements that precise figures of the susceptibility of the electorate to extreme-right parties cannot be provided. In normal circumstances it appears that most voters who consider themselves on the extreme right will give their support to non-extremist parties like the Thatcherite Conservatives in Britain, the Gaullist RPR in France, the Christian Democrats in Germany and Italy, or Liberals in Belgium or Holland. Extreme-right voters look for nationalism, ethno-centrism, anti-parliamentarism, a tough line on law and order, as well as a strong leader. Political sociologists suggest that support for right-wing extremism reflects an inability to cope with the demands of modern society. Stronger support for the extreme right is available amongst the lesser educated members of society, whether they be amongst younger or older voters. This phenomenon may be due to a sense among older voters that the authoritarian habits and fixed beliefs of their formative years are not reflected in modern mainstream parties. Impatience and intolerance may be seen both as a characteristic of older and of younger extreme-right voters. The young face the added anxiety of uncertain job prospects and future economic insecurity. In both cases lack of education appears to lead individuals to blame the system for letting them down and to look for a more promising alternative. In short, many extreme-right voters look for a stability and predictability in political life which can never, in practice, be guaranteed. The very rapidity of the process of change in the modern world, reflected by such events as immigration or European integration, which may inspire many to hope for a better world may also lead to a greater sense of insecurity and bewilderment among those who fear that these changes will be, in some way, to their cost in economic terms or in terms of their self-esteem as citizens of a particular place or country.

A global social malaise

The problem to be faced, therefore, is not merely the existence of extreme, right-wing parties, disturbing as they are, it is the overall social and political situation which their continued political relevance reflects. They are the symptom of a sickness in society. Institutional racism, oversimplification by the media, and opportunistic remarks by vote-hungry politicians can serve to make the sickness appear as something normal. Concerns about this trend have been endorsed by a series of objective non-partisan analyses. In 1980 the Parliamentary Assembly of the Council of Europe pointed to the 'need to combat resurgent fascist propaganda and its racist aspects'.[2]

This particular report was a response to attacks on Jewish, immigrant, and refugee targets, and it set these issues in their wider context. Fascist propaganda, the report stated, 'finds, in a climate of economic and social uncertainty, an audience among certain sections of the population and is even seeking, more subtly, to find a place in the ideologies of certain widely supported political parties'. Since 1980 the situation has clearly worsened, and the findings of the report remain all too relevant. It pointed out how severe economic strains on society were leading, once again, to a search for scapegoats amongst minority groups. Colour, nationality, and language are for the most-deprived groups in society symbols of dignity and supposed superiority. Ray Hill's autobiographical account of how he became a fascist dramatically illustrates how poor members of society find in political racism not just a sense of superiority but also a sense of purpose and are, therefore, particularly likely to listen to fascist demagogues. This is not the only source of support for the extreme right, but some of the aspects of the situation such as fascist activity in British schools, the rise of Le Pen and support for fascist terrorism would suggest that a perception of economic decline is one of the main explanations for the growth of the new audience for fascists. In the years of growth in the 1950s and 1960s scapegoats were not required.

It is also important to emphasise that the dangers posed to society by these developments cannot be measured simply. The social situation in which extremists operate is the real problem and not their political activities as such. The 1980 report of the Council of Europe did not find any 'major revival of fascist or racist ideology' but it still emphasised the need for positive action to combat this ideology. Even with small numbers of members and limited resources, it must be disturbing that in the time of the fiftieth anniversary of the outbreak of the Second World War, two extreme-right groups were recruiting amongst young people, as Paul Wilkinson put it in 1981, 'on a larger scale than anything experienced in the democracies since 1945'.[3] As he pointed out, such activists are not trying to become politically respectable, their aim is to bring down democracy, and observers who measure their aims and potential in terms of the traditional electoral battle are bound to misunderstand and misrepresent the situation. The neo-fascists' aim is to exploit weaknesses in the functioning of democracy and to play on unsatisfied and perhaps unsatisfiable aspirations. The continuing strength of the extreme right may, therefore, be partially due to its ability to feed on public concerns which are to some extent insoluble in the sense that law and order is as much a social problem as a political problem; immigration is a fact of economic and social life, and bad housing in big cities is not a sudden new phenomenon. If citizens really expect that politicians can 'solve' such 'problems', then the extreme right is correct in trying to build up pressure for the kind of action such as repatriation, or hanging muggers and rapists, which the democratic political parties will not seriously contemplate. It is precisely for this reason that giving credence or semi-recognition to the legitimacy of certain extremist demands could prove a catastrophic error. Moreover, the failure to deliver on promises made in election campaigns only fans the flames. Precisely because Chirac was much more extreme as an opposition leader or Presidential candidate than as Prime Minister, Le Pen's attacks on him were so effective. Similarly, just because the British Tories mopped up the votes of the British NF in the 1970s and 1980s does not mean that extremists could not reappear on the electoral scene if Thatcherism does, in fact, fail to deliver in terms of halting some people's perception of national decline.

In this context it must be recognised that both the democratic left and right have to be careful if they are not to play into the hands of the enemies of democracy. Too often, Conservative politicians in Britain and elsewhere echo the ideas of extremists when they ridicule the 'race relations industry' as if anti-racist activity was part of some unnecessary bureaucratic exercise. Combining such attitudes with a subtle appeal for the votes of racist sympathisers, they are in danger of making a bad situation worse. Similarly, some on the left use the word 'fascist'as a convenient term of abuse for any right-of-centre politician. There are also on the left those who have such enthusiasm for revolutionary change that they await with relish a situation in which their country would become ungovernable as the left and right confront each other on the streets. In 1982 Bill Jordan [4] therefore argued 'that the decisive move towards socialism in Britain could arise in response to the threat of a new and powerful fascist party'. He predicted that during the mid-1980s political and economic disruption will be associated with the activities of fascist groups on the right and with the organised and angry demands of workers on the left. It is difficult to know whether this is meant to be a cry of hope or of despair. In reality the situation remains far more complex. Society remains unhealthy, but there are no real signs of an imminent collapse. A more appropriate response would be to encourage the widest possible awareness of the dangers of letting present trends go unchecked rather than raising false threats of a fascist upsurge. In particular, apart from Italy, there is no evidence of close co-operation between big business in alliance with powerful groups in society and the extreme right as occurred in the 1920s and 1930s. Exaggerated comparisons, therefore, risk making it more difficult to persuade a broad sector of public opinion to join in efforts to increase awareness of present dangers and to nip in the bud the current rise of racism and fascism.

In 1985, the catastrophic incidents at the Heysel Stadium before the European Cup Final match brought home to a wider public the problem of football violence and the involvement of extreme-right groups. It is impossible and perhaps unnecessary to try and define the precise extent to which the extreme right was responsible for what occurred. Football violence is itself a reflection of deeper social problems and, therefore, the activity of fascist agitators can be seen as part of the problem. Racial abuse and the singing of racial chants from football terraces are phenomena apparent right across Western Europe. Visiting black players and blacks in home teams are often assailed by racist abuse and insults. In Western Europe most of the persistent and vocal support for football teams comes from young men who have to face daily the effects of the decline in economic and social prospects of their city or their region. Why football should provide the occasion for such dramatic expressions of anger or violence is not clear. Even in the same city football violence is not always emulated by fans of other sports. It is, none the less, clear, as James Wallis[5] has put it, 'in times of marked industrial decline and major urban decay in the areas from which the game of football draws its support, many of the tensions, frustrations and antipathies of local life are likely to find expression in local football'. He adds that other forms of popular culture reflect the same tensions in society. It is hardly surprising that in a period of economic difficulty young and energetic people will become frustrated and angry. A particular sign of changing times is available to passers-by in Carnaby Street in Central London. This street was once the home of flower-power and the movement which thought that a new era of peace and love had actually arrived. In the 1980s it became a centre for fashionable fascists from all over Europe. It is the symbols of the SS, the records fo the white power movement, taped speeches of Hitler, and obscene racist publications which now attract people to cross Europe just to go shopping in Carnaby Street.[6] The growing market for Nazi paraphernalia, the racist slogans on the walls of buildings in Carnaby Street, and so many other streets in Europe are the visible confirmation of the political phenomenon revealed in votes for Le Pen or the social phenomenon revealed by the Economic and Social Research Council's report about political attitudes amongst young people in Britain. That thousands of young people should be attracted to concerts by groups with an openly neo-Nazi message is not a phenomenon to be ignored. Propaganda songs with titles such as 'Master Race' or 'Strength through Oi' (a play on the Nazism 'Strength through Joy' slogan) are designed to strengthen this dangerous trend in society. Given that the background problems of urban decay and mass unemployment are not about to disappear, it is impossible to imagine that the political consequences will be any more temporary.

As well as avoiding the use of exaggerated comparisons, the left must also be careful not to feed the flames of anger and frustration. In Italy and France the strengthening of the extreme right has come after periods of relative success for centre-left parties. Their failure to live up to expectations can create an even more chronic situation. The left needs not only to develop a careful critique of the nature of the present dominance of neo-conservative policies but also to develop an alternative vision and set of policies which can both attract electoral support and deal with the problems of society. Similarly, the functioning of political parties and trade unions must be at fault if among the poorer sections of society young people are looking to the extreme right rather than to the democratic left for solutions. The rise of the extreme right has to be fought on a political level. Parties should strengthen their ability to represent minority groups at the same time as they strengthen their roots in society, particularly amongst the young. In Western European democracies political parties should be the main channels of political action and if they fail to represent important sectors of opinion and society then the democratic system risks failing to function properly. If, as has occurred in Britain, the youth sections of the two main parties fall into the hands of extremists, then something has clearly gone seriously wrong. The official leadership of both parties cannot escape their responsibility for these situations, and should consider how best to develop the capacity for democratic politics to attract the involvement of young people with a·genuine interest in democracy rather than in undermining it.

In the face of alienation, the obvious strategy is to seek dialogue. Where, however, extremists are at work, dialogue between politicians and activists of mainstream parties clashes with the priority of denouncing each other rather than solving social problems. At the same time an unsavoury competition to produce the most stringent policies on immigration has, as we have seen, a damaging effect on the development of political attitudes to minorities. The growth of racism is a test of the health of Europe's body politic. If Europe is to pass that test it must show itself capable of producing an adequate response to this sickness and creating a political climate in which extremists cannot use racism for political ends. As well as the positive measures which can be introduced through legislation, the main way to defeat this sickness is by genuine popular rejection of racism. The activities of the trade unions should be part of that response. Official declarations, legislative and educational measures must be supplemented by the work of voluntary grassroots organisations. The spontaneous growth in France of 'SOS-Racisme' is perhaps the most interesting example of the possibilities of such a response to racism. The rapid emergence of 'SOS-Racisme' showed that there is no copyright on anti-racism. It can take many forms, of which a media-orientated form is only one of the various possibilities.

'SOS-Racisme', which shot to prominence in France in 1985, was formed as a response to racial murders which were seen as the tip of the iceberg in a society where the extreme right was gaining ground and racism was becoming an everyday experience for many French people and immigrants. The leader of the movement and its symbol was a young man, half-Algerian, a black Frenchman called Harlem Desir.[7] In co-operation with Parisian intellectuals such as Marek Halter and Bernard Henri-Levy, he turned the idea of a simple badge into a mass movement. The response to racial attacks was a simple one: 'don't touch my buddy'. Within weeks of its appearance the simple hand-shaped badge bearing the French words *Touche pas à mon pote* became known throughout France as literally millions of young people chose to wear it, to take part in marches, to organise concerts, meetings and discussions on the rise of racism in France and how to combat it. Le Pen and his followers responded by openly sneering at the Jewish element in Desir's background, but could not match or undermine the appeal of the movement that had developed. It was particularly significant that many of Desir's followers put themselves forward as Frenchmen campaigning in the finest traditions of freedom and equality. They received all-party support, celebrities flocked to take part in their events and for a time they appeared to put traditional human rights or migrant workers groups into the shade. Desir gave evidence to the European Parliament's Committee of Inquiry and was present in Strasbourg in January 1986 when its findings were endorsed by the Parliament's plenary session. On the positive side 'SOS-Racisme' showed that, with a simple message combined with skilful use of the media, the best instincts of the French people could be mobilised and the extremists could be isolated. They proved that racism was far from gripping the whole of France. In a party political sense they made it all the harder for Le Pen to appear as just another politician looking for votes. The massive demonstrations and wide-ranging support which followed Desir's success showed that France's political system was not about to succumb to extremism and provided an encouraging sign of the limits of Le Pen's advances.

'SOS-Racisme' did not, however, defeat Le Pen. It did not stop racist murders. It did not stop politicians like Chirac and Pasqua seeking to cut the electoral ground from under Le Pen. It did, however, make it impossible to ignore racism as a social problem and an electoral issue. This itself was a substantial achievement, as in many countries a consensus has developed that really racism is a marginal problem affecting only minorities, not an issue of national concern. Of course, 'SOS-Racisme' did not enter a situation in which no-one else had noticed the problem or campaigned actively for a response. Many migrant organisations such as the 'March of the Beurs' refused to co-operate too closely with 'SOS-Racisme' because they feared that such a massive media-orientated exercise could not actually give the voice and recognition for which migrants had long been campaigning. The importance of such conflicts should not be over-estimated. Inevitably, migrant groups have tended to represent particular groups such as Turks, Moroccans, or Zairois. Jewish and human rights groups have had different objectives and problems. The principal achievement and problem for 'SOS-Racisme' was that it had in its ranks Jews and Arabs as well as others, such as homosexuals, who felt targetted by Le Pen's hateful demagogy. Moreover, while traditional human rights groups such as MRAP and LICRA had for some time been denouncing the extreme right and the rise of racism, they were more or less out of touch with life in the poorer quarters of the big cities where the main day-to-day problems of racism and xenophobia have to be faced by various minority groups. 'SOS-Racisme' may well go out of fashion, but it showed that the simple ideals of solidarity and unity as strength can mobilise and inspire millions of people, and overcome traditional barriers to co-operation. That, in itself, was an historic achievement which others would do well to try and emulate.

By early 1990, the movement was becoming openly critical of the Socialist Government's immigration policy and seemed to have lost both momentum and clear objectives. One of the main criticisms of 'SOS-Racisme' has been that it is non-political, in the sense that while its leaders clearly sympathised broadly with the Socialist Party it accepted support from across the political spectrum. Indeed, because of anti-Semitism some of the most brutal language of the Front National is reserved for non-socialist leaders like Simone Veil. By not taking on an overtly party political label 'SOS-Racisme' was probably able to reach a wider audience. Leaders of the centre-right were certainly slower to rally to its activities but it did nominally enjoy all-party support and encouragement.

This contrasts with the only large and even loosely similar group that has emerged in Britain: the Anti-Nazi League (ANL). This was formed in response to the political campaigns of the National Front in Britain in the 1970s. The group had a left-wing stance and it has been criticised as having been dominated by revolutionary socialists. It undertook an important task of alerting a wider public to what was happening in society and worked with others in an educational effort to resist the rise of racism. Its strategy of taking the law into its own hands did, however, undermine its credibility with many people who, whilst they would never dream of going to a Nazi rally and would abhor the National Front's aims, could not see what was gained by attempting to prevent fascist meetings taking place. A counter-demonstration is something quite different from a direct intentionally planned physical confrontation in which the police are inevitably placed in the position of defending the rights of fascists to hold rallies or undertake marches. The ANL did succeed in waking up a lot of people to the chances of a possible Nazi revival in Britain and in openly challenging it could be seen to be contributing to protecting democracy. The ANL has most impact at a time when the NF was electorally strong before the emergence and then dominance of Mrs Thatcher. By targetting the NF as the main political enemy of the left, some revolutionaries appeared to be making not only an error of political judgement but also underestimating the possibility of an authoritarian government, with a populist policy on immigration and law and order profiting from the circumstances created by both the racists (the demand for immigration controls) and left-wing demonstrators (the demand for tougher police powers). The ANL was, however, particularly important because no other political party had been prepared to take the lead on this issue. As Stuart Hall[8] has put it: 'People now have much less confidence in the organised political parties and in their capacity to represent the real forces in British politics. The parties seem so bureaucratically removed from where the daily nitty gritty of politics goes on.' In such a context, groups capable of organising, educating, and responding at local level fill a huge void. Legislative action and action at the level of national, European, or international bodies cannot really fill the gap even if such action is equally necessary. Similarly, the work of independent bodies like the Runnymede Trust or Searchlight in Britain, which closely observe the effects of racist and fascist developments in society, cannot really be replaced by official bodies. As the political climate evolved in the 1980s even non-partisan anti-racist groups felt themselves to be operating in a cold climate, where the authorities prefer to ignore the real dimensions of the problem. As the new right gained influence, the left wing parties preferred to give a marginal role to their anti-racist stance. A particularly unhealthy situation is in danger of evolving whereby racism becomes increasingly endemic and those who feel themselves the targets do not feel that they have legitimate sources of response or even defence. As institutional racism comes to pervade parts of the police force, a dangerous spiral of race riots, racist propaganda, anti-democratic demagogy by extremists, and a lack of confidence in the state by minorities could get out of control and contribute to a further weakening of what should be a democratic political culture, where citizens rely on the law for security and for redress. Such trends in society cannot be ignored if a social malaise facing Western Europe is not to turn, sooner or later, into an open challenge to democracy.

Banning the extreme right

Alongside educational and cultural action there are various possible legislative responses to the activities of the extreme right. Having accepted its right to stand at elections or hold rallies on the grounds that freedom cannot be defended through measures based on repression and intolerance, the problem remains as to whether groups which openly abuse democracy in order to undermine its should have the same tolerance extended to them by the law, as they would wish to deprive others.

Different countries have different legal provisions for dealing with political extremism.[9] The differences reflect differences in history, different legal concepts and traditions, as well as differences with regard to the scale of the problem. The various mechanisms range from formal bans on fascist and Nazi parties to vaguely worded provisions against threats to democracy in general. Article 1 of the 1949 Basic Law of West Germany concerns the organisation of parties in accordance with democratic principles. The twelfth transitional and final provision of the constitution of the Italian Republic prohibits the Fascist Party.

Under Article 29 (1) of the 1975 Greek Constitutions it is laid down that political parties must contribute to the untrammelled functioning of democracy. Under Article 6 of the Spanish Constitution parties are required to be democratically organised and exist as an expression of political pluralism.

For historical reasons West Germany and Italy have constitutional provisions which are supposed to prevent the re-establishment of fascist or Nazi parties. These measures had some impact in the 1950s. In West Germany an annual report is produced by the 'Office for Protection of the Constitution', which carefully monitors the membership of extremist groups, racial attacks, the circulation of propaganda, etc. The legislation has not been useless, but it may not be quite as effective as would be hoped. Banning an organisation from regular political activity forces it into underground activity such as terrorism. Imprisoning activists can create martyrs or heroes for those who see the activists as their spokesmen. In recent years there has been some controversy following a weakening of a law in West Germany which had been designed to prevent the circulation of propaganda denying the holocaust. Since much right-wing extremist activity is a reflection of deeply rooted social problems, it is a complete illusion to imagine that the solution lies through legislation. As a new generation emerges it is very hard to accuse people of refounding a party which was destroyed decades before they were born. In the meantime, however, the legislative apparatus appears to have been marginally useful and there would, therefore, not appear to be any case for simply dismantling it. Certainly, when some kind of ban is introduced it should be part of a concerted effort by the authorities. The absence of such an effort was apparent in the weeks following the Republican Party's breakthrough in Berlin early in 1989. Chancellor Kohl's attempts to give a lead, by declaring that immigrants are to be treated as fellow citizens, or *mitburger*, were immediately challenged by other Christian Democrats who insisted that foreigners be treated as guests an not as citizens. Franz-Josef Strauss's successor as leader of the Bavarian CSU, one of the coalition parties in power, insisted that West Germany should keep its identity. The new CSU leader, Max Streibl, rejected the idea of a multicultural society. Such statements inevitably reduced the impact of the Interior Ministry's decision in February 1989 to ban the Nationale Sammlung, a neo-Nazi group whose leader, Michael Kuhnen, was standing for the Frankfurt City Council. Such bans will not stop the spread of racist poison so long as those like Max Streibl continue to appeal to xenophobia, and controversy rages over the issue of voting rights for migrant workers and entry rights for people seeking political asylum.

In Italy the constitutional provisions against fascism were supplemented in 1952 by a law providing for legal sanctions against attempts to recreate the Fascist Party. On the occasion of the celebration of the fortieth anniversary of Italy's present Constitution, it was argued that the time had come to delete from the Constitution those provisions which prevent the reformation of a fascist party. This argument was not put forward by Fascist sympathisers and the controversy that continues in Italy on this subject is relevant not only for the light it sheds on the relative value of legislative action but also on the problem of how Europeans face up to their past and look at their current political problems. In an article in *Corriere della Sera*,[10] Renzo De Felice, one of the principal experts on Italian fascism, argued that the time had come to abolish those parts of the Italian Constitution and law specifically intended to prevent the recreation of a fascist party. He argued that the Italian political system operated satisfactorily even with an openly fascist party like the MSI participating not only in elections and parliamentary activities but also in state bodies such as the managing boards of the Italian broadcasting authorities and the nationalised industries. The fact that the MSI operated openly in spite of the provisions of the law proved that legal bans of this kind were 'grotesque and ridiculous'. He added that in reality these provisions merely made the whole Constitution seem ridiculous. Whereas in the 1940s the main political issue in Italy had been the struggle between fascists and anti-fascists, this could no longer be considered as so overwhelmingly important as a line of division in Italian policies and society. Anti-fascism, which had been fundamental to the re-establishment of democracy in the 1940s, no longer had the same meaning in public consciousness. Asked whether he was aware of the trauma that such comments might cause, De Felice argued that since it was not directly responsible for the holocaust Italian fascism could be considered as 'better' than its French, German, or Dutch equivalents. He also considered that since Italy did not face the same problems of mass immigration as France there could never be the same sort of racist political movement of the kind which had provided support for the extreme right in France in the 1930s and 1940s and again in the 1980s.

That such a prestigious historian should make remarks of such remarkable superficiality and short-sightedness merely confirms that resistance to fascist and racist tendencies is too important a matter to be left to specialists, whether they be political activists or academics. If Italian fascism was so special and the MSI was merely a harmless *piccolo borghese* party containing no serious threat to democracy, one has to ask why Giorgio Almirante should in 1984 have led his party members in the European Parliament into a group chaired by the racist Le Pen and containing a Greek member who openly supported the totalitarian regime of the Greek colonels. In Italy De Felice's view was, naturally, strongly challenged from the historical point of view by those who pointed out that fascism in Italy had served as Hitler's inspiration and model in the 1920s, and that although Mussolini had not ordered a holocaust, his regime did participate in the rounding up of Jews, some of whom were then killed. The point was also made that from the late 1940s, when the MSI first sent representatives to the Italian Parliament, the dominant issue had been the clash between the Communist Party (PCI) and the other parties, there being an unwritten consensus that the PCI would never be allowed into the government. Indeed, it was precisely the fear of the communists in the 1940s which allowed the likes of Licio Gelli to recommence political activity and in the crisis years from 1960 onwards it was the growing strength of the communists which provided the moving force behind attempted coups, terrorism, and co-operation between police and right-wing extremists.

De Felice's remarks were naturally welcomed by the MSI but were denounced by representatives of the families of those killed or injured by fascist terrorism in recent years. Generally, the reactions to what De Felice proposed were negative. Even Christian Democrats and centrist politicians argued that whilst anti-fascist rhetoric might be outdated, it would be wrong to appear to legitimise an ideology which had totalitarian objectives, or, as Norberto Bobbio put it, to deny that democracy and dictatorship are two totally different systems. He ridiculed De Felice's comment that Italian fascism could in some way be considered as better than other variants of fascism, arguing that no citizen of a democracy would actually prefer the replacement of democracy by even the best of the dictatorships.

This controversy was partly sparked by a meeting between Bettino Craxi, the leader of the Italian Socialist Party, and Gianfranco Fini, the then leader of the MSI — the first meeting of its kind for seventy years. The meeting took place at the end of 1987 and was one of a series of consultations Craxi has undertaken to seek support for his proposals for constitutional reform, such as the direct election of the President of the Italian Republic. Craxi's meeting with Fini seems, in fact, far less controversial than the reflections it inspired on the part of one particular historian. The controversy was perhaps partially enflamed by the fact that it coincided with those raging about the remarks of Le Pen on the holocaust, and the exposure of Kurt Waldheim's past. Forty years after the war most people would still appear to feel the need to underline the fact that the regimes and the crimes against humanity committed in their name cannot be dismissed as merely a part of history. Rejection and condemnation of fascism remain necessary. This is not to deny that circumstances are now quite different and that the threat of a totalitarian regime is extremely limited, but to argue that anti-fascism is somehow no longer relevant is to deny both the basis of democracy and the nature of certain contemporary political trends. It is this which gives the various articles of the Italian constitution banning the Fascist Party their continuing relevance and validity. That they should have been acted upon with more determination, particularly in the 1940s and 1950s, is equally clear.

One of the problems in countries like Spain, France, and Italy has been the fact that not only has the law not been used to prevent fascist political activity but that fascist or their sympathisers are present in the ranks of the police and intelligence services. It is, therefore necessary to ensure that these individuals are not left free to cause enormous damage. Experience in Italy has shown how a few fascists can block investigations, manufacture evidence, or blame the left for right-wing attacks. Their activities only partially explain the fact that even in a democracy the law can operate in a way that is 'blind in the right eye', but it is clearly necessary to ensure that all kinds of terrorism are pursued equally ruthlessly and that policemen not loyal to democracy are removed from the force because of the damage they can do to the public order which they are meant to protect.

Another aspect of this question of banning the extreme right has been a subject of controversy in Britain, where many have argued that the law or political action through marches or sit-ins should be used to prevent fascist access to any political platform. In many universities in Britain there have been violent demonstrations as anti-fascist activists have tried to prevent fascist speakers being heard. As Bhikhu Parekh has pointed out, [11] those who use this tactic and those who insist on the inviolability of the principle of free speech both have a point. Demonstrations of this kind are, however, little more than symbolic gestures, with little relevance to the fight against the extreme right which does not generally see the university campus as a particularly propitious context for its political campaigns. Moreover, the 'no platform' policy is not effective in the sense that it does not appear to achieve the desired result of weakening the influence of fascist ideas in society. As Parekh puts it, the policy, in fact, produces a 'a new breed of professional martyrs' who go around drawing attention to themselves, presenting the left as authoritarian and intolerant using the political opportunity which the counter-demonstrators seem willing to provide, and in so doing give the impression of the extreme right as the voice of some kind of uncomfortable truth which society and the political establishment conspire to ignore or suppress.

Legal provisions against racism and discrimination

The law cannot solve all the problems of society and the political system, but it can provide both a symbolic and a punitive restraint on the activities of political extremists, especially as they attempt to recover political respectability. Le Pen always fights in the courts when he considers he is being insulted. Often he wins his cases, on other occasions he loses, such as when he thought it was unfair for him to be described as an '*adepte*' or follower of Hitler. The law has not, however, significantly restrained his rhetoric and certainly not that of many of his followers who use words at meetings they would not expect to see reported in the press.

Following the report of the European Parliament's Committee of Inquiry, the Commission sponsored a detailed study of the different approaches in the EC countries to the problem of protection against racism and xenophobia. Studies were undertaken in each member state and a general report, never officially published, was drafted by the Runnymede Trust in London. The report quoted the British Commission for Racial Equality (CRE) that the law is best seen as a catalyst which can contribute to better practices and can also provide a source of relief for minorities facing discrimination. Racists often face prosecution, fines, and imprisonment in various countries for violence or incitement, but the operation of the law does not alter the political and social climate and indeed the CRE itself has emphasised that lasting change requires popular support which can be built up only through 'education, persuasion and time'.

British law in this field could serve as a model for other countries since civil remedies in most of the EC member states are relatively underdeveloped. Denmark and the Netherlands have developed their criminal law to combat racism. Germany, Luxembourg, Greece, and Belgium have laws against incitement. Discrimination can be combatted through the law in Belgium, Denmark, and the Netherlands. The situation is clearly fairly patchy, but prosecutions regularly take place in all these countries. Immigrants, however, find it harder to make use of the law to defend themselves than other citizens who are part of a visible minority but face no danger of deportation. The British law may be the most comprehensive but no one, least of all the CRE, is claiming that it has really solved fundamental social problems. Given that we are dealing with a problem of European society, it would be appropriate for certain common guidelines for national legislation to be agreed. The report submitted by the Runnymede Trust to the Commission made numerous proposals for practical action which could serve as a brake on the activities of right-wing extremists. These included the following:

Incitement to racial hatred should be prohibited as a threat to public order. The civil law should provide individuals with the right to sue for damages when they are the object of the publication of false or inflammatory propaganda.

Governments should provide accurate and objective information concerning aliens and minority affairs.

There should be the implementation of laws against discrimination, particularly in employment, housing, and access to services, including effective sanctions against those who practice discrimination.

There should be provision of a legal responsibility for local authorities to contribute to the elimination of racism and discrimination.

There should be a prohibition on threatening and abusive language at meetings, in publications, and in broadcasts.

There should be the provision of a civil remedy against expressions of racial or religious hatred.

Efforts are now being made through the European Parliament and some of the member governments of the EC to ensure that European guidelines for national legislation are agreed. In 1985 the Council of Ministers did, in fact, call for the co-ordination of national laws across the EC to combat racism and xenophobia. It remains necessary to campaign for effective action to follow these positive declarations of intent. The fact, however, that the European Community institutions should have felt impelled even to undertake these first hesitant steps confirms the importance of the problem. In the present political climate the strengthening of laws against racism would be precisely the kind of lead which governments should give to society. It is, however, extremely unlikely that many of them will take such action for fear of losing some votes. The CRE's proposals for strengthening the British arrangements have not been acted upon by the government.

The role of the law is at best limited, but whatever progress can be achieved is bound to be be minimal so long as Governments and state authorities do not give a lead. When politicians play on xenophobia to win votes at election time they undermine all the work of legal or non-governmental bodies trying to combat racism. Moreover, unless the police also give a lead at local level, the value of legal provisions is extremely limited.

In 1981, following the Brixton disorders of 10–12 April, an inquiry was undertaken under Lord Scarman.[12] Witnesses told the inquiry that the riots had, in their view, been provoked by harrassment of black people by a racially prejudiced police force. It was alleged that officers pick on black people, especially young black people, when exercising, for example, stop and search powers. The inquiry rejected the view that the police were 'the oppressive arm of the racist state' but accepted that there was a problem with some officers. It rejected the view that since policemen are a cross-section of society some officers are bound to be racially prejudiced. Police standards have to be higher, not just because they are a model for society but also because provocative action on their part can have such massive repercussions in society. The reports of everyday racism heard by the European Parliament inquiry show that experience in Britain is mirrored elsewhere. It is also clear that right-wing extremists find more than average support in certain sectors of the police force, particularly those who feel they should have a freer hand to exert authority. Indeed, the problem of racism amongst police or other authorities supposed to protect citizens' rights or ensure public order is not entirely separate from that of policemen in Spain or Italy who openly sympathise or co-operate with fascist groups. The dimensions of this should not be exaggerated; the problem is that a racist or fascist policeman can have a disproportionate influence: by letting racial attackers go unapprehended or appearing to legitimise brutal treatment of minorities he can contribute enormously to creating the kind of situation in which right-wing extremism thrives. The kind of highly publicised effort by London's Metropolitan police, which, in February 1989, launched a campaign against racial attacks is certainly an example of what can be done if the will is there.

A multiracial Europe

Multicultural societies are not a particular twentieth-century novelty and certainly there is no valid historical reason for considering such societies as inevitably in decline. The appeal to patriotism is a perfectly valid policy or sentiment, but massive migration has been a constant theme of world history, whether as result of economic or political reasons. The idea that Britain or Europe is not, by definition, multi-cultural is quite odd. The monarchy itself dates back to various wars and invasions and the Royal Family has more European relatives than most British families. This is not the place to analyse the phenomenon of nationalism and its constitutional offspring the nation-state. Empires, dictatorships, and democracies can just as well be based on monocultural nations as on multinational or multicultural groupings.

It is also clearly apparent that Europe's economic need for immigration is a continuing reality. Demographic trends in Western Europe are leading to labour shortages in certain industries and regions. Immigration is, therefore, not a result of overpopulation in Africa or elsewhere, or of growing demands for political asylum, it is very often a response to the demands of the labour market. This reality was recently dramatically confirmed by a German business magazine which had the slogan 'Foreigners In' on its front page, illustrating that business has no reason to feel sympathy with anti-immigration campaigns.[13] The magazine described migrant workers as the motor of the economy. Such an approach does not mean that migrants can expect fair wages or a warm welcome in German society. It does, however, confirm that we are dealing with a phenomenon which will grow in political and social importance if present demographic trends continue and especially if the 1992 programme does speed up economic growth in Europe.

The development of a multiracial and multicultural Europe is now a political necessity as urgent and necessary as the political development of Europe which has come to be widely accepted as historically inevitable. Just as politicians have learnt to talk positively about the need to build up Europe's independence and economic strength rather than be obsessed with loss of world power status and sovereignty, so they must learn to see and encourage acceptance of the political and social reality of a multiracial Europe. As the European Parliament's Inquiry concluded in 1985, the new situation 'requires the formulation of a new global policy which will ensure that the new minorities can find their place in the social fabric of European nations and that these national societies develop harmoniously in understanding and respect for democratic values'.[14] Ignoring this reality is likely only to exacerbate problems. The bold talk of European union or of the development of a citizens' Europe cannot ignore that this new Europe will be as multiracial as it will be multinational. To argue that this is unrealistic is as appropriate as it would have been in the 1940s to assume that after two world wars Frenchmen and Germans could not live in peace inside a common political and institutional framework. The development of a citizens' Europe actually becomes a more interesting and attractive prospect if it is associated with the strengthening of equality and individual citizens' rights.

In April 1985 the European Trade Union Confederation (ETUC) made a timely call for the old-fashioned concept of solidarity to be revived. On 15 April their Executive Committee stated that mass unemployment was 'causing ruptures in social solidarity'. The fight for scarce job opportunities was seen to be at the source of a dangerous escalation from xenophobia to racism and discrimination. The trade unions committed themselves to a positive approach based on the reality that 'European countries have become multi-ethnic societies'. In an earlier resolution of January 1985 the ETUC pointed that in the period of growth after 1945 there had been 'a systematic utilisation of foreign labour by the economies of the highly industrialised countries of Western Europe'. They pointed out that the possible social and political consequences of this policy were ignored as economic and political leaders concentrated on ensuring that the labour force was large enough to promote economic expansion. In some cases illegal immigration was more or less tolerated because it contributed to expansion. Since the mid-1970s legal and illegal immigration has generally been restricted, and arrangements for family regrouping have been tightened up accordingly, but in reality 'the myth of the temporary nature of European or extra-European migration has been gradually destroyed'. In campaigning for a positive response to this reality, the trade unions could set an example for society as a whole.

If extreme right-wing and racist ideas are not to become a permanent feature of European society and political life this positive approach must be adopted. This means openly accepting a multiracial future, giving minorities the opportunity to participate fully in society, and challenging the prejudices and ignorance amongst young people in particular with a positive alternative vision of how society can develop.

Improved community relations, as American and British experiences have shown, cannot come about without first giving ethnic minority groups access to every level of decision-making. It is an illusion to expect peace and harmony in multi-ethnic communities if the minorities do not feel they have any real power over their own future. Racist and fascist groups are particularly opposed to suggestions of this kind, and that is why it is necessary to press ahead with them. In France, for example, special elections have been held to elect representatives of migrant workers to sit as co-opted members of local councils. The Front National has held demonstrations when these elections have been taking place, but it is better to have a confrontation of this kind in defence of a positive vision of society than to always be in the position of responding to racial attacks and speeches, or challenging racial discrimination in the jobs and housing markets. Many of the minorities have a perception of society in which racism and xenophobia permeate the framework and the legal system in which they live. What they are entitled to expect is a secure economic and political status, safe homes, and opportunities for educating their children. Their aspirations are not really very special, but political reality is influenced by the way they are perceived by the majority of their fellow citizens.

Part of the response to racism must, therefore, be to extend the civil rights of the minorities. In most European countries the right to vote is based on citizenship, and problems arise about giving the right to vote in parliamentary elections for some migrants. The situation at local level is different since it is inappropriate to deprive immigrants of the right to vote in situations where they are contributing to, and participating in, society in the same way as their neighbours. It is also quite unhealthy for a democratic society to develop with a substantial number of people living in a country but not enjoying full civil and political rights. This is why the European Parliament and Commission are pressing for the right to vote, at least in local elections, for migrants. The adoption of numerous declarations on human rights by European bodies would be meaningless if the development of a multinational and multiracial Europe actually led to a reduction in certain people's rights. This is not the place to deal in detail with problems of political refugees, nationality laws, and the inevitable differences which different categories of migrants face. Europe must deal with these issues not as if they were an unpleasant unexpected problem but as an inevitable result of policies in the past which encouraged migration, and as an inevitable fact of modern European life. In giving such political prominence to the 'problems' which these phenomena create, politicians give the wrong lead to society and encourage extremists to outbid them with appeals to xenophobia.

One of the key proposals of the report of the European Parliament's Committee of Inquiry was, therefore, the creation of a 'Migrants Forum' with direct access to the decision-making bodies of the EC. The forum could also monitor the effects of the economic situation on minorities, undertake comparative work on community relations at local and national levels, and develop practical proposals for actions to be undertaken to combat racism. The value of such a forum would be that it would provide an input for minorities to participate in discussions on European legislation and a vantage point from which to view the problems they face. Such a forum already exists for youth organisations and this could serve as a model for a migrants' forum. Since the European Parliament reported, talks on the establishment of the forum have been going on with non-governmental bodies trying to come together to make a proposal for the most effective way in which the numerous different minority groups at national and Community level can be made able to work together. The ethnic minority citizens of the EC represent a bigger group of people than many of the individual member states and the creation of a forum would, in symbolic and practical terms, confirm that the political message of the extreme right runs counter to the very nature of a democratic Europe.

In this context a number of initiatives have been taken which, it is hoped will bear fruit in the years ahead. In October 1988 MIGREUROPE was formed to provide an organised framework for

> non-governmental organisations dealing with migration issues in Europe as well as for associations of immigrants, refugees, exiles and foreign students to develop contacts among themselves and with the European institutions in order to struggle more effectively against racism and xenophobia and for an amelioration of the rights and economic, political, social and cultural situation of these people.[15]

Similar movements are developing in various countries to defend the right of political asylum and avoid the development of 'fortress Europe'. The Refugee Manifesto published in 1989 by the British Refugee Council and the *Whose Europe* publication by the Refugee Forum are examples of work going on in Britain to meet the objectives of organisations like MIGREUROPE. To achieve success and influence public opinion, such groups must combine local and national activities with the expression of a coherent message at the EC level. This is by no means an easy task, given the varying circumstances in different countries and regions, and the different particular problems faced by ethnic minorities, refugees, and migrants.

In December 1988, 'SOS-Racisme' organised in Paris the 'States-General of Youth for Equality'. As with other 'SOS-Racisme' activities these may turn out to have more impact on public opinion and the media than the grassroots organisations represented within MIGREUROPE, but it was clearly an effective continuation of efforts for a Europe-wide movement against racism. The Paris meeting emphasised the campaign for the civic rights of migrants but its significance was much wider. As President Delors told the meeting which was held at the Sorbonne: 'I am in charge of making the businessmen's Europe, you will do the rest.'[16] The meeting was presided over by Glyn Ford, MEP. Such contacts between the institutions of the European Community and popular anti-racist movements could prove particularly effective as new forms of political mobilisation become necessary in a more integrated Europe. The situation faced by different minorities in different countries clearly varies considerably. Most importantly it would be quite wrong to describe black British citizens as migrant workers. On the other hand, Harlem Desir, like Bernie Grant MP, is a black political activist, a citizen of a European country but also a representative of a part of society whose equality of opportunity is by no means certain. Moreover, both represent a part of society against which the extreme right is intent on mounting a political attack. The particular vision of Europe to which the extreme right is committed must be clearly and unequivocally rejected, and in this sense the declarations of the EC institutions and the close co-operation between them and the organisations representing immigrants and fighting racism is a welcome development.

The basic aim of the extreme right is the rejection of pluralism in both the democratic and the racial make-up of society. As Roy Jenkins put it in the British context, in 1966, integration was not a flattening process of assimilation, but of equal opportunity accompanied by cultural diversity in an atmosphere of mutual tolerance. Integration of different peoples and the abolition of inequalities, pluralism of ideas and cultures should be the strengths of modern Europe, defended and extended in a positive fashion.

Historically racism has been the cause of innumerable international conflicts and it is, therefore, appropriate that in the post-war world, particularly with the establishment of the United Nations (UN), countries should attempt to work together to eliminate racism. Clearly, such action is not going to eradicate the problem, but given the way that racism develops from people's instinctive fear of strangers and foreigners, it is certainly valuable for countries to be seen working together in the face of racism. Racism was at the origin of the world's most destructive conflict, the Second World War, and the fact that since 1945, countries who fought each other now join together in condemning racism is certainly a positive development. Since a first resolution in 1946 the UN General Assembly has regularly felt it appropriate to condemn racial persecution and discrimination. Indeed, the fact that it has felt necessary to do so is a confirmation of the intractability of the problem. The year 1971 was designated as the International Year of Action to Combat Racism and Racial Discrimination. The various resolutions of the UN have concentrated on certain points: condemnation of discrimination, respect for human rights, combatting discrimination. The UN puts a particular emphasis on the need to end colonialism, which itself is a power relationship built on racism. The commitments undertaken within the UN give the lie to the idea that racism is somehow an inevitable fact of life rather than something which people are taught and can, therefore, be taught to reject. A 1981 report for the UN Institute for Training and Research[17] concluded that 'it would seem that man is indeed contaminating and doing his utmost to destroy this shrinking world as much by his racism and racial discrimination as by all the pollutants with which he befouls the earth and the atmosphere. The circumstances call most urgently for a consciousness of the world's solidarity.' The report put the emphasis on the need for action through education and the media, on the need to help minorities recover from the inferiority complex which results from long periods of discrimination, and on the need for international co-operation for world development. In this sense, Europeans can at least be proud that with the Lomé Convention, they have provided the most advanced form of international co-operation between white and black, rich and poor countries, developing not only trade and aid policies but also joint meetings of Ministers and parliamentarians. This is a small step in the right direction.

The reports by the Council of Europe and the European Parliament also serve to confirm the fact that racism remains a major social issue. Whether it is appropriate to speak of an upsurge of racism and fascism is not really the issue. It is all too clear that race is a major and explosive political issue in many European countries, and that extreme right-wing political forces are ready and willing to profit from the situation. The detailed proposals endorsed by the European Parliament are annexed to the end of this book. The fact that they were endorsed almost unanimously by the European Parliament in January 1986 does not mean that their implementation will not be controversial and difficult. In fact, the initial response to the report by the Commission and Council has been extremely non-committal and the efforts within the European Parliament have so far produced little more than a series of well-meaning declarations of intent. Unless these first steps are followed with concrete action they will inevitably produce disillusionment amongst those who wish to see the new Europe act effectively against racism and not just condemn it. In June 1986 all the EC institutions agreed in a joint declaration that the rise of racism and xenophobia required an effective response but since it had not been acted upon, the European Parliament decided, at the end of 1989, to establish a new inquiry committee into the implementation of this declaration.

Three years after this joint declaration, the Commission, which proposes all EC action to the twelve governments represented in the Council of Ministers, finally produced some proposals.[18] This document certainly represented a recognition that the fight against racism and xenophobia should be seen as part of the general question of protecting basic civil rights which is one of the main aspects of identity and the movement towards integration in the Community. The Commission proposed:

— the encouragement and improvement of legislative measures against racist groups and racial discrimination;
— the involvement of associations fighting discrimination and racism in order to reduce the potential for conflict;
— efforts to improve health, housing, education and employment opportunities for migrants and members of minority groups;
— continuing studies of racism and the 'perception of democratic values' in the framework of Eurobarometer;
— improving the training of public servants coming into contact with immigrants;
— promoting the teaching of languages and culture of the countries from which immigrants have come;
— promoting a European dimension in education.

These proposals were far less ambitious than the European Parliament and the Runnymede Trust reports had proposed and were put forward in the form of a non-binding resolution. They received almost unanimous support in the European Parliament, which did, however, point out that the issue was important enough to 'require truly effective Community action in the shape of legislation'.[19] In March 1989 the Parliament organised a special colloquy with representatives of the twelve national parliaments as well as the commission and the European Court of Justice. Even at that meeting, the Council of Ministers representative was not able to announce if and when the draft resolution would be adopted, let alone commit his institution to effective legislative action. Such events and the parliamentary debates they lead to, do at least underline the exclusion of the extreme right and prevent their access to political respectability. It was precisely for this reason that a few years earlier Le Pen had seized on Commissioner Ivor Richard's suggestion that racism could not be considered as a part of the policy framework of the EC. The proposals now under consideration at least provide a basis on which to work. This basis was itself, as we have seen, part of a conscious response to the emergence of extreme right in the European Parliament in the mid-1980s.

Many experts refer to the need to encourage awareness of history so that young people see the deadly dangers lurking behind a certain type of political appeal. In the first decades after 1945 this was a relatively straightforward educational task, but as new generations grow up it will become all the more difficult. The strength of the appeal of the extreme right to the young is a confirmation of this problem. Young left-wingers in the 1960s were generally unimpressed when parents or professors referred to their sacrifices for freedom in the 1940s, and in the 1980s young people seem even more sceptical of the progressive message which the people who were young in the 1960s thought would become the natural approach to life for future generations. Such idealism may have been admirable but it would be absurd and dangerous to believe that the appeal of the extreme right will be countered only with appeals to idealism.

Another sign of changing times is the evolution of opinion within Israel and of opinions in Europe towards Israel. The saddest proof of the universality of the racist danger can be seen in the 1980s in Israel itself. Not only has an extreme-right party, basing its appeal on violent racism, succeeded in getting people elected to the Knesset but also a fanatical ultra-nationalism seems to have entered the mainstream of Israeli politics through such leaders as Begin. The expansionist policy which was initiated during his period as Prime Minister is based on a belief in the right of one people to a particular piece of territory and on a sense of racial superiority towards those who previously or currently live in it. This approach justifies violence and creates a cycle of hatred clearly based on a conflict between races. Developments in Israel not only create dangers for the international political situation, they will also make the fight against historical revisionism and therefore anti-Semitism and neo-Nazism all the more difficult. Events surrounding the exposure of the truth about Waldheim or the reaction to Le Pen's remark about the holocaust show that although there is enough health in Europe's body politic to face up to the realities of history, it would be quite unreasonably optimistic to assume that this will be the case in the 1990s and into the twenty-first century. If Israel is seen as a country with a brutal and oppressive government, the old ghosts of anti-Semitism could be easily reawakened. This would be doubly ironic. First, because the memory of the holocaust has been one of the main barriers to any major revival of the extreme right; and secondly, because Israel itself chose to co-operate closely with the racist apartheid regime in South Africa, which itself has provided a haven for European neo-Nazis during the lean years for Europe's extreme right. The self-destruction of Israel's moral standing could have negative consequences for the development of political attitudes in Europe, and in this context educational work will be all the more difficult. To put it bluntly, it will be hard for teachers to awaken a new generation's awareness of the holocaust if the Israeli government gives the impression of itself operating a racist expansionist policy in its internal and foreign policies.

Another extremely dangerous development has been the international crisis resulting from the publication of Salmon Rushdie's novel *The Satanic Verses*. Mr Rushdie has been for many years a leading campaigner for tolerance and understanding between the different peoples within Britain's own multicultural society: 'Britain is now two entirely different worlds, and the one you inherit is dependent upon the colour of your skin,' he had written. His words have been confirmed by numerous reports of discrimination in the legal profession, in job opportunities, and so on. His receipt of the Booker Prize was itself a sign of his own acceptance within a multicultural society. That the book he wrote should then be burnt in public in a horrendously symbolic gesture by Muslims in Bradford is as deplorable as it is ironic. That the almost unbelievable sight of a distant Ayatollah announcing that Rushdie had been sentenced to death should be considered as acceptable to even a small minority of the author's fellow British citizens in an issue too important to be ignored by those who have been concerned at the rise of racism in Europe. The City of Bradford, where Rushdie's book was burnt, had itself recently been taken over by local Conservatives who had skilfully exploited populist feeling against race relations initiatives and, on taking office, had moved quickly to postpone the appointment of extra teachers of English as a second language in schools with a high proportion of Muslim children. The Rushdie affair has, according to the local Labour MP, Pat Wall, led to the high risk of a racist backlash.[20]

Within weeks of the book-burning incident the Monday Club had distributed thousands of leaflets in the city, using the affair to call for an end to immigration. The difficulties which this issue raised were symbolised by the open disagreements within the leadership of the Labour Party. Local MPs and the party's deputy leader felt it appropriate to express sympathy for the offence apparently caused to Muslim people by the contents of Rushdie's book. Black Labour MPs and activists were also divided. It was argued by some that the non-publication of the book as a paperback would somehow assuage Muslim feelings. Others, including party leader Neil Kinnock, considered that the basic right to free speech could not be the subject of compromise. In contrast, Roy Hattersley appeared to feel that obliging Muslims to accept the consequences of living in a free society which allowed their own and other religions to be ridiculed was itself a form of racism. The discomfiture and division of the Left in Britain was a fore-runner of the controversy in France's Socialist Government over the 'Chador' by Muslim schoolgirls with the same concern being expressed that religious fundamentalism and resistance to Western influence by the Muslim religion was itself the source of oppression, particularly of women. The Commission for Racial Equality itself expressed concern at the effects on public opinion of the Muslim response to the publication of *The Satanic Verses*. Some observers criticised the failure of the authorities to prosecute those Muslim leaders who publicly called for the murder of Rushdie. The problems for the Labour Party in 1989 were further complicated by its refusal to adopt a black candidate for a by-election in London's Vauxhall constituency. This led to Hattersley himself being accused of racism, by some black activists. In France Le Pen used the Rushdie affair during the March 1989 municipal election campaigns to argue that the Ayatollah's murderous forces had entered France and that the whole incident showed the danger of allowing Muslim immigration into France. This confirms the way in which extremism breeds extremism. If intolerance, authoritarianism, obsession with the protection of a particular culture are to be deplored and resisted when they are part of European racist and extreme-right politics, a similar response is appropriate when the same kind of politics offered by Jewish politicians in Israel or Muslim leaders in Britain and elsewhere. The Rushdie affair, in particular, confirms the need to spare no effort for greater understanding of different people's culture and history. The book had been written partly with the intention of challenging the complacency of many who believe that multiculturalism has been painlessly implemented. The harsh and less-comforting reality could not have been more dramatically illustrated by the events which followed the publication of Rushdie's book. The Rushdie affair came, however, at a time in which anti-racist educationists could not agree on the issue of the Muslim authorities' right to run their own schools. Arguments that this would work against the development of a multicultural Britain were rejected as racist by some Muslim leaders.

In spite, or perhaps because, of these problems education clearly remains a key area of response to the threat of racism. It is particularly disturbing to see how in the past local authorities have appeared to be unaware of the extent of extremist activity within schools. Whilst any attempt at anti-racist 'indoctrination' could prove unproductive, it should be possible to be tough with those who use schools as a place for political propaganda. There is controversy surrounding the activities of certain local authorities in Britain but in fact the national government should be giving a lead in this area of policy instead of sneering at attempts to combat prejudice and providing encouragement to extremists with exaggerated attacks on local councils with complex problems simplistically referred to in a way that makes people all the more comfortable with their prejudices.

In resisting the rise of racism the state must set the right example. Ministers in their speeches, policemen on the beat, immigration officials all set an example which the rest of society is likely to follow. As the *Guardian*[21] put it in 1986, treatment of black immigrants at Heathrow Airport compared with American, Canadian or Australian immigrants represents 'the apotheosis of a squalid policy' and indirectly signifies that voting, tax-paying citizens who are also immigrants are 'second class'. So long as state authorities, encouraged by a raucous popular press, behave in this way, the situation in which the extreme right has developed its strength will not change.

What kind of Europe

The great issues which led to massive bloodshed in twentieth century Europe have all been linked to the nature of the development of Europe. The clash between different monarchs and ideologies has not just been about which country would dominate, it has also been about the kind of society which should develop. Lenin and Hitler had a vision for Europe, as do modern conservative, liberal, socialists and social democratic politicians. The difference now is not only that European society is much more homogeneous with similar economic, social, and institutional problems in most Western European countries. It is also more and more apparent that interdependence has led to the slow development of a supranational structure. Even the extreme right has based its appeal since the 1950s on the appeal to Europe as a whole. Contacts between extreme-right groups have not just been exercises in mutual moral or logistical support. Whilst nationalism of a kind may be seen as hampering the rapid development of some kind of European political union, the kind of nationally based racism of Hitler is something quite different, since it assumed the domination of Europe by one single country. The co-operation between France and Germany in the post-war era is, therefore, the principal bulwark against a return of the phoenix from the ashes, and the EC's very existence is a proof that alternative frameworks exist to the purely national one. Spain, Portugal, and Greece joined the EC precisely because it appears as a block on any possible return to fascism. It will, however, be necessary for the EC to live up to its ideals if its institutions are not themselves to be poisoned with the influence of Europe's extreme right. There is bound to be a nationalistic response in some quarters as the pace of political integration quickens. Mrs Thatcher's speech at the College of Europe in Bruges in October 1988 was clearly intended to present an alternative to the ideal of political union. It is, perhaps, worth noting that whilst the style and content of her speech, which not only glorified the nation state but specifically defended the former colonial role of European countries as a benefit to civilisation, were rejected by almost all of Europe's main political leaders, the group which was formed to further her message, the Bruges Group, attracted open support from the extreme right. Yvon Blot, who played a key role in establishing a committee in France to support this group, is a former Gaullist parliamentarian elected in June 1989 to the European Parliament on Le Pen's list.

Racism in Europe was there long before the migrant workers came in large numbers and it has survived even in parts of Europe where Jews or migrants are not very numerous. Immigrants are not, anyway, the only divergent group in society, and it would be a mistake to over-emphasise their importance as a spur to racism or fascism. Most of the nation states of Western Europe contain tensions between various ethnic groups, based on language, region, class, and religion. The nation state structure as it developed at the end of the century reflected a particular economic and social situation, and one effect of this was the submergence of minorities in order to create the appearance of national unity. The extreme right has itself used regionalist or environmentalist issues not fully taken into account by parties based on the structure of the nation state. If a lasting response to racism and fascism is to be found, it cannot only be as a response to the dominant issues of the 1980s, it must take into account the very particular structure of the nation state as compared with the reality of ethnic pluralism which the political structure of Europe does not yet reflect. The place of ethnic minorities in society is, therefore, not just a question of the problem of immigration. It should also be recalled that historically the struggle for human rights and national unity degenerated in some cases into a struggle for one nation's supremacy over others.

For many years, and in particular since 1987 with the Single European Act, the EC member states have been committed to building an area without internal frontiers. The 1992 project has caught public attention, but the message transmitted has in many cases been extremely ambiva-lent. The initial nature and appeal of this project has, moreover, become less obvious with the collapse of communism in Eastern Europe and the prospect of early German reunification. Mrs Thatcher has combined claims about commitments to European unity with a renewed appeal to British xenophobia and mistrust of foreigners. If electoral circumstances justify, there is little doubt that she will try to strengthen this part of her appeal. At the same time as Europe's economy does become more integrated there is a danger that Europeans' collective sense of superiority will lead to new forms of racism no longer based on purely national ethno-centrism. The extreme right has been preaching this alternative vision of Europe for decades. If European unity is to be a genuinely attractive prospect, it must be clear from the outset that the removal of internal frontiers concerns everyone, including the 16 million people settled in the EC whose original homes are from outside the area. Unfortunately, the governments of the member states are not starting off with this approach. Not only do most of them resist giving full civil rights to immigrants but also they are already treating the whole issue as a 'problem' to be dealt with secretively alongside such other possible side-effects of the internal market as the increase of drug-trafficking or terrorism. A more positive approach must combine acceptance of the need for greater political unity with a rejection of the idea of Europe as a new form of white hegemony. The efforts of those within the EC's institutions to get racism onto the political agenda must be combined with a positive vision of citizenship for all who live in Europe as an inspiring alternative to the fear of foreigners and the rejection of a genuinely open society which the extreme right has put at the centre of its efforts for revival. The needs of the European economy which make a continuing process of migration and immigration inevitable should not be presented as some unfortunate necessity but as a further example of the kind of interdependence which lies at the heart of the whole idea of European unity.

The countries of Western Europe have lost the dominant role which together they had at the beginning of the twentieth century. Through this period of rapid and violent change not all Europeans have lost the sense of racial superiority which accompanied the economic and military superiority of a past era. Europe has not, however, fully recovered its self-confidence or sufficiently developed an alternative ideal to that of national glory. In responding to the challenge of right-wing extremism and in facing up to the dark side of Europe's history and social reality, that ideal can, and must, be developed. Racism and fascism breed on distrust and fear of the future; Europeans should defeat those threats by showing trust in all peoples and working for a common future.

Notes

1. J. Falter and S. Schumann, 'Affinity towards Right-wing extremism', *West European Politics*, Vol. 11, 2 April 1988, pp. 96–110.
2. Council of Europe Parliamentary Assembly Resolution 743, (1980) of 1 October 1980.
3. Paul Wilkinson, *The New Fascists,* Paris, 1981 p. 199.
4. Bill Jordan, *Mass Unemployment and the Future of Britain*, Blackwell, Oxford, 1982
5. James Wallis, *Football and the Decline of Britain*, Macmillan, London, 1986, Ch. 6.
6. *New Statesman*, 10 February 1989, p. 6.
7. Harlem Desir, *Touch pas à mon Pote*, Grasset, Paris, 1985.
8. Stuart Hall, 'The gulf between Labour and blacks', The *Guardian*, 15 July 1985.

9. *Evrigenis Report*, para. 3.5.2.
10. Interview with Giuliano Ferrara, *Corriere della Sera*, 27 December 1987.
11. B. Parekh, 'Without Prejudice', *New Statesman* 11 November 1988, p. 25.
12. *Scarman Report on the Brixton Disorders*, HMSO, London, 1981, Cmnd. 8427.
13. *Wirtschaftswoche*, 10 February 1989.
14. *Evrigenis Report*, para 521.
15. *MIGREUROPE*: Declaration adopted at its Constituent Assembly, Brussels 3 October, 1988.
16. *Libération*, 19 December 1988.
17. Sir Rupert John, *Racism and its Elimination*, UNITAR, New York, 1981.
18. EC Commission, Draft Council Resolution on the Fight against Racism and Xenophobia, COM (88) 318, Brussels, 22 June 1988.
19. *Medina Report*, European Parliament Doc. A2–265/88.
20. 'Race becomes a burning issue', *Sunday Times*, 19 February 1989.
21. 'Heathrow puts us all to shame', The *Guardian*, 16 October 1986.

Appendix A

From *Apocalypse 2000* by Jay and Stewart[1]

In 1994 the 'Europe first Movement', a neo-fascist racist grouping won a majority of seats in elections for the European Parliament. In a speech to his followers at a victory celebration in Florence, the Movement's leader Olaf D. Le Rith, who had campaigned as a European, arguing that Hitler was right, and that European civilisation was threatened by Russo-American global domination stated:

Thirty million Europeans have no work. The old, out of date politicians in the old, out of date national capitals have nothing for them to do. They have nothing to say to them except 'we are sorry. We are doing our best. Trust us. We hope that things will get better one day.' Thirty million sons and daughters of true-born European stock, waiting and wanting to serve, to serve themselves, to serve their families, and to serve Europe; and all that these inert, corrupt, discredited parish-pump politicians can say is 'Please be patient. We have nothing for you just now. Come back tomorrow.'

Well they will not be patient any longer. The blood is running in their veins today. Their sinews and muscles are flexing today. They will not come back to the old leaders at all, ever. They are here, now, in this great place. They are on the march. They have their feet on the threshold of every capital in Europe. Their hands are on the bars of the prisons which the old, discredited politicians have fashioned for them. The bars, like the politicians, are old and rotten; and their shoulders are young and strong. They know the truth. They know how to shrug off the insidious net of American seduction and subjugation. They know how to trample under their feet the leeches and parasites from alien races that drain their vitality. They know that to do this, two things are needed: work, and discipline. Work, for every man and woman who can and will. Discipline, which turns a rabble into an army, and without which civilization degenerates into a jungle. The Spartans and the Athenians did not turn back the million-strong army of the Persian king except with discipline. The Roman Republic did not build the greatest empire of ancient times, except with discipline; and they did not watch it decline and fall for any other reason than the loss of discipline. It is the American empire that, alone, has been built on self-indulgence, on the easy affluence of empty fertile lands, on the ignoble foundations of commercial purchase and of shameless appeal to depraved appetites, not on the honest foundations of legitimate arms or on the strong base of high principles and self-discipline. And therefore the American empire is rotten, it is resented throughout the world, and it is crumbling away before our eyes.

We, in the Europe First Movement, speak for Europe. We control the Parliament of Europe. The people of Europe have given us their trust. They have given us their mandate, their authority to carry out our programme. We will not flinch from carrying out our programme. No commission, no council of corrupt, out of date politicians, no procrastination from the old national capitals, no piece of paper waved by the very men who have brought Europe to its knees shall stand in our way. We have a job to do. We must have the tools. We will take them and we will fashion them and we will shoulder them and we will use them. A great task lies ahead of us. We are ready to begin.

Note

1. As recounted by Peter Jay and Michael Stewart in *Apocalypse 2000: Economic Breakdown and the Suicide of Democracy 1989–2000*, Sidgwick and Jackson, London, 1987, pp. 208–9.

Appendix B

Conclusions and Recommendations of the European Parliament Committee of Inquiry, endorsed by the Parliament in January 1986

5.1   Forty years after the victory over the Nazi and fascist regimes, groups and individuals in the Community and in other countries of Western Europe still proclaim their adherence to those regimes' ideologies, or at least some of their features and especially those which are racist and anti-democratic.

5.2   These groups are in general extremely small. Their multiplicity, due to ideological dissension, constant personal squabbles and occasional outlawing, can hardly disguise the smallness of their numbers and the meagreness of their resources. It may be said that the more radical their ideology and behaviour, the more peripheral these groups become.

5.3   Even when those movements all or part of whose ideology can be described as right-wing extremism manage to achieve representation in local or parliamentary bodies, their public following by and large remains very limited and is unlikely seriously to undermine the European democracies.

5.4   What is more, right-wing extremism has suffered the consequences of the fall of the dictatorships in Greece, Spain and Portugal. The Community's attitude has helped to restore democracy in these countries. The last enlargement of the Community will formally mark the end of the authoritarian right-wing regimes which emerged in Europe in the 1930s. As regards Turkey, a country in association with the EEC and aspiring to membership, the European Parliament has on many occasions expressed its concern over, and its condemnation of, the violations of human rights occurring in that country.

5.5   In recent years individuals and movements belonging to the extreme right have taken to violence, often resulting in murder, instances of which have been particularly pronounced in Italy and Federal Germany. These development are associated with the appearance of a general climate of thoughtless toleration towards violence, extremism and depreciation of constitutionality.

5.6   What is more, some extreme right-wing ideas have recently been given more explicit and perhaps broader expression than before. This is particularly the case of supposedly 'scientific' racism which, by invoking strange mixtures of ideas, false generalizations and sometimes pure myths and inventions, erects the differences between individuals and groups of people into an absolute system and on the basis of such 'theories' attempts to justify racial segregation.

5.7   Among other themes which have made their appearance or reappearance in recent years we should note: the denial of the fact of genocide perpetrated by the Nazi regime, the inevitability of a 'race war', the resurgence of 'national-revolutionary' attitudes, also called 'the third position' or 'strasserism' (a mixture of spurious neutralism with a theory of 'national socialism'), virulent anti-semitism, often disguised as 'anti-zionism', and glorification of 'purifying' or 'liberating' violence. Some of these trends have contributed to the emergence of a terrorist movement which eludes classification in traditional political terms, such classification being in any event inapplicable when dealing with phenomena outside the democratic political spectrum.

5.8   By way of pinpointing the phenomenon, it should be said that the various extremist groups often provoke each other, attempting to exacerbate opposing views and polarize attitudes. Moreover the international context, and especially reference to totalitarian and dictatorial regimes, help to dramatize clashes within democratic Europe.

5.9   Links exist between the various European extreme right-wing groupings and between these and the American continent and the Middle East, as well as contacts with extreme left-wing groupings or state services of the Communist dictatorships and others. Thanks to these links, there is sporadic exchange of material assistance as well as a certain consonance in the theories propounded by the various groups. The extent of such links is, however, limited by various differences, rivalries and incomparabilities. The supposition that these various movements pursue a coordinated international strategy is not borne out by the evidence and is hard to reconcile with the nature of the facts listed here.

5.10   There is cause for more concern over the rise of more or less diffuse feelings of xenophobia and the increase in tensions between different communities. It has a distressing effect on the immigrant communities which are daily subject to displays of mistrust and hostility, to continuous discrimination, which legislative measures have failed to prevent, when seeking accommodation or employment or trying to provide services and, in many cases, to racial violence, including murder. The situation is aggravated by the fact that, rightly or wrongly, these minorities have little confidence in the institutions on which they should be able to call to uphold their rights and offer them protection.

5.11   The development of this situation is associated with a global social malaise, the elements of which are difficult to identify and assess and in any case may vary from context to context. They comprise the time-honoured distrust of strangers, fear of the future combined with a self-defensive reflex which together often lead to a withdrawal symptom, prejudices arising from the way national and international news is presented, and occasionally, a spiral of violence in which aggression and defence are almost inextricably intertwined. All these elements can be found in crisis-ridden urban centres where physical, economic and social conditions gravely militate against dialogue and tolerance.

5.12   There are movements seeking to give radical expression to the feelings and aspirations engendered by these social and cultural changes. They would be more likely to succeed if the democratic parties were short-sightedly tempted to exploit the possibilities offered by a disturbance of the electoral balance and if they gave preference to rhetorical incantations over the search for realistic solutions in the spirit of social peace and democratic dialogue.

5.13   For the time being the climate of mistrust and xenophobia existing here and there has not weakened overall confidence in the democratic institutions. But this confidence could be eroded, not so much by the 'historic fallout' represented by the activities of groups obsessively attached to out-dated totalitarian regimes and ideologies as by the 'generation effect', whereby knowledge of the harm perpetrated by these regimes and of the pernicious nature of their ideologies could gradually become attenuated. It is the generation effect, together with the attractiveness of protest movements in general, that is undoubtedly the reason why the youngest age groups account for a large proportion of extremist right-wing militants. Moreover, an allegiance to democratic values has to face the battering to which they are liable to be subjected by every kind of extremism and totalitarian tendency beyond the traditional political classifications.

5.14 Considerable efforts have been made since the end of the war at international, European, Community and national level to draw up the necessary legal instruments to ensure both the eradication of all forms of racism and discrimination and the protection of fundamental rights. Though success in this area has been mixed and though there have been doubts and errors in the formulation of a policy on migration, particularly in the last few years, West European and Community States continue their efforts to prevent and check fascist and racist speech and action and to abolish such forms of discrimination as still exist.

5.15 Recourse by private individuals to the legal means which have been introduced is nevertheless not easy. Apart from procedural difficulties, administrative practice often puts an impenetrable screen between the intention and the deed. The first victims of such a state of affairs are precisely those whom the provisions are intended to protect.

5.16 In Eastern Europe the situation is essentially different: not only are fundamental rights and democratic values systematically denied, in a way inherent in the very nature of the regime, but there are many instances of discrimination, not to say persecution, of ethnic minorities in what has always been a very culturally mixed area. The most glaring example is the position of the Jewish community in the Soviet Union where the conduct of the authorities can justifiably be described as 'state racism'.

5.17 The success of educational policies, both as regards the eradication of all forms of discrimination and instruction in toleration and democratic values, is closely dependent on the design and performance of the educational system as a whole and of the confidence which it consequently commands. In general, civic education in the broad sense – and particularly the prevention of racist prejudice and instruction in human rights and democratic values – receives far less attention than it merits.

5.18 The information media, which play an essential role in the functioning of every democratic system, bear an important responsibility for the image of the minorities that is presented to society and, more broadly, for the mutual perceptions of different sections of the population by the way in which they succeed or fail in their task. The perception of violence depends largely on the way in which it is presented by the media. The professional ethics of the media require closer consideration in this respect.

5.19   Groups and institutions devoted to combating fascism and racism and the protection of the minorities perform a most useful task in information and representation. That task is fully accomplished when it is carried on in a spirit of dialogue and pluralism and with due consideration to the expectations and aspirations of the public at large. The emergence of new cultural forms of combating intolerance and discrimination must be recognized and encouraged.

5.20   In matters concerning the defence of human rights and democratic values, the responsibility of all citizens, and especially of leaders of public opinion, can neither be reduced nor delegated. There is no room for considerations of political expediency.

5.21   The large population movements which have taken place in recent years with the consequent entry of new communities into the social tissue of a number of European countries, the cultural changes taking place and, not least, the growing openness of societies to events throughout the world – all these call for the formulation of new global policy which will ensure that the new minorities can find their place in the social fabric of European nations and that these national societies develop harmoniously in understanding and respect for democratic values. A European policy on inter-communal relations must become part of any genuine policy for European Union.

6.   RECOMMENDATIONS OF THE COMMITTEE INQUIRY

6.   To this effect, the Committee submits the following recommendations:

6.1   *At the institutional level*

(a)   Countries which have not yet done so; must ratify the international conventions (UN, UNESCO, ILO, Council of Europe) relating to the subject of this inquiry.

(b)   Countries which had not already done so should issue declarations and perform ratifications relating to 'individual' petitions (Article 25 of the European Convention on Human Rights, Article 14 of the International Convention on the Elimination of all forms of Racial Discrimination, Optional protocol to the International Covenant on Civil and political Rights).

(c)   Commitments undertaken in virtue of international conventions must be given full implementation in domestic law.

(d) National legislation on combating political extremism, racism and racial discrimination must be continually revised and adjusted and its application in practice must be ensured. Forms of racial discrimination present in current national legislation must be identified and expunged.

(e) Effective means of legal recourse in disputes relating to racial discrimination must be established and the organizations involved must be guaranteed the right to institute civil proceedings.

(f) The legislation described under (d) above must be subject to monitoring, analysis and assessment of implementation by national administrative and judicial authorities.

(g) The benefits of genuine free legal aid and free legal consultation must be extended to proceedings in disputes relating to racial discrimination.

(h) A policy must be formulated and introduced for positive institutional measures to create at national level specialist bodies concerned with race relations, where such bodies do not already exist, to protect the victims, and prevent manifestations, of racial discrimination.

(i) In the spirit of resolutions already voted by the European Parliament, progress must be made towards the creation of a European legal area in order to prevent the activities of and collusion between terrorist and extremist organizations in the execution of their acts and the distribution of illegal propaganda material, and to defend the fundamental principles of democracy afforded by the rule of law.

(j) An effort must be made to define more broadly Community powers and responsibilities in the area of race relations by applying a teleological interpretation of the Treaties, on the basis, inter alia, of seeking the useful effect of the relevant provisions and of the European Community's implicit powers; by recourse to the procedure under Article 235 of the EEC Treaty; and, if necessary, by revision of the Treaties. Action must be taken on the communication from the Commission to the Council for a Community policy on migration, on which Parliament has delivered its opinion, and on the resolutions adopted by Parliament on the same subject.

(k) Commission initiatives must be encouraged in the area of problems identified by this inquiry.

(l)   The questions identified by this inquiry must be intro-
      duced into the purview of para-Community mechanisms,
      for instance the European Council and European political
      cooperation.

(m)   An effort should be made to draw up a declaration
      against racism, racial discrimination and xenophobia
      and in favour of harmonious relations among all the
      communities existing in Europe, to be adopted jointly
      by the Community political institutions, in accordance
      with the spirit of the Commission proposal and the
      Council resolution. Plans should be laid for a Euro-
      pean Year to promote inter-community harmony, during
      which Community funds would be allocated for holding
      conferences or arranging other events for the purpose of
      combating racism, racial discrimination and xenophobia
      and encouraging tolerance and mutual respect between
      the different communities living in Europe.

(n)   The role of the European Parliament, in its capacity as
      an organ of deliberation, debate and political initiative,
      should be enhanced in matters relating to respect for, and
      consolidation of, the democratic order, the fight against
      racism and harmonious relations among all communities
      residing in Europe.

6.2   *At the level of information*

(a)   A comparative-law study should be undertaken on the
      various legal instruments and practices introduced in the
      countries of the Community to deal with the matters
      which are the subject of this inquiry and on the effec-
      tiveness of these instruments. The European Parliament
      should encourage this project to take effect.

(b)   In each State bodies should be set up to provide infor-
      mation on the means of legal protection against dis-
      crimination, racism and incitement to racial hatred and
      violence. The means for coordinating such bodies at
      European level should be provided. Efforts should be
      made to improve the spread of information on legal
      recourse at the international, European, Community and
      domestic level, using all the available information and
      communications techniques, including in particular the
      technological opportunities afforded by telematics and
      data processing. At all points of entry into Community
      Member States directories should be provided, listing, in

the appropriate languages, the names, addresses and telephone numbers of counselling and legal advice services provided for migrants, immigrants, refugees and persons seeking a reception centre.

(c) Within the framework of Euro-barometer one or more surveys should be carried out on the present state of relations between the different communities living n Europe. It should comprise questions on the respondent's feelings about contacts with communities other than his own and also on his understanding of democratic values. The necessary funds should be provided in the Community budget.

(d) Case studies should be carried out in a number of Community urban centres where minority communities are strongly represented, or where surveys have identified a high level of racism, in order to compare both the problems that arise and the strategies adopted to deal with them.

(e) The professional ethic, of the information industry with respect to manifestations of violence, and especially of racial violence, should be carefully considered. The European parliament could take the initiative in organizing a symposium on this subject.

(f) It should be brought home to those concerned at all levels of the information industry that the mass media have an important role to play in eliminating racial prejudice and promoting harmonious relations among communities resident in Europe. The minority communities must be fairly represented in the information media.

6.3   *At the level of education*

(a) In all educational structures and policies the aim of non-discrimination must be promoted.

(b) Much more importance must be given to civic education throughout the school curriculum, with the aim of fostering allegiance to the principles and practice of democracy and pluralism, a critical approach, tolerance and mutual respect between human beings and a sense of civic responsibility. Special training programmes based on these principles should be provided for civil servants working in areas where racial tension is likely or dealing with the problems and needs of individuals belonging to minority communities.

(c)   The concerns evident in the present inquiry must be taken into account when drafts of a European civic education textbook are prepared.

(d)   Special attention should be given to the civic education of teachers. They must be given a knowledge of the principles and essential content of the legal texts relevant to the subject of the inquiry. They should be made aware of the problem of relations between children or adolescents belonging to different communities and taught the appropriate pedagogic approach; they should be alerted to the danger of racist ideas which are presented through the subtle manipulation of language.

(e)   Instruction in minority cultures and languages should be encouraged in order that societies may become more open both to these minority communities and to the world outside the Community. Full application of the Community directive on the teaching of the language and culture of children's country of origin during the normal school timetable by all the Member States should be monitored.

(f)   Contemporary history should be taught at an early age, presenting children with an accurate picture of the crimes committed by European fascist and totalitarian regimes, and more particularly of their acts of genocide. A Community initiative should be promoted for the preparation of a European textbook of contemporary history on the basis of work already done by the Council of Europe and by UNESCO.

6.4   *At the level of action by social forces*

(a)   Efforts must be made to ensure that the European countries pursue a policy designed to provide full employment and underpin social peace; this policy should be defined so as to withstand social and economic crises which put democracy itself at risk.

(b)   Institutions and associations opposed to racism, and immigrants' organizations, trade unions, professional organizations and other bodies concerned should be invited to promote the creation of an Intercommunity Forum under the aegis of the European Communities on the model of the Youth Forum. This body's main tasks should be to provide an exchange of information and improve the coordination and allocation of duties in action and research. The Forum would be financed by the Communities' budget.

(c) Encouragement should be given to European dialogue and meetings between people, institutions and associations combating racism and working for human rights. The trade unions, professional organizations and other institutions concerned should take part in this dialogue. Discussion and debate should be encouraged in the European Parliament with a view to drawing further public attention to the subjects considered by the Committee of Inquiry and the conclusions it has reached, and in particular, to the institutional response, i.e. that of the forces of law and order, to terrorism.

(d) Encouragement should be given to contacts and dialogue between different religions and persuasions, both to promote religious and spiritual tolerance and to encourage joint debate on the place of the various faiths in modern European society.

(e) Detailed consideration should be given to the responsibility of democratic political bodies in the face of the problems highlighted by this inquiry and in order to try to establish an ethic of debate on the subject. The European Parliament could play a crucial role in this.

6.5   *Guidelines for general debate*

(a) The issues raised and the solutions envisaged should have constant priority in considerations on the formulation of national and Community institutional, economic and social policies and in the fields of education, culture and information.

(b) Within the European Parliament discussion and debate should take place on the issues raised by the inquiry and political responsibilities in this area should be defined at international, national and Community level. In two years' time, and at regular intervals thereafter, there should be a review of developments in the matters considered by the inquiry, and of the extent to which the recommendations in this document have been carried out.

(c) An effort should be made to identify the areas of tension and problems in multi-community Europe and on this basis to define the political and social balance which should be attained and the strategies required for action.

(d)   The debate should be widened, with contacts being established in the appropriate international authorities with the aim of obtaining reciprocity of treatment in relations between Community Member States and third countries.

6.6   The Committee of Inquiry requests the appropriate committees of the European Parliament to study closely the ideas and the proposals set out in this document. The report and especially its recommendations can undoubtedly give rise to parliamentary initiatives, whether in the form of motions for resolutions or oral questions with debate, initiatives which could result from joint action by different groups within the Parliament, thus witnessing to a consensus that goes beyond political divisions. The committee also asks the Council, the Commission, the national governments and parliaments and all the democratic forces of Europe to study these proposals and to draw practical conclusions from them, bearing in mind not only the seriousness and urgency this further challenge facing Community Europe today but also the duty of democratic vigilance and political responsibility which lies upon it.

Index